THE
LOCAL FOOD
REVOLUTION

HOW HUMANITY WILL FEED ITSELF
IN UNCERTAIN TIMES

MICHAEL BROWNLEE

North Atlantic Books
Berkeley, California

Published by   Cover image © iStockphoto.com/Vector
North Atlantic Books   Cover design by Rob Johnson
Berkeley, California   Book design by Suzanne Albertson

Printed in the United States of America

The Local Food Revolution: How Humanity Will Feed Itself in Uncertain Times is sponsored and published by the Society for the Study of Native Arts and Sciences (dba North Atlantic Books), an educational nonprofit based in Berkeley, California, that collaborates with partners to develop cross-cultural perspectives, nurture holistic views of art, science, the humanities, and healing, and seed personal and global transformation by publishing work on the relationship of body, spirit, and nature.

North Atlantic Books' publications are available through most bookstores. For further information, visit our website at www.northatlanticbooks.com or call 800-733-3000.

Library of Congress Cataloging-in-Publication Data

Names: Brownlee, Michael, 1946- author.
Title: The local food revolution : how humanity will feed itself in uncertain times / Michael Brownlee.
Description: Berkeley, California : North Atlantic Books, [2016] | Includes bibliographical references.
Identifiers: LCCN 2016005775 (print) | LCCN 2016007048 (ebook) | ISBN 9781623170004 (print) | ISBN 9781623170011 (ebook)
Subjects: LCSH: Food supply. | Local foods.
Classification: LCC HD9000.5 .B745 2016 (print) | LCC HD9000.5 (ebook) | DDC 338.1/9—dc23
LC record available at http://lccn.loc.gov/2016005775

1   2   3   4   5   6   7   Sheridan   21   20   19   18   17   16

Printed on recycled paper

*For the angels of evolution, past, present,
and future, visible and invisible.*

If you want to build a ship, don't drum up people together to collect wood and don't assign them tasks and work, but rather teach them to long for the sea.

—Antoine de Saint-Exupéry

CONTENTS

ILLUSTRATIONS

PROLOGUE

For some time, in the local food movement, we've been hearing that our food system is *broken* and that we need to fix it. This idea gets much enthusiastic agreement, and in fact, there are many people who say they are indeed working on *fixing the broken food system.* This has long made me feel uncomfortable, but I could never quite explain why. Eventually, I began to understand that the very idea of a broken food system is the result of a particular kind of thinking, one that has helped to create our collective predicament, our evolutionary crisis.

Witnessing how nearly everyone in the global industrial food supply chain has been trained to believe and declare with near-religious fervor that their collective mission is *to feed the world,* I came to see that this is a system that has been carefully engineered, constructed, and managed. It is a brilliant enterprise; in fact, it is the largest industry in the world.

Gradually it became obvious to me that the global food system works exactly the way it has been designed. Its purpose, however, is actually *not* feeding the world or contributing to the health and well-being of our people. Instead, its fundamental purpose is to produce corporate profits and to consolidate power through ruthlessly exploiting the human need for food. Over the last seventy years or so, this system has become extremely successful, extremely efficient, extremely profitable, and extremely powerful—and very good at externalizing costs. It now controls at least 97 percent of our food supply in the United States, and it is moving aggressively toward 100 percent control. *They want it all,* and they consider the natural, organic, and local food "segments" to be trivial niche markets that they will soon subsume.

Along the way, I've also noticed that people who devote themselves to "fixing" this system often wind up somehow becoming part of it, or their energies are completely consumed to the point that they are left with nothing real to contribute to building local food systems.

❦

Our food predicament today is not unlike pre-Revolutionary America toward the end of 1775, when all discussion and debate in the colonies centered on reconciliation with the British Crown. Of course, the Crown had no real interest in reconciliation, though they may have occasionally given it lip service.

These days we hear from proponents of Big Ag that we who stand for local, wholesome food production must accept *coexistence* with their fossil-fuel-based, genetically modified, monocropping approach to agriculture. But as nearly any organic farmer will tell you, coexistence is ultimately impossible, for accepting such terms of engagement guarantees the inevitable disappearance of organic farming. The Unholy Alliance of Big Ag, Big Food, and Big Pharma is relentless in its push for total domination of the food supply, and it is even willing to risk contaminating other farmers' non-GMO crops to achieve its ends—so that the meaning of "organic" is finally obliterated.

Big Ag proudly proclaims that there is only "one agriculture" (as if all farming is equal in value), but of course, what they're pointing to is their own favored form of agricultural and economic practice. They seek to have this system institutionalized as the *only* agriculture. This amounts to nothing less than tyranny, unjust and oppressive, unrestrained by law, effectively usurping legitimate freedom and sovereignty. In this context, their slogan, "We must feed the world," can be appropriately translated as "No one but us shall be *allowed* to feed the world." We should understand that we are being asked to accept food slavery.

❦

We watched in horror here in Boulder County, Colorado, when one of our most highly venerated local organic farms lost its entire fall harvest (worth some $250,000) to an incident of "pesticide drift" from a field of sunflowers more than a mile away—difficult to prove in a court of law, but undeniable to those who were witness to the destruction. This event contributed to that farm's untimely demise, long before any token legal or insurance settlement could be reached.

Such experiences, and the educational process they stimulated, ultimately led me to articulate what has been building within me for the last few years.

❧

The idea that all farming is equal, that all farmers should be respected and revered, is preposterous. But there is a robust taboo against stating the obvious: that modern industrial farming amounts to one of the most destructive enterprises on the planet. We need to lose the romantic notion about the essential goodness of all farming and all farmers. It's simply not true.

Some farmers have told me that, because of my public stand against the use of GMOs, they consider me to be "anti-farmer." Well, I stand for farmers who work to feed their communities, who build soil, who regenerate the land, and who are dedicated to contributing to the health and well-being of the people whose lives they touch. Conventional commodity-crop farming is not about these things. It is essentially *all about the money.* Let's not romanticize it and pretend it is something other than the disaster it has become. We are easily confused about this, and we need to become clear about our priorities at this moment in human evolution.

❧

I've long understood that food localization is radical, even revolutionary, and I've been saying so over the last few years. I did not quite realize what I was saying, but I did notice that my calling it a *revolution* seemed to make many local food activists and policy makers uncomfortable. I nevertheless persisted, experimented, and kept looking deeper.

Finally, in June 2015, after participating in a conference of the Business Alliance for Local Living Economies (BALLE) in Phoenix, Arizona, I shuttered myself in a motel room in Tucson for three days to attempt to pull my thoughts together. I felt what was needed was a compelling manifesto for a local food revolution. The best I could do, I suspected, was to pen a sort of interim communiqué—a step along the way, a building block. I didn't know then that I was writing the beginning of this book and that the book I thought I had been writing for the previous three years would be utterly transformed in the process.

Since June, I've been asking myself just what a local food *revolution* actually means—what it looks like, how it might unfold, and how we might support it. This book is, first of all, an attempt to begin to answer that question and to challenge us all to become local food revolutionaries. But the book is also an invitation to explore what I am now calling *deep revolution,* which will be the subject of upcoming workshops, presentations, and perhaps a subsequent book.

PART 1

WHAT MUST BE SAID NOW

This is the true revolution: not a superficial overthrow of whatever powers happen to be, but a radically new understanding of self and world.... Why is such a deep revolution necessary?... A revolution that leaves our sense of self and world intact cannot bring other than temporary, superficial change. Only a much deeper revolution, a reconceiving of who we are, can reverse the crises of our age. Fortunately, this deepest of all possible revolutions is inevitable.... When at last the futility of controlling reality becomes apparent, when at last the burden of maintaining an artificial self separate from nature becomes too heavy to bear any longer, when at last we realize that our wealth has bankrupted us of life, then a million tiny revolutions will converge into a vast planetary shift, a rapid phase transition into a new mode of being.

—CHARLES EISENSTEIN, *SACRED ECONOMICS*

CHAPTER 1

Toward a Local Food Revolution

Hegemony: preponderant influence or authority over others *(Merriam-Webster's Collegiate Dictionary).* A form of power in which those who have power maintain their position not through force but through the elaboration of a particular world view, an ideology, a particular notion of common sense, which is infused in everyday cultural practices. The result is that people do not submit to power; rather, they consent to it, even though it might not be in their best interest.

We are a hungry people, malnourished and underfed.

Yet, for the most part, we do not suffer from a lack of food. One-third of our citizens are chronically obese. Our food is so cheap and abundant that we throw away more than a third of it (even though, as environmentalists remind us, there is no "away").

But the food that is so reliably delivered to us by the global industrial food system does not nourish us or support us. Instead, it undermines our health, degrades our environment, poisons the biota, destroys the soil, weakens our economies, and eviscerates our communities. This cannot, in any meaningful sense, be considered "food."

Meanwhile, we suffer from a different kind of hunger, a deeper, existential or spiritual hunger that is too often unspoken, unconscious, and ignored. Silently, we hunger for meaningful connection with the earth. We hunger for connection with the cycles and processes of nature, for connection with the sacredness of life. And we hunger for connection in community with each other.

Our global industrial food system has broken these connections.

It's not that our current food system is broken, for it functions very well indeed. It is more that it has broken our connections with the most fundamental relationships of life itself. Our food system has left us starved for life.

Our food system is breaking us. Participating in it disconnects us from living systems and from each other, unintentionally producing broken economies, broken communities, and broken people.

We could think of industrialized civilization today as a huge concentrated animal feeding operation (CAFO)—not much nicer than the massive feedlots that we subject our cattle to or the factory farms that house and process our pigs and chickens and lambs and fish. And, for the most part, we humans are not much better off than those poor suffering creatures. We're not raised on the open range, with free access to the foods that are natural to us where we live. Instead, we're pumped full of hormones and antibiotics and fed a synthetic diet of highly processed food-like items laced with toxic chemicals and drugs designed to fatten us up for the market of the industrial health care system. We are not encouraged to be cage free or grass fed or pasture raised. Almost everything about our diet and our lives is artificial, controlled by transnational corporations. *We are being ranched.*

There is much anguish about food deserts these days, and rightfully so. But the uncomfortable reality is that *almost all of us* live in something of a food desert, where healthy, fresh, local, sustainably produced food is available to almost no one except the relatively wealthy and those who have learned to grow it for themselves.

Amazingly, most of us have been almost completely unconscious of what is happening to our food supply and what it is doing to us. For the most part, we have passively accepted our plight. However, this is quickly beginning to change.

The way we compensate for our unmet hunger is what has come to be known as *consumerism*—a social and economic order (and ideology) that encourages the ever-increasing acquisition and consumption of products and services. We have been trained even to identify ourselves as consumers—a lifestyle that emits toxic wastes that foul our air, land, and water (to say nothing of the mental and emotional toxicities that we produce along the way). While it's amazing that we are able to "live" this way at all, it is a life that does not remotely resemble the life of which we are capable—or the purpose and meaning for which we seem to be designed.

While this sad state of affairs seems to dominate our society, something new is stirring across the land—a much-needed revolution in the way humanity feeds itself. We are beginning to take back our food supply, reclaiming our food sovereignty, and building local foodsheds.

THE UNHOLY ALLIANCE

It's necessary to understand how we got into our predicament before we can begin to see the path beyond it. Here's the backstory.

Since the advent of industrial civilization, but especially since World War II, we have become increasingly dependent on a globalized, industrialized, corporatized food system, controlled by an Unholy Alliance of transnational corporations—known by the familiar monikers of Big Ag, Big Food, and Big Pharma—all empowered by Big Banking and Big Government, and fueled (not coincidentally) by Big Oil. This industrial food supply chain is tightly intertwined and highly focused on producing profits and consolidating power above all else.

In this system, our farmers and ranchers are told that their job is to "feed the world." But this is pure propaganda, an insidious reframing of reality—for in less than a century, this Unholy Alliance has successfully colonized most of the industrialized world, almost completely displacing humanity's ability to feed itself, creating a ruthless dependency for the most fundamental requirements for life.

Altogether, the industrial food system—now by far the largest and most destructive industry in the world—burns about 23 percent of global oil and gas supplies, and is apparently responsible for more than half of global greenhouse-gas emissions and 80 percent of fresh-water resource use.

With the goal of producing commoditized food as cheaply as possible while maximizing corporate profit and control, the architects of this behemoth have put the well-being of life on this planet at risk, for it has been steadily fouling our natural environment, destroying topsoil (half of which has been lost in the last 150 years), depleting ancient fossil-fuel and fresh-water reserves, dramatically warming our atmosphere, and gradually destroying the very conditions conducive to life. Our industrial food system has become the equivalent of mountaintop-removal coal mining—to the point that it is now an overwhelming contributor to the sixth mass extinction of species in planetary history, producing what Paul Ehrlich and his fellow researchers are now calling "a global spasm of biodiversity loss," the worst planetary crisis in sixty-six million years.[1]

The Unholy Alliance has unleashed a wave of rapacious and disastrous economic growth, uprooting small farmers and converting farmlands into urban and peri-urban developments, transforming cities into human CAFOs, and making inevitable an explosion of the human population—an estimated 70 to 90 percent of whom will be forced to live in overcrowded urban environments by midcentury.

All the while, this system delivers to us food of ever-poorer quality and diminishing nutritional value, weakening our bodies and minds, causing an epidemic of diet-related diseases, decreasing our life expectancy, undermining our local economies, creating a profound economic disparity among our people, and severing our relationship with the land and with all that is sacred in life.

If left to continue, the trajectory of this juggernaut in the coming decades portends an unavoidable collapse of ecosystems, economies, and human populations.

We must recognize that the global industrial food system cannot be redeemed, for, like the fossil-fuel industry on which it depends, it is so deeply corrupt and corrupting, so morally and spiritually bankrupt, that its inevitable fate is entropic decline or even widespread collapse. As Fred Bahnson says, "You can't trust Babylon with the food supply."[2]

It is an obvious, if largely unspoken, reality that this food system on which we depend is profoundly unsustainable. Less obvious is the reality that it is also becoming dangerously unstable. The system is teetering on the brink of collapse just at the moment when it purports to be ramping up to feed a world of some nine or ten billion people by midcentury. But in fact, this global food system has itself become *the greatest threat to humanity's being able to feed itself,* and it is already beginning to fail us. How we answer this challenge could well determine the future of humanity and even the future of life on this planet.

FOOD INSECURE

> We're one disaster away from complete anarchy.
>
> —BOB DANDREW, LOCAL ECONOMIES PROJECT,
> HUDSON VALLEY, NEW YORK[3]

"America is the most food insecure country in the world," a farmer from Kenya recently told one of our young food entrepreneurs in Denver. "If the truck doesn't make it over the hill," he said, "you have no food." In his village, everyone has a garden, and everyone knows how to grow his or her own food.

With the advent of the global industrial food system, controlled by a handful of multinational corporations who operate in concert, we, as a people, have essentially lost our capacity to feed ourselves. This is especially true in the United States.

Rusty Collins, Colorado State University's extension agent in Denver, himself a local food revolutionary, reminds us that during World War II there were some fifty thousand victory gardens in that city alone. Large-scale truck farming of vegetables in the area near Denver was a major industry. But today, like most cities, Denver has only an estimated two days supply of food. And, according to Collins, less than 1 percent of Colorado's food is now produced within this supposedly "agricultural" state.

By allowing ourselves to become so dependent on the global food system, we have given up our food security. We have surrendered our food sovereignty. In effect, we have relinquished our freedom. If this continues unabated, a global food catastrophe is inevitable—and it will quickly land on our own shores. For tens of millions of our people, the truck from over the hill will simply not arrive.

Here's the principle that we are learning all too painfully: To the extent that we are dependent on distant sources and foreign powers for our essential needs, we have lost our freedom.

THE UPRISING

There comes a time for declaring that all this is unacceptable, a time for withdrawing from the current food system and building something new to regain our food security and sovereignty. There comes a time for our people to become self-reliant, to meet our own essential needs locally, beginning with food. *That time is now.*

If humanity is to have a future that is both tolerable and resilient, on a planet where life can thrive, we must regain control over our food supply. We must recover our capacity to feed ourselves. In doing so, we will regain our food sovereignty and food security, which have been almost completely lost over the last seventy years. All this is essential to secure the future of humanity and the viability of life on this planet.

For all these reasons, we can reasonably conclude that localizing our food supply is among the most important and urgent social causes on our planet today. The process of food localization has the power to reverse our downward spiral, bringing healing and wholeness to people and communities and regeneration to the land and its living systems. This requires a revolution, a great turning over. And it has already begun.

This revolution is not, however, a revolt against the global industrial food system. It is a spontaneous uprising, a coming together to build something new in the face of nearly impossible odds. We do not have the time or the resources to change the global industrial food system. Nor is this necessary. For now, what we most need to do is create an independent and parallel system.

Localizing our food supply is a radical and subversive effort that is rapidly growing from the ground up. We are forging a new pathway into the future. The project is both inspiring and daunting—and more than a little dangerous. The stakes are high.

The Unholy Alliance says that we must feed the world and that we must rely on large-scale industrial agriculture to do so. But we're not going to feed the world. Instead, the people of the world are going to learn to feed themselves. That's what the local food revolution is all about.

THE ROOTS OF REVOLUTION

When we, as a people, find ourselves embedded in systems that are beyond redemption, when we can no longer countenance our own complicity, we begin to resist. We rebel. We distance ourselves. We speak out. We begin to cobble together alternatives. Soon, especially if the existing system reacts with even greater destructiveness (which it almost always will), *something will ignite a revolution.*

A revolution is a relatively abrupt shift in social order. Tocqueville said that revolutions are sweeping transformations of the entire society that often take several generations to bring about. But once in a great while, something entirely different happens—a kind of spontaneous awakening, arising from the bottom, which rapidly changes everything: how we see the world, what we value, how we define progress and organize ourselves, and perhaps, eventually, even how our institutions operate.

One of the founders of the local food revolution is Fred Kirschenmann at the Leopold Center for Sustainable Agriculture, who, a few years ago, somewhat presciently declared, "A food revolution is definitely underway ... evidence that the era of passive food 'consumers' is over and a new era of engaged food 'citizens' is rapidly emerging."[4]

We recently heard these very words quoted by a nutritionist at Natural Grocers, a Colorado-based food retailer now opening a new store every three weeks, fueled by an IPO designed to enable them to grow to 1,500 stores over the next several years. The leaders of this company may well be revolutionaries.

Those involved in the grocery industry celebrate the steady growth of organics over the last few decades, mostly averaging a 10 to 12 percent annual growth rate. In 2014, organics brought in $39 billion. But in that same year, the local food segment—at least the part that could be roughly measured—reached nearly $12 billion. It is now growing at rates perhaps two to three times that of the organic segment and will likely eclipse organics in the next few years. Local food is a completely eater-driven industry segment, and that's something new. It's revolutionary.

ANSWERING THE CALL

Because of the stakes and the urgency, many of us are called to join and accelerate this local food revolution—which, first of all, means uncompromisingly extracting ourselves from participation in the global industrial food system. We are called to take responsibility for feeding ourselves and to assist our neighbors in learning to feed themselves. We are called to decolonize ourselves and to cease being consumers. We are called to be revolutionaries, not merely advocates or activists.

In answering this call, we are inspired to follow the example of the early American revolutionaries and commit our lives, our fortunes, and our sacred honor to building truly local food economies. We understand that we will be opposed and misunderstood, but we will persist.

What we're engaged in is building restorative, regenerative local food economies that are completely independent. We're shifting away from a global system that is killing us—declaring our independence from that extractive, exploitive system. And we're building exactly what we know is most needed—regional foodsheds that are life giving, restoring health, land, economies, and souls. We understand that this is the only real path to food security, food justice, and food sovereignty. We understand that this is radical, revolutionary.

THE VISION

The vision of this revolution is to restore food to its rightful place in our society, to bring it home again, so that it is grown on farms close to where we live, by people whom we know and trust and love; joyfully prepared in our own kitchens; gratefully shared with neighbors, friends, and family; and received into our lives in ways that nourish body, mind, and soul—so that food once again becomes sacred, sacramental, central to our communities.

Localizing our food supply is right at the heart of a vast and spontaneous bottom-up effort to bring healing, restoration, and regeneration to our troubled world, to begin to reverse the widespread destruction caused by the industrial growth society—including by sequestering carbon and mitigating the impacts of climate change. Since food is what catalyzed human civilization in the first place, it is only appropriate that our efforts to begin healing and regeneration should also begin with food. There is no issue or human activity more fundamental than the way we feed ourselves.

What is most profoundly needed in our predicament is a systemic, collaborative approach to localizing our food supply to the greatest extent possible in the briefest possible time. This requires, in Jack Kloppenburg's poignant terminology, *thinking like a foodshed*—a new and greatly needed skill set in our society.

If we are to feed our own populations to any significant degree—our *local* populations, that is—and if we are to assist people in other nations in feeding themselves sustainably, we must find ways to convert a significant amount of our current commodity-crop production and export-oriented agriculture to sustainably growing food for local consumption. This is a profound reversal of a paradigm that is deeply rooted in an economy of extraction and consumption, with no regard for the costs to the ecosystem or the negative impacts on human health. This is the agricultural paradigm that our federal government explicitly supports through the USDA and the Farm Bill. In this paradigm, they do not want us to localize our food supply, for that runs counter to their values.

But we have an opportunity to build regional foodsheds that are economically robust, environmentally sustainable, resilient, and self-reliant; that ensure food security, food sovereignty, and food justice for all our citizens; that contribute to the health and well-being of our communities; that rediscover and cultivate a sense of place; and that strengthen our local economies.

Such is the vision of the local food revolution.

CAVEATS

While all this sounds hopeful and inspiring, we must also recognize that the local food revolution faces serious challenges and obstacles.

First, let us acknowledge that the situation is urgent. More than anything else, global warming will drive us to the brink regarding food. Climate change—along with soil depletion, drought, and loss of farmland (often to "development")—is likely to result in a dramatic reduction of global food production, by as much as 20 to 30 percent, in the next two or three decades. Unless we find ways to radically increase local food production in spite of these challenges, mass starvation could be widespread—and even the United States may not be spared.

Meanwhile, the human population is, of course, expected to increase, creating 14 percent more demand for food each decade. This is a global disaster in the making.

The Unholy Alliance cynically seeks to exploit this emerging global food crisis by convincing farmers, entrepreneurs, and investors that the solutions for "feeding the world" are primarily technological—through genetic modification, application of more powerful chemicals, use of better drugs, and even the creation of artificial food.

Not only are these technological strategies unnecessary, but also, as a matter of unintended consequences, they will greatly exacerbate the global food crisis. Along the way, they will increase humanity's dependence on the industrial food system and further diminish our capacity to feed ourselves. The result could be a catastrophic reduction in human population over the next few decades.

While perhaps not agreeing on details or timelines, many of those in the forefront of the local food revolution share a common understanding and orientation: they comprehend the fundamental nature of our human predicament and are quietly doing what is in their power, often in the face of overwhelming obstacles. They are, in fact, doing the daunting work of revolutionaries, though few of them would identify themselves as such.

Meanwhile, we would do well to remember that the so-called Green Revolution[5] was not a revolution at all. A brilliant public-relations move obscured the reality that the Green Revolution was an industrial-development strategy designed by transnational agrochemical corporations to create an ever-growing market—to increase their own profits—while making much of humanity increasingly dependent on industrial methods of agriculture and food production: reliance on fossil fuels, chemical pesticides, herbicides, and genetic modification. It is no coincidence that the system of land-grant universities remains at the forefront of this development.

Indeed, the meme of "feeding the world" is essentially an exploitive and manipulative marketing strategy. It is a mantra still mindlessly and ritually chanted by nearly everyone in the industrial food supply chain—an article of near-religious faith.

In such an environment, it is not possible even to suggest that this very dependency keeps humanity shackled and enslaved solely in the name of economic growth and corporate profitability.

Real revolutions come from the bottom up, starting at the grassroots, responding to the real needs of the people. The Green Revolution was more of a coup, in that it came from the top down, from the halls of industry and academia, supported by the heavy hand of government and international banks. As a result, we have almost completely lost our capacity to meet our essential food needs locally. We have lost our food sovereignty and our food security.

We come to these realizations with great pain and humility, for we have all been complicit in this loss.

❧

How do we end our complicity? How do we contribute to this great and urgent cause? How do we ourselves become revolutionaries?

There are myriad ways to participate, of course. And there are countless courageous and innovative efforts already underway that we can join.

But perhaps we can begin with a simple declaration.

CHAPTER 2

The Local Food Declaration
of Independence

We, the undersigned, declare our independence from the global industrial food system.

We join a growing community of local eaters and local food producers who are building regional foodsheds.

Together, we are reclaiming our food sovereignty by shifting our food supply from the global to the local.

We hold local food and our foodsheds as sacred.

We pledge to eat (and drink) as local as possible.

We pledge to actively support our local farmers and ranchers who produce food for our community.

We pledge to actively support local food enterprises that source from local farmers and ranchers.

We pledge to seek the appropriate role of animals in our agriculture and in our diets.

We pledge to grow some of our own food, more every year.

We pledge to rebuild soil, more every year.

We pledge to grow our community, more every year.

To this local food revolution we commit our lives, our health, our well-being, our financial and social resources, and our sacred honor.

We will honor and nurture the sacredness of food and the sharing of food.

We will honor and nurture our lands, our waters, and the living soils from which our food arises.

We will honor and nurture the living ecosystem of plants, animals, and microorganisms that nourishes us.

We will honor and celebrate the natural cycles and seasons of life.

We will cherish, cultivate, and protect the conditions that make life possible and allow it to evolve.

We will love our living foodsheds into sustainability and resilience.

And we will do whatever we can to support our brothers and sisters everywhere who are reclaiming their food sovereignty and building their own regional foodsheds.

Together, we are the local food revolution.

CHAPTER 3

The Coming Revolution

Wendell Berry has written that eating is an agricultural act. I would also say that eating is a political act, but in the way the ancient Greeks used the word "political"—not just to mean having to do with voting in an election, but to mean "of, or pertaining to, all our interactions with other people"—from the family to the school, to the neighborhood, the nation, and the world. Every single choice we make about food matters, at every level. The right choice saves the world. Paul Cezanne said: "The day is coming when a single carrot, freshly observed, will set off a revolution." So let us all make our food decisions in that spirit: let us observe that carrot afresh, and make our choice.

—ALICE WATERS, "A DELICIOUS REVOLUTION"

SYRIA: A PROPHETIC PARABLE

The trouble that has been festering in Syria, now spreading throughout the world, began with a badly managed drought and a subsequent food crisis. We'll see this scenario played out again and again in the coming years.

The story is instructive. The worst drought in Syrian history devastates that country from 2006 to 2010. Farmers, desperate for water, begin to sink tens of thousands of new wells into shrinking aquifers.

Soon the water table drops so low their pumps can no longer lift water to the surface. Production plummets; food prices skyrocket.

In many areas of the Syrian countryside, all agriculture ceases. In other areas, crop failures reach 75 percent. As much as 85 percent of livestock die of thirst or hunger. Hundreds of thousands of farmers give up and flee to the cities, followed by millions of other rural inhabitants, who have been reduced to extreme poverty. Now climate refugees, they soon find themselves competing for scarce food, water, and jobs with an exploding foreign refugee population, including about 1.5 million people pouring in from Iraq.

Inevitably, hostilities erupt among those desperately competing just to survive. Urgent appeals to the United Nations and United States for aid go mostly unanswered.

And then the Syrian government makes the situation far worse. Lured by the high price of wheat on the world market, Assad decides to sell the country's grain reserves. This raises short-term cash, but in the following year, Syria has almost nothing to export. Beginning in 2008 and for the rest of the drought years, Syria has to import wheat to have any hope of keeping its citizens alive.

This situation creates a tinderbox, and the flashpoint comes on March 15, 2011, when a small group of people gathers in the town of Daraa to protest the Assad government's failure to help them. Assad ruthlessly cracks down on them as subversives. Riots then break out all over the country, which Assad attempts to quell with military force—but the effort fails, as the protesters are bolstered by outside help coming into the country.

This is just the beginning of the Arab Spring. The government quickly loses control of more than 30 percent of the country's rural areas and roughly half of its population.

As of today, perhaps half a million people have been killed in the fighting in Syria. Nearly eight million have been displaced from their homes, and an additional five million people have fled the country. Vast amounts of infrastructure have been destroyed, along with entire cities, like Aleppo. It's a growing disaster, a tragedy with global consequences.

We call it the Syrian Civil War, but it is arguably a consequence of global warming.

As highly respected senior foreign policy analyst William R. Polk writes, "If all that doesn't sound like a premonition of many more crises to come, I don't know what does."

For the last few years, I've been saying that what is called for is a *revolution*—a local food revolution. I'm not speaking of a rebellion or a revolt or violent extremism. I'm not speaking of taking to the streets in protest, smashing supermarket windows, blockading fast-food restaurants, setting fire to monocultured fields of GMO crops, laying our bodies down in front of an army of advancing combines during harvest, or hijacking and dumping truckloads of industrial food.

I'm *not* speaking of what in the 1960s was the rallying cry for many, coming out of the Berkeley Free Speech Movement, in the words of Mario Savio: "There's a time when the operation of the machine becomes so odious, makes you so sick at heart, that you can't take part, you can't even passively take part, and you've got to put your bodies upon the gears and upon the wheels, upon the levers, upon all the apparatus, and you've got to make it stop!"[6]

That's *not* where we're going—although at times we may be tempted.

What is needed is something far deeper and more fundamental and more effective and more generative and *re-generative* than all that.

Something is coming.

In the 1960s, Robert F. Kennedy said something prophetic that has haunted me for many years: "A revolution is coming—a revolution which will be peaceful if we are wise enough; compassionate if we care enough; successful if we are fortunate enough—but a revolution which is coming whether we will it or not. We can affect its character, we cannot alter its inevitability."[7]

A revolution is indeed coming, long overdue. And those of us working toward food localization are on the front lines of that revolution. Like it or not, we are revolutionaries.

LESSONS FROM THE AMERICAN REVOLUTION

Largely inspired by Woody Tasch's extraordinary essay of September 2014, "Commons Nth: Common Sense for a Post Wall Street World,"[8] I eagerly began reexploring the history of the American Revolution.

Tasch's essay, in the form of a modern pamphlet, began with these intriguing words: "When Thomas Paine's *Common Sense* went viral and sparked the American Revolution—more than a century before the first virus was discovered and two centuries before the term 'viral' would cause a gleam in the first blogger's eye—it set us upon a course of national discovery that produced historic benefits galore but ultimately left us short of that elusive goal: common sense."

In my inquiry, I learned that at the end of 1775—even though there was great tension and increasing violence between the British Empire and the American colonies—there was little discussion of *independence* in the colonies or in the Continental Congress. Apparently it was not considered a viable option. Almost all negotiation and debate was focused on somehow achieving *reconciliation* with the Crown.

But in January of 1776, Thomas Paine published *Common Sense,* a forty-six-page pamphlet calling for a complete break with Britain—*independence.* It was revolutionary thinking, and this publication indeed ignited a revolution. To begin, Paine published 120,000 copies of *Common Sense* in Philadelphia, which sold for two shillings each. By the time the Declaration of Independence was signed in July, more than half a million copies had been distributed—sold—throughout the thirteen colonies. That one essay changed the entire mood and direction and focus of the people; it rallied them together *to birth an independent nation.*

In those days, there was a great deal of public discourse going on in coffee houses and pubs. People came together in those very public places and vigorously debated the revolutionary ideas put forth in *Common Sense.* Others read the pamphlet to those who could not read for themselves. General George Washington even ordered copies distributed and read to his struggling troops in the field.

Common Sense galvanized a revolution and changed everything. *A publication can do that.*

As it happens, my roots are actually in the newspaper business. I grew up in Yuma, in northeastern Colorado, and went to work for our county's weekly newspaper, the *Yuma Pioneer*, when I was in the sixth grade—to the dismay of my parents. I worked there until after I graduated from high school. Later, I went to the University of Colorado in Boulder to study journalism—at a time when the journalism school had lost its accreditation (it now no longer exists). This was in the tumultuous late 1960s, and I worked for the *Colorado Daily* on campus as a photographer and copy editor. I eventually became a photojournalist, later a writer, and have been involved in publishing in many ways over the years, including helping to start a daily newspaper in New York City (which still exists today, though in another city). I think I can say that in my life I have learned something about the power of the independent press—and the power of catalytic or transformational communication, especially with my multimedia work for fast-growth corporations, particularly Apple.

EVOLUTIONARY REFLECTIONS

The evolutionary significance and impact of the American Revolution went far beyond the establishing of a new and independent nation. More deeply, it represented human freedom and sovereignty emerging on our planet—or at least *attempting* to emerge. That was the underlying evolutionary impulse, and it is still seeking its full expression today (we certainly aren't there yet).

Similarly, the local food revolution is part of something much larger and very widespread—the beginnings of an evolutionary transition on this planet. But it's still far below the radar of the media, academia, economists, developers, or planners.

For instance, when individuals pull all their money out of Wall Street, and when institutions divest completely from petroleum-based investments, that's revolutionary.

This evolutionary transition, on the other hand, is difficult to see (unless you're specifically looking for it), because our attention is constantly being diverted and even overwhelmed by the massive problems and converging crises we face—including the sixth mass extinction of species, the threat of environmental collapse, economic collapse, and even human population collapse.

The much-needed *revolution* in the way humanity feeds itself is a spontaneous uprising, already well under way, kindled by people who are discovering not only that the current global industrial food system is profoundly unsustainable and increasingly unstable but also that a truly regenerative solution is within our reach—the localization of our food supply. This is one of the most positive and inspiring and hopeful developments on the planet today.

Fundamentally, localizing our food supply is at the center of an effort to bring healing to our troubled world, to begin to reverse the widespread destruction caused by the industrial growth society. Food localization is so revolutionary because it's *regenerative*. It gets right to the heart of what needs to shift in our society and quietly goes to work.

And since food is what catalyzed human civilization in the first place, it's appropriate that the effort to *reverse* the damage our civilization has caused should also begin with food. It is the very foundation of human society. This makes localizing our food supply the most important and most urgent social cause of our time. And it's also one of the greatest *stories* of our time.

Here in Colorado, we have the great privilege to witness and even be a part of the awakening of a regional foodshed and the emergence of a true local food culture. That's a once-in-a-lifetime opportunity, perhaps once in a generation, maybe even once in a civilization!

When we hear the many stories of what's happening throughout the area, we are deeply moved—even though we are keenly aware that it's all in the early stages. In development. Under construction. *It's emerging.* And it's deeply inspiring to see.

But at the same time, we are often saddened, because it seems that so few people are aware of all this and what it means, even those who are directly involved. I have become persuaded that if we all knew more about what is emerging within our awakening foodsheds, we would be moved to come together with each other, learn from each other, inspire each other, and support each other. We would forge bonds of collaboration and deep connection that would ensure that this local food revolution would grow and prevail over the evil that has gripped our food supply and the very heart of our society.

It's also true that when we see what we're up against, what the odds are, it can seem completely overwhelming, even impossible. We're only at the very beginning of this revolution. And the revolution could fail.

PERIL AND PROMISE

This is an extraordinary moment in the history of this planet, a time of great peril and of great promise. And in this moment, many of us find ourselves being called in unexpected ways.

I sense that the conditions in this country right now are similar to what they were in early 1776, and that an enormous number of people are nearly ready to declare—en masse—our independence from the Unholy Alliance of Big Ag, Big Food, and Big Pharma that is responsible for creating the global industrial food system that is devastating the environment, destroying human health, and undermining our local economies. We understand that reconciliation with the Unholy Alliance—fixing the system—is not an option, and that *revolution is our only viable and responsible pathway forward.*

But here's what has never really been said before and must be said now:

In this local food revolution, we are not attempting to change or fix the global industrial food system. We're simply putting all our efforts into building our own food system, our own regional foodsheds.

We do not need to rise up against the Unholy Alliance. We're not declaring war; we're simply walking away. We are building something *new,* which they cannot understand and will never successfully co-opt—because it's authentic, home grown, and local. And it's exactly what people are hungry for.

We're resigning as "consumers," opting out of their system. We're leaving the field. In the past, we may have unconsciously been food slaves, but no longer. We are freeing ourselves, decolonizing. We are declaring our independence from the global industrial food system.

And this is what the Unholy Alliance fears most, for it represents how they are most vulnerable. They are losing control over our food supply, losing control over *us*. What a beautiful revolution!

This local food revolution is the front line of the struggle to preserve human freedom and sovereignty. It is here that we have the opportunity to begin reversing the profound damage that has been done to our planet and to ourselves since the Industrial Revolution began.

We could even say that food is at the heart of the struggle between the forces of goodness and evil on the planet. It's no wonder that localizing our food supply and reclaiming our food sovereignty and security are so damned difficult! There is great resistance to these efforts and even great opposition—some of it overt, but mostly covert, unspoken. Many of us working in this arena feel this opposition every day.

But this is not a war. It's a revolution, the beginnings of a great turning over. No one is telling us to do this. We simply know in our hearts that this must happen, no matter how difficult it might be, no matter how long it might take.

We understand that this is possibly a Sisyphean task, and that the odds are profoundly stacked against us. We know that the damage unleashed by the global food system is just beginning to become visible and that its consequences will accelerate and will be with us for a very long time. Climate change is *forever*. The environment will not go back to what it once was. The world will never be as it once was. And we, as a people, will never be the same.

But we also know that the process of regenerating the conditions conducive to what we know life can be begins right here, at the front lines of the local food revolution. This is where the healing begins. This is where we draw the line and declare that we're taking back our food supply. This is where we draw the line and say no to the global industrial food system. This where we draw the line and say that we are planting the seeds of our own living foodshed and that we will cultivate and nurture them until they become so deeply rooted that no one will ever be able to steal our food supply from us again. We shall become food sovereigns, secure in the knowledge that, as a people, we are able to meet our own essential food needs locally. This is freedom. And it begins right here, right now.

We've often heard it said that the local food revolution is a small part of something much bigger. I'd like us to consider that the stakes are actually much higher than that, higher than we've ever imagined. Perhaps the local food revolution is actually the *beginning* of something much larger, the beginning of a deep revolution in human civilization, coming at a moment of an evolutionary bottleneck on this planet. *And isn't it about time?*

∾

Our modern human civilization—which, in many ways, is crashing—began, ironically, with the birth of agriculture around 10,000 BCE. For many of us working in local food, this has been troubling, causing some to wonder if agriculture itself is the culprit. How could that be?

Daniel Quinn, the legendary author of *Ishmael*,[9] reports that humans had actually been practicing a sustainable form of agriculture for perhaps hundreds of thousands of years before this time. The form of agriculture that became prevalent around 10,000 BCE is what he calls "totalitarian agriculture," in which humans so dominate a particular region of land that it is capable of producing food only for humans, subordinating and displacing all other forms of life. The problem, says Quinn, is that such agricultural practices make it possible for more people to live in an area than the land can sustainably support, leading to rapid population growth and the birth of cities and creating the dynamics that inevitably lead to periodic famines.

But now, empowered by the extraordinary technological advancements of the Industrial Revolution and the information age, this kind of agriculture is the largest and most destructive industry on the planet, bringing us to Peak Everything and to the brink of global disaster and irreversible entropy.

Many scientists now argue that humanity's impact has grown to a planetary scale, to the point of beginning a new geological epoch, which most are calling the Anthropocene. Although there is some disagreement about precisely when it began, it brings to a close the Holocene epoch (the promising beginning of which was marked by the end of the last major ice age, some 11,700 years ago).

Historian and theologian Thomas Berry has poignantly noted "the radical discontinuity between the human and the non-human."[10] He sees this disconnect as the central pathology that has characterized human existence since the advent of agriculture. The cumulative effect over the last twelve thousand years—particularly the last three hundred—has even brought to an end the Cenozoic era, the long period of slow planetary recovery from the last mass extinction of species, including the dinosaurs, sixty-six million years ago.

This convergence of human forces has brought us to an evolutionary *bottleneck,* to the point where we're now facing a new mass extinction of species. We ourselves have caused it, and the survival of humanity itself is threatened. During this tumultuous Anthropocene epoch, human population will likely be significantly reduced, perhaps to preindustrial levels. Economic growth will cease. Agriculture will go through a radical transformation. We will have to adapt to the devastating impacts of climate change and environmental destruction. Collapse will become a very real possibility—ecosystem collapse, climate collapse, economic collapse, and population collapse.

If all this sounds like a hopeless scenario, take heart. One of the great environmental heroes of our time, Tim DeChristopher, helps provide some perspective here.

> There is no hope in avoiding collapse. If you look at the worst-case scenarios for climate change, those pretty much mean the collapse of our industrial civilization. But that doesn't mean the end of everything. It means that we're going to be living through the most rapid and intense period of change that humanity has ever faced. And that's certainly not hopeless. It means we're going to have to build another world in the ashes of this one. And it could very easily be a better world. I have a lot of hope in my generation's

ability to build a better world in the ashes of this one. And I have very little doubt that we'll have to. The nice thing about this is that this culture hasn't led to happiness anyway, it hasn't satisfied our human needs. So there's a lot of room for improvement.[11]

In this local food revolution, *we are not working to bring about change.* Change is coming, whether we want it or not—profound change. Food localization is essentially about preparing ourselves and our communities for the unstoppable changes of the winter of the Anthropocene. More deeply, it's about creating the conditions that will ensure a spring on the other side.

If we manage to successfully negotiate the dangerous transition of the Anthropocene, we may eventually find ourselves in what Thomas Berry and mathematical cosmologist Brian Swimme have called the Ecozoic epoch, during which humanity will live in a mutually enhancing relationship with the earth and the earth community. This would be a period of planetary healing and regeneration, a time of recovery from the damage inflicted by our industrial growth society, a return to honoring the sacredness of life. Then, perhaps, the profound evolutionary potential of the human species—which has been mostly obscured—can at last begin to become evident. That sounds like spring to me.

But what could lead us into the Ecozoic epoch? Virtually all of our great social change movements—the environmental movement, the climate movement, the social justice movement—are all sadly ineffective and in decline, essentially energetically bankrupt.

Micah White, the cocreator of Occupy Wall Street—arguably the largest global protest movement in human history—now declares that even protest is broken and that what must now arise is a revolution inspired by the Divine, a deep revolution. The local food revolution could ignite just that.

Perhaps the local food revolution could have a catalytic impact on other movements, far beyond what we usually consider.

WHAT IS BEING ASKED OF US

This local food revolution is not ideological; it's not metaphorical; and it's certainly not just a lifestyle movement. This is real. This matters, and it's happening right now.

The local food revolution opens a doorway—maybe not the only doorway, but one of the most inviting and wide open these days—and heralds the deep revolution that is soon upon us. The local food revolution is a center of aliveness in the midst of a dying civilization. It provides more than hope; it is a revelation of the deeper meaning and purpose and presence that lie ahead, emerging mysteriously out of a convergence of seed, soil, soul, and stars. Nothing could be more organic. Nothing could be more grounded. Nothing could be more connected. Nothing could be more important. Nothing could be more urgent.

This awareness is precisely what many in the local food movement are awakening to, but almost no one speaks of it—not yet. Many of us already know it at a deep inner level, but we have not allowed ourselves to think it explicitly, let alone to give it voice. But I am certain that we all *feel* it.

A real revolution is a rare thing. It asks something of us, and it will not be possible for any of us to remain neutral. It's no accident that those who signed the Declaration of Independence pledged their lives, their fortunes, and their sacred honor. And for many of them, the personal cost was enormous.

Real revolutions are not based on economics, politics, or ideologies. Fundamentally, they are driven by moral, ethical, and even spiritual values. Real revolutions are *called* into being. And the truth is that we in the local food revolution are being mobilized by something greater than ourselves. It is perhaps the greatest calling in human history, a calling that radically reorganizes our intentions, our priorities, and our actions.

In a time of revolution, we are called, challenged to respond. And then we decide whether we can support the fundamental aims and values of the revolution and whether we will become revolutionaries ourselves—that is, whether we will allow ourselves to become so aligned with the deeper evolutionary thrust of the revolution that we seek not to control it but to contribute to it, to support it, to give to it, to be connected with it in heart, mind, body, and soul. And to make whatever commitments, promises, and even sacrifices that are necessary.

THE SACRED AT THE CENTER

> An activism that is not purified by profound spiritual and psychological self-awareness and rooted in divine truth, wisdom, and compassion will only perpetuate the problem it is trying to solve, however righteous its intentions. When, however, the deepest and most grounded spiritual vision is married to a practical and pragmatic drive to transform all existing political, economic and social institutions, a holy force—the power of wisdom and love in action—is born. This force I define as Sacred Activism.
>
> —ANDREW HARVEY, *THE HOPE: A GUIDE TO SACRED ACTIVISM*

> We will never restore the ability of America's agriculture to meet the needs of people, its ultimate source of effectiveness and efficiency, until we restore its respect for life. We can never restore its respect for life until we restore its soul. Within the crisis in American agriculture is the opportunity to reclaim its spiritual roots.
>
> —JOHN IKERD

Part of the purpose of the local food revolution is to restore food to its rightful place in our society. We are moving away from a food system that disconnects us from the land, cuts us off from the natural cycles of life, alienates us from nature, hollows out our communities, and destroys our relationships with each other. The revolution will bring food home again, so that it is grown on farms close to where we live (if not in our own yards) and by people who we know and trust and love, so that it is joyfully prepared, mostly in our own kitchens; gratefully shared with neighbors, friends, and family; received into our lives in ways that nourish body, mind, and soul—so that food once again becomes sacred, sacramental, and central to the life of our communities and, in time, central to the life of our society.

There is another important reason the focus of this revolution is on food, and this perhaps eclipses all the others: food is not a commodity. We could even say that *food is sacred.* Food is what connects us with life itself. Most people today eat food that is highly processed; shipped from thousands of miles away; adulterated with chemical pesticides, insecticides, and fertilizers; and genetically modified to the point that our bodies can barely recognize it as food. And if we eat such food, we understand that it plays a crucial role in disconnecting us—every day—from life, from nature, from the land, and from our brothers and sisters.

Wendell Berry reminds us that eating is an agricultural act. Others have suggested that eating is a moral or ethical act. Perhaps it's time for us to consider eating as a *sacramental* act. For eating to be sacramental (or moral or ethical) requires our honoring awareness of the connection to life itself that food provides, and our honoring awareness of the entire process by which our food is created and comes to our table. This is not about mere physical sustenance or nutrition, but actual connection.

Food is the means whereby the gifts of sun, soil, water, and labor converge and are released into our being to make possible our life in this world. The entire process of growing and preparing and eating food could be regarded as the transubstantiation of the soul and spirit of the universe into the flesh and blood and bone of living beings, whereby all beings—literally and figuratively—become food for other beings. We all eat, and we all are ultimately eaten—if we allow nature to take its course. But we are not merely consumed; we are transmuted, transubstantiated.

We have largely lost touch with this aspect of human life and have become unconscious of the great network of relationships and processes that provides us with food. Most people within the industrial food network have lost their connection with the sacredness of food as well. In that system, only profits are considered nourishing.

Food is sacred. We need to make eating sacramental again and come to regard farming and ranching, along with preparing and cooking food, as nothing less than spiritual practice. And those of us who are involved in localizing our food supply must place this realization at the center of our work—or we ourselves, no matter how lofty our intentions, will likely only contribute to the commoditization of food and our disconnection from life itself.

Wendell Berry insists there is no non-sacred food. For him, there is only sacred food and desecrated food. Desecrated food disconnects, weakens body and mind. Sacred food connects, strengthens body, mind, soul, and spirit.

Increasingly, we all want food that brings us into connection with life, land, and community. Increasingly, we are discovering that food is about trust and relationship. Food, it turns out, is sacred connection.

Carolyn Baker eloquently speaks of this in an essay called "The Sanctity of Food."

> Something in our ancient memory understands that mindlessly manufactured and technologically tortured so-called food constitutes the most profane of substances which are unfit to be ingested in human bodies. The more deeply immersed we are in the sanctity of food and its origins, the more we are likely to be repelled by processed, genetically modified, and chemically laden foods that have been produced by way of massive resource and ecological destruction, and which deliver more of the same to our physiology.... The sacred within us instinctively resonates with the sanctity of food. Therefore, the growing, transporting, distribution, and consumption of food are sacred acts that deserve ritual and reverence from the moment the seed is planted in the earth to the moment we have washed and put away the plate on which our food was served.[12]

We're localizing our food supply, birthing a living foodshed, and restoring food to its fundamental sacredness in our society. A living foodshed provides myriad pathways for the sacred to tunnel into physical reality to bring healing, restoration, and regeneration. It is a visible manifestation of the inevitable unfolding of redemption.

This is sacred work. This is the kind of revolution of which we are a part. This is the deeper revolution that we serve.

CHAPTER 4

Note to the Reader

We find ourselves in an excruciating position, you and I. We have awakened in a magnificent and unimaginably beautiful world that is now undergoing its most devastating crisis in the last sixty-six million years—since the dinosaurs became extinct. Worse, we learn that the cause of this unfolding devastation is us—the manner and magnitude in which we have been living on the planet.

Meanwhile, human civilization itself seems to be beginning to unravel. We can see that humanity is on the brink of collapse, possibly extinction, and that we might even undermine the prospects for all future life on earth. Charting the ever-worsening trajectory of these trends can be quite disheartening. It's an unfathomable situation, and it sometimes drives us to our knees, weeping.

Mysteriously, though, we seem somehow incapable of succumbing to acquiescence or despair, for we know that we are seeing all this and feeling all this for a reason. Purpose lurks behind the scenes.

Surely each of us is culpable in our shared crisis, but there is more that blooms in our awareness these days, something far more unsettling. It is as if each of us grappling with these realizations has been sent here at precisely this moment in history because we bear some gift to deliver, something unique and necessary, something essential. Whether this will remain an unopened package remains to be seen—and the world awaits the outcome.

Meanwhile, we are caught between two worlds—on the one hand, a cloying and dysfunctional world that perhaps most of us never truly felt a part of, and on the other, a new world looming on the horizon that is by turns threatening and exhilarating. Somehow we find ourselves drawn to simultaneously hospice the old and midwife the new—and perhaps even to illuminate the choice between them. For many of us, this is often terribly disorienting.

Ironically, in the face of all this, we somehow find ourselves called to be leaders or organizers or catalysts or communicators or facilitators. Some people seem to look to us because they sense that we see something, perhaps know something—when mostly we just *feel*. We often respond to this calling reluctantly, hesitatingly, incredulous that it might just somehow come down to us after all.

But there is little choice. We know unequivocally that we have much work to do, and time is growing short. Never mind that we do not know if it is already too late. In these dark moments of a waning era, much depends on our response, our ability to find and cocreate with others who are similarly called—in whatever arena we have been drawn to.

We are *evolutionary catalysts*. There is a future that longs to be born in us and through us, a future that began in the Initial Flaring Forth nearly fourteen billion years ago, a future that has been steadily unfolding and accelerating right through to this day. We bear the seeds of that future within us. Where will we plant ourselves?

Perhaps, as systems scientist Peter Senge suggests, *if we can find our place, we will find our purpose.*[13] This book is about finding our place and delivering our as-yet-unnamed gift in that place—hopefully in time.

❧

How humanity will feed itself in an increasingly uncertain future is perhaps the single most urgent challenge of our time, but it seems that only a handful of people on the planet can currently see this. It's well known, of course, that hundreds of millions of people go hungry every day; that poverty and food insecurity are inextricably linked; and that, as human population soars toward a projected nine or ten billion people by the middle of the century, the demand for food production will rapidly increase.

Given what we now know, it is undeniable that what is urgently needed is a widespread revolution in the way humanity feeds itself. What is needed is a revolutionary movement to localize the global food supply to the greatest extent possible, starting in our own communities. This book was written to inspire, guide, and empower those individuals who are awakening to these realities and are beginning to face the daunting challenge of localizing our food supply—forging a new and regenerative way for humanity to feed itself.

The truth is that this work is far more difficult than almost anyone is willing to discuss. It's so easy to get buoyed up by all the great projects bursting into existence everywhere, from CSAs to farm-to-school programs. And they do indeed give us hope. But when we allow ourselves to look at the scale of what has actually been achieved so far (Vermont at only 7 percent food localization is a particularly stunning example—and they lead the nation), it's clear that our efforts are minuscule in the face of the immensity and inertia of the industrial food system.

What's more, as we will see, the global situation is far worse than we've apprehended. We've naively overridden our inner knowing to the point that we've accepted the claims of marketers and propagandists. There is no way to avoid the reality that converging global crises are rapidly becoming calamities. We're in for a rough ride on this planet, and there is likely no way to avoid catastrophic population reduction in the next few decades. There will be no soft landing.

Nevertheless, the work we are doing is crucial—even if the likelihood of failure is high.

ᐯ

We may have already failed, in terms of metrics. What we are attempting may turn out to be utterly impossible. But such is the realm of the evolutionary catalyst. I recall a famous quote (sometimes attributed to Winston Churchill) from an earlier global struggle: "Leadership is the ability to go from failure to failure without losing enthusiasm." So it is for us. We may completely fail a thousand times before we ever experience a systemic success. And yet we know that this is precisely how evolution works, relentlessly seeking to emerge through countless transitional entities. We ourselves are such transitional entities, and we must be willing to be used for this purpose. We serve something greater than what can be measured or even visible in this lifetime.

Do these seem harsh words? I hope not, for they are offered with deep compassion for the individuals who take them into their being. Do these seem the words of someone depressed or one who has experienced inordinate failure? While I can confirm that I have occasionally felt that way, those feelings are generally fleeting, and I am repeatedly brought back to center, with an all-encompassing perspective that reminds me that I am an integral part of the flow of evolution itself. Evolution is an unstoppable force.

One of my local heroes is Dana Miller, the founder of Transition Denver and a dynamic and successful organization called Grow Local Colorado. When we first met her several years ago, she was a former airline stewardess enjoying her retirement. Then she went to a conference in Denver called Earthworks Expo, where she heard Richard Heinberg and me give back-to-back presentations. As she tells it, she was so shaken that she went home and cried for three days. *Then she got to work.* She is now an extraordinary leader in preparing Denver for what's coming. Dana is an evolutionary catalyst. And our involvement in her activation is as mysterious to me as it is to her. So it often is with evolutionary catalysts.

❧

The primary consideration for planning this book is a single question: what do local food revolutionaries need?

- We need *context,* concise but comprehensive perspective that connects the dots and makes sense out of a complex global situation. We need to understand the advent of the global food system and its catastrophic impacts on human society and the entire biosphere, because seeing the present systemically is crucial to creating the future. And as environmental activist and Buddhist scholar Joanna Macy says, seeing the deeper pattern that connects many different problems is crucial if we are to move beyond piecemeal reactions and create far-reaching transformation.

- We need *meaning,* confirmation that the nagging sense we feel of being drawn to this issue is real and rightful and important, a revelation that we are, in fact, evolutionary catalysts with a significant contribution to make.

- We need *hope,* to be able to see that a revolutionary and evolutionary process is unfolding in unexpected ways. We need to see that the local food revolution is indeed emerging and that it is far bigger and is moving far more quickly than almost all of us had realized. We need to feel that localizing the global food supply is both necessary and possible—even inevitable.

- We need *inspiration,* examples of what is possible, other catalysts who are innovating and creating pathways that we can follow.

- We need a *vision* of the revolutionary impact that food localization can have, and we need a sense that this is perhaps the most important social cause on the planet today, an opportunity to contribute meaningfully and strategically at the most crucial moment in human evolution. We need to see what's possible. We need to learn how to simultaneously hold inspirational visions of a positive future and the uncomfortable truth about current reality.

- We need a *detailed map* of the process by which food localization can be accomplished, along with guidance in implementing that process.

- We need a *pattern language* for food localization, a way to visualize and talk about the deeper patterns of present reality and the emerging future, which will open the way to learning how to think together in the process.

- We need *guidance* in collaborative, cocreative, co-learning group process. The work will require passion and patience, for we will be moving together toward aims that have deep meaning for us and opening ourselves to ideas that may seem foreign and even threatening. And it requires the courage to act without having all the answers, moving beyond the usual approach of figuring out the answer and then implementing it. The collaborative process is, above all, a learning process, which calls us to venture into difficult and uncharted territory with openness and humility, continually discovering the pathways forward.

- We need *motivation* to develop necessary skills, especially in seeing and thinking systemically, cultivating the ability to see

systems and creative process as natural and essential comple-
ments to one another.

- We need the *clarity* and *discernment* to tap into what we truly
want and what is truly needed. In other words, we need to cultivate the *discipline* of being evolutionary catalysts.

- We need *confidence* in our own power and purpose; and with
this confidence, we need courage and determination.

- We need a *way to begin* right where we are, the beginnings of a
plan that emerges from the core of our being.

- We need *choices* that we can make immediately, actions we can
take now, as well as others we can work our way up to.

- We need *connection* with other evolutionary catalysts.

- We need *access* to informational and inspirational resources,
along with tools, processes and programs we can implement in
our communities. As Buckminster Fuller said, "If you want to
teach people a new way of thinking, don't bother to teach them.
Instead, give them a tool, the use of which will lead to new ways
of thinking."

- We need an *experiential sense* that we are part of something
revolutionary, that we belong to this, that this represents who
we truly are.

- We need *wisdom* from those who have gone before, from elders
of the tribe of evolutionary catalysts.

These are the things that *The Local Food Revolution* attempts to
offer. What is pointed to here can't fit between the covers, so please
consider this book a doorway to an expanded universe, a doorway to
deep engagement.

ॐ

Peter Senge says that *problem solving* is about making what you don't
want go away and that *creating* involves bringing something you care
about into reality. If this is true, then what is *catalyzing?* We could say
that catalyzing is an evolutionary strategy that calls for serving and
aligning with what is attempting to emerge in us and through us—both
what is needed and what is truly wanted.

❦

The heart of this book, part six, "Field Notes for the Emergence of a Foodshed," is a very preliminary exploration of the process by which a regional foodshed comes into being. Learning to see food localization as an emergent process of healing and regeneration liberates us from the crushing enormity of what we face. It is easy to feel overwhelmed when we come to grips with the magnitude of the challenge of localizing our food supply and beginning to reverse the trajectory of decades of domination by the global food system.

In seeing the underlying structure of this localization process—which mirrors emergent processes in nature—we can learn to identify where we are, regionally, and to begin to chart pathways through the complexities of the work, anticipating what will be needed in the future. We learn there is a kind of seasonality to all this, just as there is an appropriate time for soil building, for planting, for cultivating, for harvesting, and for celebrating.

This section of the book is inspired in no small measure by the breakthrough work of renowned architect Christopher Alexander, whose book *A Pattern Language* has, for nearly forty years, been a classic for designers and builders of many different disciplines, particularly for practitioners and teachers of permaculture. This foundational text led to our beginning to map a kind of pattern language for food localization. But Alexander's magnum opus, a recent four-volume series, *The Nature of Order,* more completely informs the deeper nature of our work, as we explore how humans can collaboratively shape systems and structures that generate wholeness and aliveness. We apply these principles to the creation of a localized foodshed.

We see that the awakening of a foodshed is an event of great historical and planetary significance. We discover that food localization can be seen as the evolution of the universe itself at work in us and through us. In these troubled times, there is perhaps no arena of life where the potential for human evolution—and restoration and regeneration—is more timely or holds more meaning and potential.

I would even say that localizing our food supply is right at the leading edge of human evolution. In one sense, it is a battleground, a matter of survival. But in another sense, it's an opportunity for the human community to rise to an occasion that can only be considered an evolutionary crossroads.

⟧

The essence of all these patterns is *relationship*, relationships of a particular quality. What is emerging through the process is a network of relationships that forms the underlying structure of an emerging foodshed. Everything that happens toward the building of the local foodshed is in service of these relationships. And the structure of everything that is created along the way is to catalyze and facilitate and nurture these relationships. This is how community is rewoven into a society where it has been absent for so long that we can scarcely recognize it.

Perhaps the reason that local food work is so attractive and so satisfying is that it is really about recovering our very humanity and all else that has been lost with the rise of industrial civilization.

⟧

We're a long way from achieving a significant degree of food localization in Colorado. But we're on the path. Things are moving, and I'm astonished at what's emerging in our midst. It is my hope that what we're doing here can become something of a whole-systems demonstration project, which can serve as a model for a food revolution in communities and foodsheds everywhere.

We don't know, however, if food localization will happen in our area quickly enough or at significant enough scale to avert disaster. We just don't know. It's something of a Hail Mary pass. We're moving as quickly as we can, paying attention as best we can, and catalyzing the emergence of food localization in every way we can.

It's such an adventure, such a joy to be involved in this effort. And it's by far the most difficult and challenging thing we've ever done in our lives. But it's happening. We are part of it, deeply implicated. It's a privilege to give our lives in this way.

And we look forward to working with you. You, together with us and many others, are the foundation of emerging localized foodsheds. Together, we are igniting the revolution in how our society feeds itself.

PART 2

THE MAKING OF AN EVOLUTIONARY CATALYST

I do not have the credentials for writing this book. Nor do I know anyone who does. But someone had to give it a try.

—LESTER R. BROWN, PREFACE TO *PLAN B: RESCUING A PLANET UNDER STRESS AND A CIVILIZATION IN TROUBLE*

CHAPTER 5

Beginnings: The Convergence
of Global Crises

In early 2005, I was sitting with Marshall Vian Summers (then a virtu-ally unknown spiritual teacher) in his backyard in Boulder, Colorado. In the midst of a casual and pleasant conversation, he suddenly became very serious and said, "What do you know about peak oil, and what are you doing to prepare?" A strange question from a spiritual teacher!

His words stung, and my mind snapped to attention. I knew that this was going to be one of those moments in which everything would change.

I was embarrassed to admit that I knew little about the topic, although I had seen it discussed peripherally during our exploration of the Y2K crisis. "I suggest you do your homework," he said flatly. Clearly he had done his own—and he wasn't talking about just fossil fuel depletion, but a host of related issues that together amounted to an evolutionary threshold for humanity.

I left his home reeling, with nothing to do but share this directive with Lynette Marie Hanthorn (my decades-long partner and cocre-ator),[14] remembering that Marshall once had said, "The purpose of a spiritual teacher is to throw the student into chaos."

We knew how to do our homework by then; we had most recently honed those skills as we researched the possibility of a cascading system breakdown after Y2K. We had learned enough in 1998–1999 to know Y2K was a real crisis, that major corporations were spending hundreds of millions of dollars in a race with the clock, and that programmers around the world were terrified that they might not be able to get the job done in time. We had learned just how fragile the systems were that ran almost everything in our modern world and how warnings about this computer flaw had been ignored for decades until it was very likely too late to fix it.

Y2K turned out to be a nonevent, but it had been a close call. The lessons of this near-disaster had been swept away by a tide of ridicule and relief. Ironically, nary a book was published on how the Y2K bug had been fixed (an army of eager and poorly paid programmers in India rose to the occasion—and birthed the outsourcing industry in the process).

In the run-up to Y2K, we had a quiet but persistent intuition that a catastrophic breakdown would be averted, even though we didn't quite know how. But this premonition was accompanied by a much more disturbing feeling: that our learning, our preparation, and the workshops we created were somehow all part of a warm-up exercise for something much bigger, yet to be revealed. This feeling never left us, and when the clock struck midnight at the end of 1999 and virtually nothing happened, we realized that we were entering uncharted territory.

Along the way, we had developed a weekend workshop, "Y2K: The Opportunity of a Lifetime," which was designed to move people through their unconscious fears about change and get them out of paralysis and actively reconnected with their life purpose. Many found this workshop useful. We had even published a book, *Just in Case: Dispatches From the Front Lines of the Y2K Crisis,* an anthology of essays from some of the most important thinkers of the day, including Tom Atlee,[15] Meg Wheatley,[16] and U.S. Senator Robert Bennett.

So yes, we knew how to do our homework. But confronted with peak oil, we were starting nearly from scratch. We dug deep and wide, and it didn't take us long to realize that fossil fuel depletion was merely the presenting symptom of a world careening into catastrophic crisis, a converging set of circumstances for which there was no solution and instead demanded radical and urgent adaptation. The more we learned, the worse the situation appeared. Of course, it was not just peak oil; it was Peak Everything—an unprecedented convergence of global crises. This was, we realized, the overarching crisis for which we had been preparing all our lives.

One of the seminal pieces of journalism we were moved by in those days was Dale Allen Pfeiffer's 2003 essay "Eating Fossil Fuels."[17] Actually, a friend of ours, architect and private pilot Harry Jordan, had sent us a battered printout of the essay in 2004, but somehow we had never taken the time to study it thoroughly. This time, however, we were paying attention.

Some brief excerpts from Pfeiffer's essay:

In a very real sense, we are literally eating fossil fuels. However, due to the laws of thermodynamics, there is not a direct correspondence between energy inflow and outflow in agriculture. Along the way, there is a marked energy loss. Between 1945 and 1994, energy input to agriculture increased 4-fold while crop yields only increased 3-fold. Since then, energy input has continued to increase without a corresponding increase in crop yield. We have reached the point of marginal returns. Yet, due to soil degradation, increased demands of pest management and increasing energy costs for irrigation ... modern agriculture must continue increasing its energy expenditures simply to maintain current crop yields. The Green Revolution is becoming bankrupt....

The U.S. food system consumes ten times more energy than it produces in food energy. This disparity is made possible by nonrenewable fossil fuel stocks....

Former prairie lands, which constitute the bread basket of the United States, have lost one half of their topsoil after farming for about 100 years. This soil is eroding 30 times faster than the natural formation rate.... Soil erosion and mineral depletion removes about $20 billion worth of plant nutrients from U.S. agricultural soils every year. Much of the soil in the Great Plains is little more than a sponge into which we must pour hydrocarbon-based fertilizers in order to produce crops....

As the population expands, an estimated one acre of land will be lost for every person added to the U.S. population. Currently, there are 1.8 acres of farmland available to grow food for each U.S. citizen. By 2050, this will decrease to 0.6 acres. 1.2 acres per person is required in order to maintain current dietary standards....

Does our present lifestyle mean so much to us that we would subject ourselves and our children to this fast approaching tragedy simply for a few more years of conspicuous consumption?

Pfeiffer's question haunts me to this day. And from an objective viewpoint, today's answer is not especially hopeful.

Michael C. Ruppert, author of *Crossing the Rubicon: The Decline of the American Empire at the End of the Age of Oil,* who originally published the essay on his website, *From the Wilderness,* called it, "the single most frightening article I have ever read and certainly the most alarming piece that [we have] ever published."

Pfeiffer himself wrote at the end of his essay,

> This is possibly the most important article I have written to date. It is certainly the most frightening, and the conclusion is the bleakest I have ever penned. This article is likely to greatly disturb the reader; it has certainly disturbed me. However, it is important for our future that this paper should be read, acknowledged and discussed. I am by nature positive and optimistic. In spite of this article, I continue to believe that we can find a positive solution to the multiple crises bearing down upon us. Though this article may provoke a flood of hate mail, it is simply a factual report of data and the obvious conclusions that follow from it.

We would come back to this essay (and the book it later inspired[18]) again and again over the years. But I must admit that at the time, the essay, even with its discussion of food, did not immediately compel us to focus on food. We felt that localizing the food supply would simply be a part of a much broader relocalization effort. I would even say that we initially overlooked the significance of what Pfeiffer was pointing to. It would take us some years to come to realize that food localization is perhaps the most urgent and important issue of our time and, furthermore, that addressing it opens the pathways to resolving our collective human predicament.

∾

Because of what we were learning in early 2005, we almost immediately began reorganizing how we lived, reducing our carbon footprint, downscaling, and simplifying. We even moved from the large suburban home we were renting to a mobile home in Boulder.

We also dusted off our emergency Y2K rations, which we had bought from a writer friend in early January 2000—she had convinced herself that there was no longer a reason to be prepared, that it had somehow all been a huge mistake.

After a few months of reorganizing our lives, all the while deepening our research, we felt a terrible tension building. It was apparent that peak oil was but the beginning of what would be a massive course-correction in human evolution, and we struggled to understand how we might be able to respond in any truly meaningful way. We sensed that something greater than lifestyle changes could be asked of us.

Several months later, I had a follow-up conversation with Marshall. With all the passion I could muster, I explained what we had been learning and what we had been doing to make new arrangements in our lives to prepare for the coming crisis. He listened quietly, not even nodding—with no reaction at all. I had expected that he would be pleased.

He waited patiently until I finally stopped talking. "That's fine," he said quietly. "But what are you doing to prepare your *community?*"

I may never be able to explain what happened for me in that moment—the burning in my chest, the flood of images from childhood dreams, memories of intimations of this time, the regret of missed opportunities. But that moment in Marshall's backyard was a profound turning point in our lives.

The rest of that conversation remains lost to me, and I don't even remember going home to tell Lynette Marie what had happened. But I do know that we immediately united our lives around this calling. I'm sure we talked for days, attempting to grasp what it all meant and how we should proceed.

Marshall had suggested that we might form some sort of organization to begin the process of preparation, focusing on developing public education, creating a community plan, and producing a replicable neighborhood preparation model. But because we were in Boulder, a mecca of environmental activism, we felt that a better strategy might be to join one of the many local groups who surely were already working on it. To our dismay, we quickly learned that apparently no organization in Boulder was even discussing peak oil or converging global crises, let alone preparing for what was coming. This was a terrible shock, for we realized that we would have to form a group to begin organizing a massive preparation effort in an environment where almost no one was talking about these issues. We felt inadequate to take on such a challenge.

Failing to find a local group, we began searching online for a national or international organization focused on these issues and quickly stumbled upon the Post Carbon Institute in Vancouver, Canada, founded by Julian Darley. To our delight, not only was Darley developing an international Relocalization Network, but he was also the coauthor of *Relocalize Now! Getting Ready for Climate Change and the End of Cheap Oil.*[19] Darley's words were encouraging.

> Bearing this knowledge on one's own is a heavy burden. If we are to have any chance of changing the course of civilization, we must work together to build a global and locally grounded movement. The outpost program offers a way for you to collaborate with people in your community and in a worldwide network to raise awareness and work for a better, more local future. Should you decide to take this on, our intent is to support you in making an immediate positive difference in your community and having an enjoyable and rewarding experience. It won't be easy, but the potential upside—a future worth living for ourselves, our children and life on the planet—merits our every effort and deepest commitment.

Little more than a year later, prolific peak-oil writer Sharon Astyk would say, after she met Julian Darley, that he seemed like "one of the most overextended people in human history." That certainly described him well. "Despite that," she wrote to us, "he's very nice. Much, much,

much nicer than I could be if I had as many balls in the air as he did, and as many people who want to add more balls. And he handled his overextension astonishingly well—not only are all these balls in the air, but he's juggling with both hands and feet." I have come to identify with that description a little.

We were also encouraged to read that Richard Heinberg (author of *Powerdown: Options and Actions for a Post-Carbon World*) had proclaimed Post Carbon Institute to be "clearly the first medic on the scene, the first organized response to Peak Oil."[20]

We quickly connected with Darley and his wife, Celine Rich, and began exploring how our nascent organization could form an official affiliation with the institute's Relocalization Network. The tag line for their organization in those early days was "Reduce consumption, produce locally." Some took that as a kind of tough love. This early movement was driven by people whom Darley called "the walking worried."

The literature of peak oil in 2005 was rich and provocative. One of the key themes was expressed by James Howard Kunstler in an interview about his book *The Long Emergency*.

> There are at least two major mental disturbances in the collective American mind these days that can be described with some precision. One is the Jiminy Cricket syndrome—the idea that when you wish upon a star your dreams come true. This is largely a product of the technological achievements of the last century, which were themselves a product of cheap energy: namely, things like our trip to the moon, combined with the effects of advertising, Hollywood and pop culture. We have now become a people who believe that wishing for things makes them happen. Unfortunately, the world just doesn't work that way. The truth is that no combination of alternative fuels or so-called renewables will allow us to run the U.S.A.—or even a substantial fraction of it—the way that we're running it now....
>
> There's another mental disturbance that Americans are suffering from. It's the idea that it's possible to get something for nothing—unearned riches, free energy, perpetual motion—and it's

exemplified by Las Vegas. Combine the Jiminy Cricket syndrome and the idea that it's possible to get something for nothing and you end up with a population that's thoroughly deluded and unable to deal with reality. That's precisely where we're at.[21]

The concept of the Jiminy Cricket and something-for-nothing syndromes gave us a handle on grappling with the overwhelming *denial* we knew we would experience as we moved into the work. For us, Kunstler remains one of the true thought leaders in the relocalization movement, and his *World Made by Hand* novel series continues to stimulate productive contemplation and discussion among his readers.

In those early days of our peak-oil journey, a crucial source of in-depth information, which we relied upon almost daily, was *The Oil Drum,* a massive website "devoted to analysis and discussion of energy and its impact on society," founded (we learned much later) by Kyle Saunders, a political science professor at Colorado State University, who wrote under the pen name "Prof. Goose." We were particularly struck by what he wrote in an essay in July 2005.

> People will never spontaneously take action themselves unless they receive social support and the validation of others. Governments in turn will continue to procrastinate until sufficient numbers of people demand a response. To avert further problems will require a degree of social consensus and collective determination normally only seen in war time, and that will require mobilization across all classes and sectors of society. For all these reasons, the creation of a large and vocal peak oil movement must be an immediate and overarching campaign objective. People will not accept the reality of the problem unless they see that others are engaging in activities that reflect its seriousness. This means they need to be confronted by emotionally charged activities: debate, protest, and meaningful, visible alternatives. Anyone concerned about this issue faces a unique historical opportunity to break the cycle of denial, and join

the handful of people who have already decided to stop being passive bystanders. The last century was marked by self-deception and mass denial. There is no need for the 21st Century to follow suit.[22]

This was helpful, for we were beginning to realize that a major part of the job ahead would be breaking the cycle of denial that held our society in its grip—especially in the United States. However, we were skittish about the prospect of debate and protest; we would later carefully consider those confrontational avenues and reject them to focus on what Prof. Goose called "meaningful, visible alternatives."

Worth remembering: "Peak oil and climate change put a mirror up to our lives and the society around us, enabling us to grasp that what we had seen as being permanent and real is in fact a fragile illusion, dependent on long supply lines and an uninterrupted flow of cheap oil. When you see the illusory nature of the world around you, it can leave you feeling bewildered."[23]

About a month later, as Hurricane Katrina was roaring through the Gulf of Mexico toward New Orleans, a handful of volunteers (Marshall Summers among them) fanned out into a north Boulder neighborhood with flyers inviting residents to attend "a special educational Peak Energy event" presented by the newly formed ad hoc group Boulder Valley Relocalization. This group was a new "outpost" of Post Carbon Institute's Relocalization Network, which was convening "an ongoing global conversation on relocalization strategies and action among and within communities" (we were the fourteenth organization in the world to join, as I recall). The invitation of our flyer said, "Join North Boulder neighbors as we explore the end of cheap energy, the end of the 3,000-mile Caesar salad—and the future of Boulder Valley."

About thirty people showed up at the meeting hall, across the street from a run-down trailer park colloquially known as Dogpatch. They were treated to poignant clips from the startling but little-known documentary, *The End of Suburbia: Oil Depletion and the Collapse of the American Dream,* which was largely inspired by James Howard Kunstler's blockbuster 2004 book, *The Long Emergency: Surviving the Converging Catastrophes of the 21st Century.* We also presented a hard-hitting video interview with prominent researcher Richard Heinberg, describing a path of self-restraint, cooperation, and sharing: "the comprehensive downscaling, rescaling, downsizing, and relocalizing of all our activities, a radical reorganization of the way we live in the most fundamental particulars."[24] For several people in the audience, the evening was a life-changing experience.

At that first meeting, we were able to fairly accurately predict the sudden escalation of oil and gasoline prices that Katrina would cause, which perhaps made us seem like prophets. But in reality, we were simply following the data, tracking the hurricane's path through the Gulf of Mexico, carefully watching the projections of weather experts, petroleum geologists, and market traders, and noting the systematic shutdowns of oil platforms and refineries well in advance of the storm.

We had no real way of knowing what would happen after this first gathering, of course, but early on we decided we would hold regular public meetings to discuss the implications of peak oil and peak energy and to begin mounting a community response. We asked attendees to bring friends, neighbors, and coworkers to subsequent meetings, and by the end of September, we were able to attract more than two hundred people to a public awareness event at the University of Colorado's Fiske Planetarium. It helped greatly that Katrina had knocked out much of oil production in the Gulf—just as we had predicted—driving gas prices to $6 per gallon in some places. Our keynote speaker was Steve Andrews, one of the cofounders of the U.S. branch of the Association for the Study of Peak Oil (ASPO), which was preparing to host a World Oil Conference in Denver a couple of months later.

In the audience that evening was the eminent Al Bartlett, a retired physics professor from the University of Colorado, who we discovered had a reputation for giving more presentations about peak oil and related issues than anyone else on the planet. I felt both intimidated and honored by his presence, but mostly I was rattled to have him there.

At the end of the evening, Steve Andrews introduced me to Bartlett, who said, "You didn't talk about the population problem." This was exactly the kind of feedback I was dreading, and I tried to explain that it was just not possible to address every important issue in such brief public presentations.

Bartlett was unrelenting. "You don't understand. You need to talk about population in *every* presentation you give!"

Later, when I had gotten over my defensiveness, I realized he was right. Population is the issue that we are most reluctant to take head-on. I made a commitment that I would do my best to follow his admonition ever after.

A month or so later, Bartlett sent out an email with a warning.

A SELF-EVIDENT TRUTH
If any fraction of the observed global warming
can be attributed to the activities of humans,
then this constitutes positive proof
that the human population, living as we do,
has exceeded the carrying capacity of the Earth.
THIS SITUATION IS NOT SUSTAINABLE!
AS A CONSEQUENCE,
IT IS AN INCONVENIENT TRUTH
THAT ALL PROPOSALS OR EFFORTS TO SLOW GLOBAL WARMING
OR TO MOVE TOWARD SUSTAINABILITY
ARE SERIOUS INTELLECTUAL FRAUDS
IF THEY DO NOT ADVOCATE
REDUCING POPULATIONS TO SUSTAINABLE LEVELS
AT THE LOCAL, NATIONAL AND GLOBAL SCALES.

In my own presentation that night, I introduced the theme that would form the foundation of our work for years to come.

This is a defining moment for our species, for our communities, and for each of us individually. Our legacy—and the future of our planet—will be determined by how we respond to the challenges and opportunities of peak oil and peak energy.

What's at stake here is human freedom and sovereignty. If we are dependent on distant sources and foreign powers for our essential needs, we will have no choice but to pay whatever price we must in order to survive. Thus freedom will be sacrificed for survival.

The only viable alternative is to learn how to meet our needs from our own local communities; the process of developing community self-reliance is called relocalization. In the face of the energy crisis (and the attendant crises it has spawned), this process has now become necessary. It's an awesome task, and it will require making it our first and foremost priority.

This is not simply about changing lifestyles or becoming more energy-efficient. This is about moving from species adolescence to adulthood, beginning to accept responsibility for life on this planet, understanding that our collective life has purpose and meaning.

How we spoke about relocalization and the human predicament was markedly different from most other writers and speakers at that time, although I don't think we realized just how great that difference was. We were informed by a perspective that included an ethical, moral, and spiritual framework that was largely missing from public discourse.

CHAPTER 6

Going Local! A Coherent Community Response

Buoyed by the initial response to our work and feeling compelled to quickly expand our efforts, in January 2006 we held a daylong conference, "Going Local! Preparing for the Accelerating Energy Crisis," on the University of Colorado campus, which was attended by more than four hundred people (on a day when the Broncos were playing in nearby Denver). The event promised "to inform citizens about options for preparing for near-term disruptions and to encourage participating in the strategic planning process for achieving long-term community self-reliance in energy, food, and economy." Julian Darley was a featured speaker, along with Al Bartlett, who—with a stack of aging overhead transparencies (he never used PowerPoint)—once again patiently explained how failure to grasp the exponential function could drive humanity to the brink of collapse. Another speaker was Megan Quinn from Community Solutions in Yellow Springs, Ohio, who introduced the national premiere of the film *The Power of Community: How Cuba Survived Peak Oil*.[25]

Instead of designating myself as a speaker, I chose to be the conference's "weaver," providing context, as well as introducing and bridging between the speakers. For instance, I tied the issue of Y2K into the current challenge.

We sometimes get comments from people that go like this: "Isn't peak oil just like the so-called Y2K crisis, a bunch of people predicting doom and gloom and then nothing happens? We got all worked up about Y2K, and it turned out to be nothing! How do we know this isn't the same kind of thing?"

Well, what's important to know about the Y2K problem is that the reason "nothing happened" is that nearly half a trillion dollars was spent around the world in an emergency effort to remediate the problem and prevent cataclysmic cascading system breakdown. We almost didn't make it, because the remediation effort began very late; and because it began so late, it cost a lot more than it should have. But we were *successful* in preventing a serious problem from becoming a global disaster. We did a good job with Y2K, and you can thank the people who risked their reputations and careers to raise the warning and draw attention to the issue when almost no one wanted to hear about it.

As Matt Simmons[26] likes to say, "A crisis is a series of problems ignored until they become terminal." Y2K was ignored for forty years. Peak oil has been ignored since Jimmy Carter.

Aldous Huxley said something very similar: "Facts do not cease to exist because they are ignored." Peak oil is a fact. It's geology. We should be very wary of economists who deny or ignore the reality of peak oil.

So yes, the situation with peak oil is in some ways similar. Today, people in communities around the world are stepping forward to ensure that the *energy crisis* does not become an unnecessary global disaster. It takes awareness, it takes commitment, and it takes concerted action. This is an issue that cannot be ignored any longer. We don't know if we can get the job done in time, but we're going to do our very best.

A month after this initial conference, we gathered more than a hundred volunteers into several working groups (we were uncomfortable with the idea of *committees*) to explore various aspects of relocalization, including renewable energy, transportation, food production and distribution, manufacturing and employment, parallel economic infrastructure, local currencies, health care, and crisis preparedness. With all this momentum, we felt we were well on the way toward developing a viable community-based plan for Boulder County to become resilient and self-reliant, able to meet its essential needs locally. We were naive, of course.

While the planning process was getting started, we continued to hold public meetings—speakers, films, presentations—because we were convinced that public education and awareness were job one. And from these meetings, our working groups grew to a total of somewhere around 125 people. This sounds great, but actually it was a disaster. We quickly learned that it's not possible to do strategic assessment and planning in such a large group, with people who have widely divergent understandings, are at different stages of commitment, possess greatly varying skill sets, and often have limited time to devote to the process.

As the working groups launched into the daunting task of developing a comprehensive plan, things quickly fell apart. To our dismay (and despite our best efforts), most of the groups essentially abandoned their work by the end of that first summer. Few people had the time or discipline to contribute productively to the process. And it became painfully clear that no one *anywhere* knew how to relocalize a community—and that, as near as we could tell, it had never even been attempted before. We were confronted with the reality that the process was going to be much more difficult than we had hoped and that it would likely take much more time than we thought we had left before collapse was upon us. Our initial excitement dissolved into doubt and depression.

We had thought that we were building an organization that would be taking on the responsibility of relocalizing Boulder, or at least of leading the effort. But the problem was that building the organization and dealing with all the drama of the organizational growth issues—the endless cycle of forming, storming, reforming, and norming—was consuming our time and energy. The real work wasn't getting done.

Somewhere along the way, it occurred to us that perhaps we shouldn't be attempting to build an organization at all. Maybe we should focus on being a catalyst for relocalization in the community—or maybe even just a catalyst for community.

After making that mental shift, two things happened. First, the strain of building an organization went away; the load lightened.

Second—and surprisingly—our impact in the community increased dramatically.

Meanwhile, gasoline prices settled down, and lots of people got comfortable again and started falling asleep. We knew the lull would be temporary. We also knew that as global warming began to dawn in the public consciousness, attention would be diverted away from peak oil, and that we were going to face a lot of business as usual.

But, this being an emergency—a Long Emergency—we knew that we couldn't slow down. In fact, it was clear to us that we needed to greatly accelerate our efforts. We didn't have a big organization, since we had stopped trying to build one, but we did have a large opt-in email list, which had grown to over a thousand people—which may sound good, but represented less than 1 percent of Boulder's population.

In early July 2006, I stepped off the cliff and finally quit my day job in order to focus 100 percent on the challenges and opportunities ahead, and I spent many hours in meetings with our core group to sketch out strategies. And I continually studied the work being done in other communities—both overseas, in Kinsale, Ireland, and Totnes, England, and in the United States, in Willits, CA; Sebastopol, CA; Portland, OR; Seattle, WA; Bellingham, WA; Tompkins County, NY; and on and on. Meanwhile, Post Carbon Institute's Relocalization Network had been growing rapidly—to more than 150 communities in something like fourteen nations. I also began exploring the incredible work being done by the Business Alliance for Local Living Economies (BALLE). After a while, I began to get the sense that something very big was happening around the country—and perhaps all over the world—that was invisible unless you went looking for it.

"We all need to go looking for it," I wrote for a public talk. "It's there, a renaissance of the human spirit that's manifesting as what we called 'A Renaissance of Local.' We need to study it, connect with it, become part of it."

Today, Al Gore's film about the challenge of climate change—*An Inconvenient Truth*—began playing in theaters. Early reviews are surprisingly respectful and supportive. Meanwhile, on June 5, one of the world's most respected voices on climate change—Australia's Tim Flannery[27]—will speak in Boulder.

With unprecedented media attention to climate change, people are beginning to feel especially uneasy. *Time* magazine uncharacteristically warned on its recent cover, "Be worried. Very worried." And Boulder Book Store recently hosted James Howard Kunstler, who exhorted his audience to awaken to the realities of "the Long Emergency" of converging crises, including peak oil and economic instability.

We are finally coming to understand that we're in serious trouble on this planet. That's good, but the next step is to realize that sustainable solutions do not lie in technology or even policy, but in ethics and morality.

—An entry in my journal, May 24, 2006

Our efforts to create an organization to relocalize Boulder had largely been abandoned, but one of the early working groups had been remarkably robust and productive: the local food working group. Composed of several experienced and metrics-oriented gardeners who had been growing most of their own food for years, in 2006 the group estimated that with the current state of agriculture in Boulder County, only about twenty thousand people could be fed from locally sourced food. This was a shocking realization—our population was around three hundred thousand—and it underscored our food insecurity. But they then looked at the upside: at what could happen if we converted all available farmland to growing food for local consumption, if we converted all the lawns and golf courses and parks to food production, if we got people to raise as much food in their yards as possible—that is, if we did *everything* we could think of, including utilizing the best bio-intensive production methods and reducing our calorie intake to about two thousand calories a day. If we did all that, we might be able to feed as many as 185,000 people—62 percent of the county population.

These tentative numbers—that is, the perspective they gave us, along with our understanding of how peak oil (later dubbed Peak Everything by Heinberg) was inevitably going to impact our local food supply— helped to convince us that we needed to focus our efforts on food localization in Boulder County.

Focus on local food may be our best immediate opportunity to unite and prepare our community; food is a universal issue and is an urgent priority for us all.
—My proposal for a single working group, October 12, 2006

By the fall of 2006, we knew that the impulse to relocalize our community was simply not going to work. Our best alternative, we suspected, was to focus solely on localizing our food supply in Boulder County. We proposed to the remaining members of Boulder Valley Relocalization a single self-organizing working group for this purpose. We also outlined some specific short-term projects that the group could focus on, based on real needs that we had come to recognize. These included

- increasing the number of gardens in our community by 100 percent;
- working with local farmers to increase community supported agriculture (CSA) subscriptions by 100 percent;
- enrolling two hundred people in permaculture courses;
- developing three new community greenhouses; and
- organizing volunteering at local farms to increase production and reduce labor costs.

By that time, many Boulder Valley Relocalization members were experiencing burnout. For them, these projects seemed far too overwhelming, simply out of reach. Leadership tensions splintered the group, and in the fall, we knew that Boulder Valley Relocalization had utterly failed and would be no more. What we could not see was that the seeds for accomplishing the goals we envisioned had already been planted and that the work would be done in ways that we could not foresee.

❧

Meanwhile, Lynette Marie and I found ourselves facing a greater sense of urgency than ever before, but no organization had coalesced to take on the task of leading our community forward. As winter set in, we knew only that we didn't know what to do but start over.

Faced with the challenge of reinventing our organization, we were driven by a stark realization that came from beyond the world, in a teaching delivered through Marshall Vian Summers: "Your work here now is to preserve human freedom and to establish yourselves in the universe as a free and independent race. If you fail, then all that humanity has accomplished will be lost. All the teaching, all of the true spiritual understanding, all of the art, all of the culture, all of your advancements can be lost. Impossible, you say? Well, think of all the human cultures that have disappeared even from your world. All that they established is lost, leaving only a few traces." In our innermost being, we knew this to be true.

We also recalled the story of a longtime student of Buckminster Fuller. Sometime in the last few years of Fuller's legendary life, the student asked, "What do you see when you look out into the future?" Bucky replied, "Unprecedented hardship."

In presentations, we had often shown a cartoon that featured two young boys, seriously overweight, downing pizza and cola in front of a television set (or computer monitor). One of them says to the other, "What do you want to be *if* you grow up?"

We knew that something was being asked of us that we had not quite grasped. We were on the threshold of something we could not quite see.

❧

It's significant that somewhere along the way, Julian Darley came to view our organization as the leading example of a relocalization effort in the nation and wanted to promote us as such. This was flattering, in a way, but it was also terribly unsettling. If we were the strongest example of a relocalization initiative, the movement was certainly in as much trouble as we feared.

∾

Our new strategy was to do the unthinkable, maybe the impossible. Our goal was a man-on-the-moon project—a relocalized economy in an energy-constrained future. We thought it might take a decade and formed a for-profit social venture that would spearhead a county-wide effort. With an ambitious business plan in hand, we were able to secure a small amount of startup capital from an angel investor and some initial sponsors, which made it possible to put a few of us on staff with a salary (a victory for sustainability).

We launched our campaign—Boulder County Going Local!—on March 15, 2007, at a big downtown event at a facility lovingly called Republic of Boulder. We expected maybe seventy-five to one hundred people, but more than 250 people came out that night. We had thirty speakers, each given two minutes—our early partners, supporters, and sponsors—and I outlined what the campaign was all about.

> Behind this campaign is the understanding that we must learn to reweave the fabric of fundamental connections and relationships that have been at the heart of human civilization from the beginning. We must learn to reconnect with the earth, with the seasons, with our biosphere, with each other. We must rebuild our relationships with those who live in our neighborhoods, with those who grow our food, with those who produce and sell the goods we need, with those who supply the services we require. And we must do it all locally as much as possible, rebuilding local living economies. Only through profoundly local living can we curtail our profligate consumption, end our contribution to global warming, and restore balance and sanity to our planet.
>
> Our communities are being called to quickly become largely self-reliant, to develop the capacity to produce locally our most essential needs. The longer-term vision is that such relocalized communities will naturally trade their surpluses interdependently

with surrounding relocalized communities, forming self-reliant bioregions that trade surpluses with each other. This will be a radical and welcome shift from the tangled web of codependent relationships that we call a globalized economy.

This transition to a local living economy will take some time, even though we don't have much time. We are all called here to make this transition possible.

CHAPTER 7

In Transition: A Movement Dies, Another Is Born

I'm reminded of the old shopman's rule that you don't actually know how to use a tool until you are ready to name at least three ways it can be abused and at least three situations where it's the wrong tool for the job.

—John Michael Greer

The primitive Relocalization Network had grown surprisingly rapidly in its early phase. At its peak, probably early 2007, there were reportedly some two hundred Post Carbon Institute outposts in about a dozen nations, and founder Julian Darley predicted in an interview I conducted that the network would continue to grow exponentially—to perhaps thousands of communities by 2010.[28] But it didn't happen. Even as Darley was saying this, I knew the network was already beginning to collapse, although he couldn't see it. Local groups were disbanding, giving up, finding the challenge too great. By the end of 2007, there were probably no more than fifty active local groups. The Relocalization Network itself turned out to be unsustainable, partly (perhaps) because it lacked a replicable process for relocalization, a methodology. It is also true that the Post Carbon Institute failed to create an adequate system to support local groups.

This experience of witnessing (and being part of) an important movement as it fell apart provided us a healthy skepticism about social movements in general. It also gave those of us working in Boulder County a profound experience of confusion, frustration, disappointment, and sometimes even despair—for while we understood that relocalization was urgently needed in our community (and in every other community, of course), we were painfully aware that we didn't know what we were doing or how to do it. And to our dismay, we gradually discovered that no one else knew how to do it either. We were attempting to pioneer something that was absolutely necessary but maddeningly difficult, and we often found ourselves vacillating between inspiration and despair.

As in all relocalization efforts, we had been trying our best to discover how to prepare our communities for a crisis that was just over the horizon but had not yet quite arrived—and we were attempting to do this without being seen as doom-and-gloomers or alarmists inciting fear and anxiety. We had done our best to follow the principles and guidelines that flowed from Post Carbon Institute, Richard Heinberg, and the early Post Carbon outposts, most notably in Willits, California. But while we continued our work, constantly adjusting and recalibrating, we could not escape the feeling that we were merely dabbling at relocalization and that we were floundering, grasping at straws. Some days, we felt that we were failing utterly.

Meanwhile, we were also watching what was happening in Ireland and England—what a permaculture teacher named Rob Hopkins was doing. Hopkins had been tapped to teach the world's first two-year permaculture course at a community college in Kinsale, Ireland. For the first class meeting, Hopkins decided to show the newly released documentary *The End of Suburbia* and to invite Colin Campbell (who lived nearby) as a guest speaker. Campbell was a celebrated petroleum geologist who was among the first in the industry to sound the alarm about the looming energy crisis.[29] He was also the founder of an international group of petroleum-industry experts, the Association for the Study of Peak Oil.

That first class, providing a clear glimpse into the depth of the looming disaster, was life changing for Hopkins and his students. It was, Hopkins said later, his "peak oil moment." What subsequently unfolded in Kinsale was a class project that would reverberate around the world. Hopkins and his students decided to devise a plan for the town of Kinsale (population eight thousand) to be able to weather the coming storm. They envisioned in detail what a resilient, self-reliant, sustainable Kinsale might look like in 2025, and then, through a process of backcasting, began mapping the myriad steps that would need to happen along the way. They called the resulting map the "Kinsale Energy Descent Action Plan." It was an inspiring piece of work, and many of us in the peak oil movement were grateful to have access to it.

Almost as an afterthought, the class felt compelled to share their plan with the Kinsale city council. Surprisingly, the council decided to adopt the students' energy descent action plan as *the* plan for the city of Kinsale—and, as legend has it, that plan continues to be implemented there today. This was truly a breakthrough moment in the history of the relocalization movement, and it gave many of us a much-needed sense of hope that more was possible than we had imagined.

But things apparently did not go well for Hopkins. Shortly after the initial success in Kinsale, he seemed to disappear from the scene and abandon the effort. Later I learned that Hopkins's home—made of straw bales and cob (an earth-and-straw building material), which his students had helped him build—had been burned to the ground. Arson was suspected, but Hopkins was apparently so badly shaken that he decided Kinsale was not where he wanted to raise his family.

Sometime in 2006, we heard that Hopkins had moved to Totnes, in southwest England, where he was apparently prototyping a community-wide Transition process to achieve local resilience and self-reliance. It seemed ambitious, but possible. We eagerly awaited news.

Hopkins would later say that he had no intention of starting a movement. His interest was simply the relocalization of Totnes, a beautiful market town of some eight thousand people (which reminded me of Carmel, California). But as he rolled out his new Transition effort in Totnes, people in other communities were watching, as we were. When it became clear that Hopkins was experimenting with a process similar to what had occurred in Kinsale—this time driven by community citizens on a grassroots level—other community groups quickly began emulating his process. It appeared that Hopkins had stumbled onto something important, which just might be the key to achieving relocalization in communities anywhere.

Transition was rooted in a grand vision, as Hopkins later wrote: "Inherent within the twin challenges of peak oil and climate change is an extraordinary opportunity to reinvent, rethink and rebuild the world around us."[30]

From internet reports, it quickly became clear that a robust, seemingly viral movement was springing up around the Transition process in Totnes, and we soon learned that Rob Hopkins was even writing a book, *The Transition Handbook: From Oil Dependence to Local Resilience*, to help foster the movement.[31] I wondered if this might be the much-needed book that Julian Darley had failed to complete.

Shortly after *The Transition Handbook* was published, I read it on a plane to the United Kingdom, on my way to see for myself if the burgeoning Transition movement really lived up to the glowing reports we had been reading on the internet. I had to know if it was actually working and to somehow gauge whether the movement could possibly be sustainable.

My first stop was Dundee, Scotland, to take the two-day Training for Transition from Sophy Banks and Naresh Giangrande, two of the cofounders of Transition Town Totnes and the creators of the Training for Transition. My experience there was entirely unexpected. Somehow Transition just *landed* in me, in my heart. I saw that Transition was alive—and, inevitably, alive *in me*.

Afterward, I made the long train ride down to southwest England to make my pilgrimage to the birthplace of the movement, Totnes. And there I was able to spend some time with Rob Hopkins and his chief coconspirator, Ben Brangwyn, who headed up the international Transition network. I got to see the movement on the ground, not only in Totnes, but also in several other communities in England. I witnessed that Transition had indeed become a household word in the United Kingdom, and that the movement was indeed spreading virally. It looked like this was going to work.

I came back to the States deeply inspired, carrying the fire of Transition, determined to ignite the entire nation around the project of relocalization.

❧

To my dismay, both Hopkins and Brangwyn had candidly admitted to me that they had considered Transition in the United States, but they felt it was too daunting a task. This country seemed unimaginably large to them—and too difficult to deal with. They had figured that they would just forget about America. There were no plans to bring Transition to the United States, but I felt it was essential. After all, I told them, the United States was by far the world's greatest consumer of fossil fuels and the largest producer of greenhouse-gas emissions. We needed Transition in this country, and we needed it to work—for everyone's sake.

I was deeply inspired by Hopkins's "cheerful disclaimer" that Transition was a social experiment on a grand scale. We really didn't know whether it would work or not. We moved forward with the conviction that if we waited for governments to act, it would be too little, too late. And if we merely acted as individuals, it would certainly be too little. We believed that if we acted together—as communities—it *might* be just enough, just in time.

As I shared this cheerful disclaimer with audiences and initiatives across the country—along with the context for Transition (our collective predicament) and a brief description of the essential elements of the Transition process—people responded with great enthusiasm. For many, this was the most hopeful development they had seen in a time of growing darkness in the world.

Boulder County has an opportunity to break new ground. Perhaps in a couple hundred years, people will look back at the beginning of the twenty-first century as a crucial time, as the fading moments of the Oil Age, the time of the Great Turning. Perhaps people will tell stories about what happened in Boulder County. And perhaps this evening will be something that is the beginning of one of those stories.

—From my talk at the Transition Boulder
County Initiation, June 5, 2008

On May 1, 2008, our relocalization organization—renamed Transition Boulder County—became the first officially recognized Transition initiative in North America (number fifty-three in the world, and the fifth outside the United Kingdom), and in September of that year, Lynette Marie and I conducted the first American Training for Transition, with sixty-one people participating. These first efforts resulted in the birth of several local initiatives in Colorado, five of which became officially recognized. That spurred us (prematurely) to become Transition Colorado, the first statewide Transition Hub.

As certified Transition trainers, Lynette Marie and I subsequently held Training for Transition sessions for hundreds of people all over the country, and we conducted numerous Transition clinics, both online and in person.

During that period, I made frequent plane trips to California for Transition United States board meetings. There was a particularly memorable board meeting in 2009, at the organization's headquarters in Sebastopol, California. Pamela Grey (an intellectually formidable scientist and entrepreneur) set the tone by saying that from her recent research she had come to the conclusion that the global situation—particularly regarding climate, energy, and the economy—was far worse than almost anyone had imagined, and it was deteriorating rapidly. Near-term systemic collapse seemed inevitable, and the economic unraveling of 2008 seemed to be the beginning of global economic disaster. She worried that the effort to organize Transition initiatives across the country was moving far too slowly, that the movement could fail spectacularly. Board member Richard Heinberg, who by this time had become a senior fellow of the Post Carbon Institute,[32] confirmed that Grey's sense of unfolding realities was dead-on accurate, that disaster could soon be upon us. We all felt a great sense of urgency and frustration, as well as bewilderment as to how to move forward.

We were greatly concerned that an energy descent action plan, like the one originally designed by Rob Hopkins's students in Kinsale, developed by any community would be far too little, too late. The process would take years to complete, let alone implement. We felt that global conditions were changing far more rapidly than Transition plans could accommodate.

Shortly thereafter, a few of us met with Transition network leaders (including Hopkins) at an international gathering in London. I was intent on learning why Transition in the United Kingdom seemed to lack a sense of urgency. It appeared that the economic crisis did not seem all that serious to them, and in fact, they had consciously decided (after some debate) to leave the economy out of the discussion in Transition trainings and in public presentations. This seemed inexplicable to us, and dangerous.

We explored various potential collapse scenarios with our British counterparts, but it was clear that there was a gulf between us in our understanding of the seriousness and urgency of our collective situation. This was driven home by Hopkins himself, who passionately expressed his conviction that if things got really bad, the British government would step in to make sure that people were well taken care of. We were incredulous, having witnessed the complete incompetence of the U.S. government in the face of Hurricane Katrina. But we could see that somehow, in the United Kingdom, there was a firm belief that the government could be relied upon to provide a safety net for its people. We in the United States suffered no such delusion.

Both optimism and pessimism trick me into judging life and betting on the odds, rather than diving into life with my whole self, with my full co-creative energy. I think the emerging crises call us to transcend such false end-games like optimism and pessimism. I think they call us to act like a spiritually healthy person who has just learned they have heart disease. We can use each dire prognosis as a stimulant for reaching more deeply into life and co-creating positive change.

—Tom Atlee, "Crisis Fatigue and the
Co-Creation of Positive Possibilities"[33]

Later that year, after a board meeting back in the United States, I arranged for a private meeting with Richard Heinberg. He invited me to his home in Santa Rosa, where he and his wife, Janet Barocco, had transformed a modest house on a small suburban plot into an oasis of food production and sustainable living. In the small straw-bale studio they had built in the backyard, Richard and I settled in for a long and candid conversation.

I had come to regard Richard as the most reliable researcher and most courageous communicator on Peak Everything issues. For me, he was one of the most important elders of the human tribe, an anchor of sanity in a world gone mad. I told him that I was well aware of his increasing sense of urgency about the human predicament and that I had decided to seek his counsel, since he seemed to know more about the realities of the coming cataclysm than anyone. He had pointed to the likelihood that collapse would soon land in the United States, and I wanted to know how he thought it would hit us first, where we would experience the greatest pain.

"Well, of course, it's food," he said matter-of-factly. *Check—confirmation of what we had been feeling back in Boulder.*

"When will it hit us?"

"Well, it could be next year or the year after. But probably no more than three years or so." *Damn! We'll have to move much faster!*

We talked for maybe an hour after that, but I can scarcely recall anything else from the conversation, for I knew (as I had suspected) that I would have to return to Boulder and focus all our relocalization efforts on food. I'm sorry I couldn't have recorded that meeting, but I had asked for a candid and off-the-record conversation.

༄

We had been deeply committed to relocalization in the place where we lived and to assisting wherever else we could. We had understood what was at stake, and we had viewed the Transition movement as the viable pathway forward. At the same time, something deeper was happening in our own understanding and experience, which was quite different from the Transition model as it was being practiced. And this eventually drew us in a radically different direction and focus. In late 2010, I was finally compelled to speak publicly about it.

CHAPTER 8

The Evolution of Transition
in the United States

Excerpted from my presentation at Xavier University's Lecture Series on Ethics, Religion, and Society, November 7, 2010.

TOWARD AN AMERICAN TRANSITION

There are now seventy-seven officially recognized Transition initiatives in the United States, along with seventeen in Canada (and none in Mexico). But this is a nation of some three hundred million people. Canada has about thirty-five million.

The United Kingdom claims 170 officially recognized initiatives, with a population of just over sixty million. Granted, the movement in the United Kingdom has been ongoing for a couple of years longer than in the United States, but the rate of adoption does seem noticeably slower here. To approach a similar level, we'd need to somehow get to nearly four hundred official initiatives over the next eighteen months. That would be truly extraordinary growth, and I'd really like to see that happen.[34]

Sadly, however, the rate of adoption in the United States seems to be slowing. Transition is hardly a household word in this country, and the mainstream media have given the movement scant attention. What's happening here?

I don't know if ever there will emerge a coherent and robust and truly viral Transition movement in this nation. I do know that we need it urgently. But today the movement here seems to me to be somewhat fragmented. Surely there are inspiring and important things going on in a number of communities—as in Sandpoint, Idaho—and truly I'm grateful for all of that. But in several other communities, the effort for relocalization has already essentially stalled. For many, it just seems too difficult, too big a challenge.

But we need Transition to work here, especially in this nation—because the United States is ground zero for the Long Emergency. We are the world's largest user of fossil fuels. With less than 5 percent of the world's population, we burn about 25 percent of the world's oil (two-thirds of which we have to import). We are also the largest producer of greenhouse-gas emissions, responsible for at least 25 percent of the total. Some would have us believe that China is the biggest contributor of greenhouse-gas emissions, but this ignores the fact that much of what China produces is for consumption in the United States. In fact, one-third of the world's industrial products come to the United States.

We are the world's most significant contributor to fossil fuel depletion, environmental degradation, and global warming. And now, with the entire globalized economy based on the U.S. dollar, which is based on an abundant supply of cheap oil, we are also the world's greatest contributor to economic decline—which is likely to soon become economic collapse, or at least long-term economic depression.

Make no mistake—the United States is the belly of the beast. Given this situation, it's hardly surprising that it's challenging to get Transition to catch fire here. There may be no other nation on the planet where denial and greed are more deeply rooted.

I appreciate the assessments of David Orr at Oberlin College, who observes in Derrick Jensen's *Listening to the Land:*

> Conventional wisdom maintains that we are slowly recovering from a recalcitrant recession. As we are now entering at least the third year of real economic contraction, continue to reel from the predations and corruption in a financial sector the federal government treats as sacrosanct, are in the sixth year of a plateau in worldwide oil extraction, and climate change is essentially unmitigated, it should be obvious that American society is arrantly

unsustainable—ecologically, fiscally, economically, politically, and ethically.... We've got a whole culture locked in the first stage of Abraham Maslow's five stages of human development: infantile self-gratification.[35]

But we have a unique history and heritage here in the United States, and in many ways a painful legacy, and all this needs to deeply inform our approach to Transition.

Self-declared "geologian" Thomas Berry helps us to understand our particular predicament here.

> When we came to this continent, we saw ourselves as a people with the most sublime spiritual insights ... as the most intellectual people of the world ... as people with the most human political traditions of the world, with our democratic political commitment; as a people, through our technologies, most able to deal with the daily needs of the world for food, clothing, and shelter. Now, after four centuries we find the North American continent toxic in its air, its water, and its land and gravely diminished in the variety and abundance of its living forms. We must ask ourselves what happened? The answer is simply that we have lost our awareness that the human community exists only as a component of the larger Earth community. Instead of an intimate presence on an abundant continent that could inspire our minds and imaginations while providing for our practical needs, we became a predator people on an innocent continent.[36]

The widespread destruction that has resulted from our presence has been enormous, as Berry laments, "The North American continent will never again be what it once was. The manner in which we have devastated the continent has never before occurred.... It is clear that there will be little development of life here in the future if we do not protect and foster the living forms of this continent. To do this, a change must occur deep in our souls. We need our technologies, but this is beyond technology. Our technologies have betrayed us."[37]

What we are learning is that what has gotten us into our collective predicament is a deep disconnection from the natural world, from life itself. And this separation between humans and the earth and the fundamental processes of life is nowhere more dramatic or more devastating than right here in the United States.

"You and I are not people who live in communion with the earth," says ecopsychology pioneer Chellis Glendinning. "We exist instead dislocated from our roots by the psychological, philosophical, and technological constructions of our civilization, and this alienation leads to our suffering: massive suffering for each and every one of us, and mass suffering throughout our society."[38]

As Americans, we will need to come to own all of this, to allow it to sink deep into our conscious awareness, and to learn to heal from it together.

TRANSITION IN TRANSITION

In his cheerful disclaimer, Rob Hopkins candidly and humbly admits that Transition is a massive social experiment and that we really don't know if it will work. Well, with the stakes as high as they are, I think we need to explore finding the ways to help ensure that it *will* work, especially here in the United States.

I do think the Transition model or process is a revolutionary development, one of the most important we've seen to date. But we should recognize that Transition itself is now undergoing radical change, one that is most especially needed in the United States.

The important thing to acknowledge here is that Transition is evolving very quickly—based both on what has been experienced in communities all over the world and on what is seeking to emerge in and through this movement. You could say that Transition is in transition. And perhaps the most visible sign of this evolution is a radical reframing of the Transition model by Rob Hopkins himself.

To his credit, Rob Hopkins was horrified to see that his early attempts to articulate a Transition process became regarded as a sort of catechism for emerging Transition initiatives, so he is now in the early stages of a valiant attempt to sweep away the rapidly forming accretions of tradition—how is it possible for a movement to establish "traditions" in a scant four years?—and to replace them with a reconception of Transition as something called "a pattern language," following the example of famed architect Christopher Alexander.

Shortly before the international Transition network conference in England in June, Rob sent out this message, which took many by surprise: "In the interests of promoting non-attachment to ideas and enshrining the principle that none of us really know what we are doing, as encapsulated in the 'Cheerful Disclaimer', for the *Transition Handbook 2.0,* I am taking the original Transition model and throwing it up in the air, using 'A Pattern Language' as a way of re-communicating and reshaping it."

With some excitement, we had learned early this year that Rob was heading in this direction. And now we see he is slowly writing *The Transition Handbook 2.0,* pattern by pattern, on his blog, inviting input and feedback.[39] It's an ambitious and creative project. Not everyone is happy about this reframing, however, including some of Alexander's longtime students—but it's on its way nonetheless.

What is the meaning of all this? What is emerging in the Transition movement? And what is all this about pattern language?

Pattern language is about discovering the inherent patterns that bring aliveness, wholeness, and healing to our communities. This is potentially an extremely potent development for the Transition movement, for underlying the Transition process is the healing impulse. In fact, it's the same impulse that's underlying permaculture.

In the United Kingdom, this bold reconception is being delivered under the banner of "Assembling Transition," and Hopkins has taken to calling the patterns he has identified as "Transition Ingredients"—as if Transition is some sort of recipe to follow, a kind of cake we can just cook up. Unwittingly, Hopkins may be condemning Transition to the same kind of fate that has befallen a mechanistic view of nature and the universe.

Language matters here. It's not trivial. Brian Swimme laughs at earlier scientists who imagined that the universe had somehow been assembled from parts—and imagined that the human had no integral connection with the process. As I delve deeper into all this, I find myself suspecting that Rob may be ignoring the deeper aspects of Christopher Alexander's work.

THE EMERGENCE OF DEEP TRANSITION

One of the core principles of permaculture has to do with valuing what's happening at the edges of a system. As David Holmgren says, "The interface between things is where the most interesting events take place. These are often the most valuable, diverse and productive elements in the system."[40]

For the last two years, we've been exploring some of these edges at Genesis Farm in northwestern New Jersey, where—after thirty years as a center for the study of "Earth Literacy" and "The Great Work" of Thomas Berry—Sister Miriam MacGillis has opened the door to a profound exploration of how to help foster the Transition movement in this land, how to regain within it the sense of sacred energy revealed through the story of the emergence of the universe itself and the evolution of our own earth, and how to cultivate a truly bioregional context for reinventing and relocalizing our way into the future (in other words, becoming native to our place).

At Genesis Farm, in a rich and deeply supportive environment, working with Miriam MacGillis, Seanna Ashburn (another Transition trainer), and others, we've held dialogues, presentations, and an ongoing series of two- and three-day workshops for Transition leaders.

Out of this exploration, several key themes have emerged.

Seriousness and Urgency

First, there is a growing and indisputable recognition that our collective predicament is far more serious and more urgent than many of us had been willing to actively contemplate. This is being increasingly reflected in the larger Transition movement, sometimes to the apparent dismay of its founders. Part of the discomfort, of course, is the unavoidable recognition that, as John Michael Greer tells us, the situation we face is not a problem that can be solved, but a predicament of our own making to which we must now quickly adapt. It's important to name our predicament, and to name and express how it's impacting us, what we are feeling about all this. And with this comes the realization that while the long-term process of energy descent action planning is essential in our communities, we must also quickly develop short-term plans to respond to likely near-term events—things like breakdowns in food or fuel supply chains, or a sudden collapse of the stock market, or a weather catastrophe, or even a widespread health crisis. Richard Heinberg has been pleading for this kind of emergency planning for years now as a core part of every resilience program. Few in this country have listened, and now time is very short.

Emergence

Second, we're beginning to learn about *emergence*—or what Christopher Alexander calls "unfolding," the evolutionary process by which the universe itself self-organizes, finding profound and practical lessons in how to catalyze Transition in our communities. We're learning about what is emerging in the Transition movement itself. In our communities, we're learning about what it is that's wanting to emerge there, far beyond our hopes and fears and desires. And in ourselves, we're discovering what it is that's wanting to emerge in us—and through us.

Self-Organization

Third, in a closely related way, we're also beginning to learn the meaning of *self-organization,* which is actually a core principle of Transition, though little discussed. We're discovering that catalyzing self-organization of a community around relocalization or Transition is entirely different from community organizing.

Permaculture Principles and Ethics

We're also beginning to understand how essential the principles and ethics of permaculture are to the Transition process. These have not been translated explicitly into the Transition literature, and yet they are fundamental to Transition. This translation will become increasingly important over time, because permaculture is based on a deep understanding of how life works.

New Cosmology/Universe Story

We're also diving deep into the story of the evolution of the universe, of the earth, and of life itself. As Thomas Berry explains, this New Cosmology "explores the contemporary, scientific story of the origin, nature and function of the Universe from its beginning, through its galactic phase, its supernova events, the shaping of the solar system, Earth, life, human life and self-reflective consciousness as a single, unbroken series of events."[41] It's often framed in terms of Earth Literacy, because we humans are so illiterate about the place where we live and how we got here. But the New Cosmology is helping us to recover our sense of the sacredness of life itself, and our fundamental connectedness with the processes that make life possible.

When people hear the word *cosmology* they sometimes automatically think that it's somehow religious. But in reality, it's based on a deep understanding of science, the story of the evolution of the universe. And, surprisingly, it brings us to a profound sense of the sacredness of life.

This perspective is even embedded in the preamble to the Earth Charter,[42] which says: "We are part of a vast, evolving universe. Earth, our home, is alive with a unique community of life." This is not a mere metaphor.

In an interview with Derrick Jensen, Creation Spirituality's Matthew Fox says,

> I maintain that the best, most profound mystical literature today is coming out of science. The new creation story is that everything—each of us—is mystery. What we're finding is that the smallest part of the atom is mystery. It's dancing. And then of course the macrocosm is a mystery. In the previous scientific worldview, mystery was "just what we don't know yet. We'll solve it." It's not that way. Death is not something you solve. Love is not something you solve. A broken heart is not something you solve. It's something you experience. It's Moses on the mountain. Moses had his

experience with the burning bush. We're learning that every bush is a burning bush, burning with photons and photosynthesis and this amazing cosmic process that was invented a few billion years ago, a process that goes back to the original fireball.[43]

This perspective is deeply enlivening.

Pattern Language

As an important adjunct to the New Cosmology, we're beginning to discover the importance of the patterns of evolution itself—and patterns of wholeness and healing. That's certainly possible with Rob Hopkins's infusion of Christopher Alexander's extraordinary work into the Transition process. We'll see. What's happening at Genesis Farm is that we're finding that our understanding of how Transition works and how real community works are being radically reshaped by our understanding of how the universe itself evolves—how life evolves and how life works.

Inner Transition/Heart and Soul

Finally, we're beginning to appreciate the centrality of Inner Transition, what is frequently called Heart and Soul work in the Transition movement, a recognition that Transition in the outer world cannot occur without an Inner Transition. Holding the space for this—including the psychology of change; the whole broad field of ecopsychology; dealing with grief, anger, and despair; and Joanna Macy's "The Work That Reconnects"[44]—is to me one of the most refreshing and endearing aspects of the Transition movement. This may turn out to be a more powerful attractor to the movement than the issues of peak oil, climate change, and economic decline.

As Sophy Banks in Totnes reminds us, "Part of the human condition is an experience of inner woundedness or brokenness. We want to be whole again, and some part of us knows how to do that. We yearn for wholeness and integration." And her partner, Naresh Giangrande, says, "Transition work is a manifestation of the healing impulse. We're making a plea to bring love into Transition."[45] These things are not often openly stated in the Transition movement, but they are being uttered in Heart and Soul groups that are meeting even in the most unexpected places.

It's a long and intense process, but we're beginning to see (and communicate) how the New Cosmology, the Universe Story, permaculture, Heart and Soul, and Christopher Alexander's work are closely related—and how they're just beginning to land together in the Transition movement. What this means to me is that we're finally beginning to understand Transition itself as an evolutionary process, one of the most intriguing and promising processes to emerge on this planet. And it's all absolutely integral with the 13.7-billion-year process of the unfolding of the universe—which, of course, is a continuing, emergent unfolding.

In short, at Genesis Farm, we're beginning to catalyze the infusion into Transition of new perspectives and leading-edge processes that are absolutely necessary in order for Transition to be ultimately successful. The emergence of these new perspectives is encouraging and inspiring. To me, these are all signs that Transition is working....

Alastair McIntosh gives us some wonderful context for all this in his book, *Hell and High Water,* where he writes about climate change (but he could just as well be speaking of our total predicament). He says, "To mitigate climate change—and even to adapt to its consequences—without losing our humanity, there needs to be a radical reactivation of our inner lives."[46]

He continues, "Inner climate affects outer climate because inner hubris drives outer hubris in a spiral of mindless economic frenzy." That's very powerful.

"I perversely hold out hope for humanity," he says, "not in spite of global warming, but precisely because it confronts us with a wake-up call to consciousness. Answering that call of the wild to the wild within us all invites outer action matched by inner transformation."

And that's part of what we've been attempting to cultivate at Genesis Farm. We're exploring these things out of a deep and urgent sense that these perspectives, these tools and processes, will be absolutely essential for Transition leaders as we move into a very uncertain future.

We're finding that this perspective about the inner work is fundamental to Transition, and it opens the door to what we've begun calling Deep Transition.

While these things may not be a "traditional" part of the Transition orientation, Deep Transition represents an opening where breakthrough understandings and processes can readily emerge and make significant contributions. After all, since no one anywhere has yet successfully relocalized a community, it is quite likely that approaches both ancient and new will be needed.

As David Orr says, "industrial civilization destroys communities."[47] And at its core, Transition is about healing and regenerating community. This is deep and profound work, and it is the very epicenter of the Transition process, even though we haven't talked about it publicly much—yet.

This is what Alistair McIntosh calls the cycle of belonging—where we help one another to re-member what has been dismembered, to re-vision how things could alternatively be, and then organize to re-claim what is needed to regenerate and heal community. This cycle of belonging offers meaning and direction in generating the responsibility necessary for community regeneration and healing.

But in the long run, I feel our Transition efforts may not be sustainable or resilient or self-reliant unless we place the Sacred at the core of our work and at the center of all our activities.

For Transition is not a movement for bringing about change. Change is coming, with us or without us, whether we want it or not—profound change. Transition is a movement for preparing our communities for the changes that are coming. And our preparation is likely to crumble unless we are able to connect with and cultivate the aliveness, the wholeness, the healing, and the sacredness that underlies the Transition process.

Buried deep in the Transition literature, there is a reference to core principles that should guide the practice of permaculture and, presumably, Transition itself. These are not discussed at any great length, but perhaps we can sense that they are fundamental.

- A sustainable human presence on the planet must align its systems with how life works.

- As long as our human culture is based on unsustainable assumptions, those systems will fail.
- A reinvention of a sustainable human culture must be in alignment with the rest of life.
- The laws of life can be seen and experienced in the natural world and many indigenous cultures.

There is aliveness here, and great wisdom. I propose these as foundational principles for Deep Transition.

I remember Christopher Alexander saying that aliveness and wholeness begin with something small. If it's authentic, truly alive, it spreads or unfolds—often in mysterious ways. It's eerily contagious—and uncontrollable. This is not something to be "organized." Instead, it grows—organically. This is as true for a community as it is for an organism.

The challenge for those of us involved in Transition is to be able to see such pockets of aliveness and wholeness in our communities, to support them, to protect them, to lovingly shine the light of day on them, to cultivate them, to catalyze their replication—and then to see what's possible and needed next. This is how communities are healed and ultimately made whole.

We're learning that none of us can make Transition happen in our communities. But we can surely be a catalyst for this emergence. All it takes is seeing what is possible and beginning right where we are.

With thanks to Mike Ruppert, I'd like to close with an authentically American perspective, from the late Floyd Red Crow Westerman, speaking from the Native American tradition.

Time evolves and comes to a place where it renews again. There is first a purification time, and then there is renewal time. We are getting very close to this time now.

We were told that we would see America come and go. And in a sense, America is dying—from within—because we forgot the instructions of how to live on Earth. Everything is coming to a time when prophecy and man's inability to live on Earth in a spiritual way will come to a crossroad of great problems.

It's our belief that if you're not spiritually connected to the Earth and understand the spiritual reality of how to live on Earth, it's likely you will not make it.[48]

I think that's true for each one of us, for this nation, and for the Transition movement itself. We need to regain and reclaim the sense, as Red Crow proclaims, that everything is spiritual, that this planet, this universe, this continent, and this movement are all about the Sacred. Perhaps this is ultimately the only thing that will truly ignite the Transition movement in America and the only thing that will enable this land and its people to fulfill our common destiny.

CHAPTER 9

Diving into Food

When we eat from the industrial food system, we are eating
oil and spewing greenhouse gases.

—MICHAEL POLLAN

As our focus in Colorado turned exclusively to localizing our food supply, we began moving away from the standard Transition model of
creating a community-generated energy descent action plan. It was the
latest in a series of such organizational shifts in identity and form. Since
the beginning, we've experimented and invented and reinvented—and
we've evolved in unexpected ways. Even the name has changed: from
Boulder Valley Relocalization to Boulder Going Local, then Boulder
County Going Local, Transition Boulder County, Transition Colorado,
and finally to Local Food Shift Group.

In this latest change, we even left our own organization behind us, in
a way. We decided to stop being community organizers and simplify our
core mission by focusing on being *catalysts for food localization,* both
directly and by helping others become catalysts as well. In the last few
years, we had been increasingly compelled to gather what we've been
learning and building and to make it all available to other individuals and communities, to empower them in their own process of food
localization.

As we experimented with different approaches, we had successes as
well as failures and setbacks, the latter especially in the realm of bringing
significant capital to new food and farming enterprises. While there may
be value in sharing some of those stories, painful or inspiring though

they might be, such an exploration doesn't seem appropriate for this particular book.

In any case, our own story is far less important than what we have been learning and who we are becoming in the process. We have learned what it means to intentionally be a catalyst for food localization during the early stages of an emerging foodshed. These days we're in the process of discovering what a local food *revolution* actually means, how it might unfold, and how we might support it. While this is radically different from the role we initially adopted, I would say, in hindsight, that the transition has been a natural and emergent process of evolution.

Through all our work over the last ten years, especially in the latter stages of our journey, we gradually came to some fundamental priorities. They are

- to learn to be a catalyst for food localization in our own region;
- to empower other foodshed catalysts;
- to discover the patterns by which food localization can naturally occur within an awakening foodshed; and
- to share what we have learned with other individuals and communities who are entering into this process.

In the background, these were (and still are) the primary priorities of all our work, whatever forms it took. Meanwhile, we were also trying, sometimes a bit desperately, to discern what organizational structures we should utilize (for instance, nonprofit or for-profit), who should be fulfilling what roles in our organizations, whom we should invite to work with us, and what daily activities we should be engaging in within our emerging foodshed.

We could find no precedent for what we were attempting to do, and we often struggled to explain our work to potential strategic partners, investors, and advisors. What we actually accomplished over the years was rarely measurable. Nevertheless, we knew that we had profoundly touched the lives of many individuals and had significantly (if indirectly) impacted the work of several other companies and organizations.

That's why this book is not just the story of what we did and didn't do, but much more about what we have learned and who we have become.

❧

Despite all our experience over the last several years, I hasten to say that we're not experts in food localization. No one is. Food localization has never been achieved to any truly significant degree in any region in this country. No one can honestly say they know how to do it. Besides, how food localization unfolds in any particular region will depend on uniquely local characteristics and circumstances.

But what I can say is that we've been learning about food localization in three primary ways. First, through on-the-ground experience in Colorado over the last several years. Second, by learning from others who have been experimenting and innovating all over the world. As you might expect, we've been taking a lot of notes along the way. But the third way we've been learning is a bit different, and it will unfold throughout this book. We've been attempting to apply to the process of food localization several core principles from different disciplines, including

- permaculture, from Bill Mollison and David Holmgren;
- pattern language, from the revolutionary architect Christopher Alexander, particularly found in his books *A Pattern Language* and *The Nature of Order;*
- presencing, as explored in Otto Scharmer's *Theory U;* and
- evolutionary emergence, embodied in the work of Brian Swimme and Thomas Berry, first described in their book *The Universe Story.*

Together, these related disciplines have formed for us a systemic, holistic, process-oriented perspective.

❧

We had learned from the Transition movement—and from the relocalization movement that preceded it—that any localization process begins with a small group (the catalysts) and that their first task is to raise awareness, to provide education, and to get people in the community engaged in the process.

We started our new focus on local food by launching a fairly ambitious campaign—Eat Local!—inserting a new meme into the community, into the local culture. Perhaps a little naively, we saw it as a ten-year project. We organized conferences, brought in guest speakers, and showed a series of documentaries. We hosted gleanings at local farms, all-local potluck dinners and celebrations, and even a couple of "Open Space" processes[49] exploring how Boulder County might feed itself after the age of cheap oil.

The mission of the campaign was to catalyze a more resilient local food system for Boulder County, based on deep ecological principles and a more connected populace, with far less dependence on fossil fuels.

The Eat Local! campaign presented positive ways of engaging citizens, communities, businesses, and local governments to take the far-reaching actions that are required to strengthen the local food system. The campaign was designed to promote close connections between community members and those who grow our food, as well as to expand the capacity of our local food system.

At first, we understood that fundamentally this was about increasing demand for local food. Boulder County was at less than 2 percent food localization, and we chose to set a rather arbitrary goal of 25 percent—which seemed plausible.

❧

As we got into this, we realized that the local media did not take us seriously (probably because we were unhesitating in talking about the local impact of global crises), and we had a hard time getting coverage of the campaign. We had to create our own media.

One of our first moves to create visibility in the community was to produce a small magazine, the *Boulder County Eat Local! Resource Guide and Directory*. The directory was inspired by a local food map produced by BeLocal in Ft. Collins, Colorado (a BALLE chapter), though, after some months of research, we realized that our county had many more sources of local food than could fit on a map. The resource guide had content educating people about the importance of local food sourcing. Our first issue was twenty-four pages long, and we printed twenty thousand copies; for our third and final edition, we went to forty-eight pages and distributed thirty thousand copies throughout the Colorado Front Range. The publication was a key part of our Eat Local! campaign and was supported by advertisers and sponsors.

We learned that having an independent print publication can be very powerful. It helped change how we were seen in the community. The directory turned out to be appreciated by almost everyone—it was absolutely the first of its kind in the area—and people regularly told us they read the publication from cover to cover. Accompanying the magazine was a new website—www.eatlocalguide.com (which has since been renamed www.localfoodshift.pub). We had realized that, as useful as the magazine was, a website could more easily provide a steady stream of new content—both local and national (and even international) in this rapidly changing environment.

The launchpad for all this—a kind of "Great Unleashing," Transition-style—was a three-day county-wide conference, festival, and expo in the fall of 2007, "A Renaissance of Local!" which drew about nine hundred people. We had twenty-eight speakers, around forty workshops, and lots of exhibitors. On the last afternoon we brought it to a finish with a feast celebrating slow food. Three hundred people enjoyed the finest in local food, an experience that people still fondly remember.

The festival and the magazine—we circulated the first edition of our Eat Local! guide during the run-up to the festival—helped create a lot of attention to the issues of local food, and it launched the Eat Local! campaign with significant exposure and momentum.

This campaign was the primary focus of our relocalization efforts for some years. We found, however, that simply providing people with the reasons to eat local and a list of sources of local food wasn't enough. They also needed incentive. We formulated it as a challenge—the 10% Local Food Shift Challenge and Pledge—asking individuals, families, and businesses to commit at least 10 percent of their food budget to local sourcing.

As a result of all of these efforts, demand for local food has certainly increased over the years. When we surveyed restaurants in Boulder

County in 2007, we found that only eight of them sourced locally to any significant degree. By 2011, there were about eighty! The 10 percent pledge resulted in more than $8 million being shifted to local food purchasing during its four-year run. We've simply lost track since then, but the numbers are still increasing.

ॐ

Of course, when demand increases, supply also must increase.

For years, farmers told us, "I sell everything I produce."

We often asked, "Could you produce more?"

"Yes," they would say, "but I'd have to know that the demand is going to be there."

Well, it's difficult to predict future demand, but we know that in Colorado, demand for local food is now significantly outstripping supply. And this is also true nationally—a seemingly good problem for an emerging industry. In fact, by early 2012 studies showed that eaters were beginning to prefer local food over organic. That was significant, a real milestone.

As local food producers have seen that a lot more people want local food, they've expanded their operations, and they've done this in the way that made the most business sense: selling directly to consumers via CSAs, farmers markets, and farm stands. This is an effective means of stimulating production capacity. Through direct marketing—and without relying on middlemen—they were able to maintain high profit margins. Some of them were even beginning to make a living at farming.

As a result, over the last several years we've seen significant growth in local food consumption and production. Again, this is true across the nation. It's a healthy growth curve. And the emerging local food segment may be one of the few industries in the world where growth is actually needed!

In recent years, however, we've seen this growth curve begin to flatten out. Sales at farmers markets in Boulder County have seemingly plateaued, though CSA sales are still on the rise. As we'll see later, we're bumping up against the limits of current production capacity.

Our farmers market in Boulder is visited by some six thousand people on a typical Saturday (during the season). It's a robust and vibrant market. But a few years ago, we learned that an entire season's sales at our Boulder County farmers markets (in both Longmont and Boulder) could feed the population of the county for less than two days. For all the growth happening in the local food scene, we were barely scratching the surface.

Along the way, we also realized that the media talked about local food as some kind of hip lifestyle choice—even when they described it as a responsible or sustainable choice, the focus was on it being alternative or fashionable. Many eaters certainly saw it that way. It was a little disconcerting to us that Boulder had been recognized by *Bon Appétit* magazine as "the foodiest town" in the whole country. Local food had become cool. But all that coolness only takes food localization so far. Direct marketing only takes food localization so far.

ॐ

Along with producing the Eat Local! guide and organizing the festival, we had also been working behind the scenes to help increase local food production in Boulder County. People had to learn new skills, because shifting to lower-carbon, mixed-farming organic systems that are less dependent on oil and chemicals requires a lot more people with the right skills working on the land again.

We began conducting an ambitious *reskilling* program (inspired by the Transition movement)—providing instruction in the basic practical life skills that modern society has largely lost: growing, cooking, and canning food; raising chickens and bees and goats; and saving seeds and saving water. These are skills that everyone needs. We delivered more than ten thousand people-hours of instruction through this program in the first couple of years. Soon we were delighted to discover that many farms and organizations began offering reskilling workshops themselves, which allowed us to gradually phase out our own offerings.

We also began offering people real training in various approaches to food production, especially permaculture. In 2007, we realized that a full permaculture design course hadn't been taught in Boulder County in at least ten years. We recruited a couple of teachers—Sandy Cruz, who had basically retired, because she felt no one was interested in permaculture any more, and Marco Lam, who had been teaching permaculture in other countries, but not locally—and organized and promoted a certification course. Many such courses soon followed, and today there are several hundred certified graduates in the area, along with more than one hundred certified permaculture teachers.

In 2008, we cohosted a local food summit in Boulder County, bringing farmers and citizens together with key decision makers and policy makers to discuss local food issues and to coalesce an increased level of support for the vision of a local, organic food economy.

Also in 2008, the county commissioners formed the Food and Agriculture Policy Council, and I was selected as a founding member, along with several of our key allies—including two of our board members. The commissioners, who understood at least some of the realities of Peak Everything, gave this group the mandate to find ways to convert 10 percent of the county's seventeen thousand acres of publicly owned open space agricultural land to food production for local consumption by 2012. They also asked us to develop or change policies to support and encourage local agriculture.

Our organization also encouraged people—especially young people—to consider farming as a viable and sustainable career choice. As part of that, we catalyzed and supported the Boulder County Farmer Cultivation Center. Under a mentorship program, in their first year, new farmers farmed a half acre of land and grew a variety of market vegetables; in their second year, they farmed one full acre and began to focus on the kind of farm operation they intended to start. The center also assisted program graduates with finding land to farm, arranging startup loans, and securing a spot at a local farmers market. With land to farm, eager customers, startup capital, and years of local farming experience, these graduates were given a great start. (Colorado State University's extension service also has launched a Building Farmers training program, which requires the development of a solid business plan and connects graduates up with an experienced local farmer as a mentor.)

Little by little, we also began working with Boulder County and municipal governments as they reconsidered their comprehensive plans and land-use policies, to ensure that local food and agriculture were supported by those plans and policies.

❧

A few years ago, we saw that our role in all this was beginning to change. We had learned from the experience in Iowa's Woodbury County that revitalizing local food and farming could become an essential strategy for economic development—rebuilding local economies. Among the public, few people considered how food localization could have significant economic benefits, though many could easily relate to many of the other benefits of localizing food—from reducing local greenhouse-gas emissions to improving children's health through farm-to-school programs.

It's no secret that there's a lot of wealth in Boulder County, and there are quite a number of wealthy individuals. But almost all their money is invested "out there" somewhere, zipping around the world. Slow Money founder Woody Tasch calls this *fast money,* money used to make as much money as possible—and quickly. And often the best way to do this is to invest in the very companies that are directly contributing to our predicament. This fast money was directly implicated, of course, in the crash of 2008.

And at the end of February in 2012, as part of the Eat Local! campaign, we held a two-day conference on how relocalizing food can lead to new economic development. The title of the conference was "Our Local Economy in Transition: Food Localization as Economic Development."

At around the same time, we were also learning about the work of community economist Michael Shuman (whose book *Local Dollars, Local Sense* had just been published). Shuman had studied the potential economic impact of food localization in New Mexico and in the greater Cleveland area. We asked him to study what the economic impact would be of 25 percent food localization in Colorado. What came out of that study gave us a whole new way of seeing and communicating about food localization.

Shuman demonstrated that just 25 percent local food in Colorado would produce thirty-one thousand new jobs and add more than $2 billion a year to the state GDP—in a state where, of the $12 billion of food we consumed each year, all but about 2 percent was imported from outside the state.[50] Shuman's report was both inspiring and grounding, and we began using his numbers to shift the conversation about local food. As he said in the report, "It is hard to find any economic development proposal, past or present, that would have as significant an impact as the 25 percent shift." (And this, by the way, was the genesis of the phrase "the local food shift.")

We thought that these numbers would get the attention of the county and state economic development folks, but even today, they seem blind to it. We have yet to have any success in getting it on their agenda.

But, thankfully, *someone else* has been paying attention: entrepreneurs and investors. In an emerging industry, where demand outpaces supply, opportunities abound. It was obvious we needed new farms and far more new farmers than the current programs could produce, massive additional acreage devoted to food production for local consumption, along with all of the food processing, storage, and distribution businesses necessary to support this local food shift. And there was a great need for restaurants and retail stores and schools to source locally, as they could reach a much bigger market and meet the growing demand.

But we knew that this expansion of the local food supply chain would require huge amounts of capital. In fact, according to Shuman, getting there would take $1.8 billion in capital investments. It was staggering.

Since reading Shuman's study, we've been deeply engaged in the process of learning how to move capital—especially local capital—into the project of rebuilding a foodshed. (Not surprisingly, it turns out that, as a society, we've become as unconscious about what our money is doing as we have about how we feed ourselves. Food localization is all about becoming conscious and deliberate with both.)

Significantly, the $1.8 billion in capital needed to get to 25 percent food localization represents only one half of 1 percent of the money that individuals in Colorado have in nonlocal stocks, bonds, and investment funds. So we know the money is there—we just have to find the way to get it to flow into local food and farming.

Slow money—a grassroots food and farming investment movement pioneered by recovering venture capitalist Woody Tasch—has become an essential strategy in this effort. In fact, the advent of slow money has arguably been the single most decisive factor in moving the local food movement toward the emergence of a viable local food industry.

Woody has been helping us understand that the economic downturn is exactly what you can expect when the relationships between money, community, and the land are broken—disconnected.

Woody wrote a most extraordinary book, *Inquiries into the Nature of Slow Money: Investing As If Food, Farms, and Fertility Mattered.* These new forms of local investment are key to relocalization—forms of investment "that catalyze the transition from a commerce of extraction and consumption to a commerce of preservation and restoration."[51] This means, especially, investing in local farming and in the enterprises that are needed to support a healthy food and farming system.

Woody speaks of *restorative economics,* economics based on the core principles of carrying capacity, cultural and biological diversity, sense of place, care of the commons, and nonviolence. This may be one of the most significant economic visions to land on this planet in recent decades. It's truly revolutionary. It's pure inspiration—and highly poetic.

To move local capital into local food and farming enterprises, local investment structures must be created. We've helped catalyze four slow money investment clubs in Colorado, and we are now exploring replicable online lending or investment platforms to democratize the movement of capital into local food economies. Such platforms could make it possible for other local communities to create their own crowd-sourced loan funds. In the future, we hope to see the launch of a business development company (BDC) capable of pooling community investment funds of up to $50 million. Ultimately, we would like to help catalyze the implementation of Michael Shuman's vision of a Local Food Authority supported by public bonds. But these things are not our responsibility.

Meanwhile, a backlash had been growing in response to the industrial-ized global food system, as millions of people were becoming aware of the fundamental value and importance of wholesome food and were waking up to the widespread damage to health and well-being big agri-business has directly caused. This backlash had its origin in the coun-terculture movement of the 1960s, an alternative lifestyle that had an emphasis on organic and homegrown food. This has evolved into a robust $39 billion per year organic food industry (half of the "natural foods" segment), and it is now growing at a little less than 10 percent per year. Yet in the United States, the total organic market amounts to less than 5 percent of total U.S. food sales.[52]

Several forces have converged to accelerate and amplify this backlash against the Unholy Alliance, what Wenonah Hauter (founder of Food and Water Watch) calls *foodopoly*.[53] Chief among them has been the emergence of a global grassroots movement toward localization—com-munities rebuilding their capacity to meet their essential needs locally, thereby greatly increasing economic resilience and self-reliance. And in the forefront of localization efforts (as seen in Transition Towns, Resil-ient Communities, Business Alliance for Local Living Economies, 350. org, the Post Carbon Institute, and so forth), there is a persistent—if inadequately organized—focus on food. As a people, we are beginning to understand that we must localize the food supply as much as possible, beginning in our own backyards and communities.

This local food revolution is emerging spontaneously in communities everywhere across America, rising to become a national movement to reclaim our food sovereignty, to shift control of our food supply away from the clutches of agribusiness, and to bring it back down to the community level, where it belongs. Still in its infancy, the movement is fragile, often chaotic, rarely organized, lacking resources, and facing overwhelming odds.

For now, many of these changes in our local food and farming sys-tem may seem "alternative" or optional. But in the coming months and years, their inevitability will become more clear, as will the reality that implementing these changes sooner rather than later will help to ensure food security and economic sustainability for all the citizens of our communities.

At the moment, it may seem that Peak Everything looms in some far-off future, a future that some of us may hope that we will never live long enough to see. But if we look carefully, if we make the effort to do the research and connect the dots, we will see that these events are much more imminent than that. Indeed, they are already beginning to unfold in our world, and we can even begin to map their trajectories.

For those who are already waking up to these realities, the triggers for this revolution in food and farming and our involvement in them are somewhat different. What moves us most are the opportunities we see

- to restore some measure of balance and fairness in a world of imbalance and injustice;
- to restore our connections with the place in which we live, our home;
- to heal the land that we have so profoundly abused;
- to heal and regenerate community;
- to rebuild our collective self-respect and our confidence in our ability to meet our own essential needs locally;
- to regain a sense of meaningful purpose;
- to ensure human freedom; and
- to experience the deep joy that comes from wholeheartedly contributing to the future of life on this beleaguered planet.

In the last decade, demand for local food in the United States has grown dramatically, perhaps exponentially. Across the country, farmers markets have increased to nearly eight thousand, with a current growth rate of nearly 10 percent. By early 2012, we saw the first industry surveys indicating that eaters were beginning to prefer local food over organic. However, demand for local food significantly outpaces supply, creating gold-rush conditions that herald the emergence of a local food industry, the dimensions of which cannot yet be fully measured.

This growth in demand has been driven by eaters who are willing to go far beyond the supermarket shelf to find their food. These are people who—thanks to authors like Michael Pollan, films like *Food Inc.,* and a plethora of conferences, workshops, and festivals around the country—want to know where their food comes from, who grows it, how it is produced, and how the land, animals, and farmworkers are treated.

Today we are living in a moment of historic transition. We are moving from a food and farming system that erodes soil, wastes water, diminishes biodiversity, wastes fossil fuels, spews carbon, relies on mechanization, modifies genes, pollutes water and air, poisons the land, depletes the spirit, destroys community, and creates economic disparity … to a food and farming system that restores and rebuilds soil, recycles and conserves water, increases biodiversity, sequesters carbon, produces its own energy, relies on human labor, breeds for resilience, saves seeds, purifies the water and the air, heals the land, feeds the spirit, builds community, and creates economic parity.

We are moving from a food system that enables only the rich to eat well to one that makes a wholesome, healthy diet a basic right for all citizens, where this is taken as a responsibility and not a luxury.

This local food revolution is already beginning to happen and *will* ultimately happen everywhere. It is a course correction that has become not only necessary but also inevitable.

The overarching vision is that our health will improve greatly, especially the health of our children. We will feel more connected, more alive, more engaged, living more meaningful and satisfying lives. Our local farmers will be able to buy the land on which they farm. We will transform the landscape, rebuild the soil. Our agricultural land will mostly be used for food production for local consumption. We will produce thousands of new jobs; our local economies will be robust! We will dramatically reduce greenhouse-gas emissions and environmental degradation. We will be sequestering carbon in the soil, in plant growth. We will have plans and food stores in place to feed all our people in times of crisis or emergency. We will all have a far greater degree of food security and food sovereignty; major corporations will no longer be in control of what and how we eat. Our local foodsheds will be resilient.

A kind of evolutionary wisdom is emerging from the heart of our cities and rural communities that is calling for a revolution in the way we humans feed ourselves. This is not so much a lifestyle movement as it is a genuine grassroots evolutionary response.

A new industry is arising to meet the growing demand for local food. It is growing quickly. Earnest pioneers are pouring sweat, tears, passion, and money into innovative visions and cherished dreams. Farmers, chefs, eaters, and food entrepreneurs across the continent are restoring soil, redefining nourishment, and reinventing business and investment models, disrupting the established order with bold new experiments and strategies. Creative investors and financial institutions are finding new ways to fuel this revolution with capital.

These are but the beginnings of the local food revolution. Like every frontier, the local food revolution is *emergent*. It is dispersed and self-organizing, decentralized, grassroots-to-grasstops, unpredictable, and generally rather messy, even chaotic. As we will see, it is populated by a wide spectrum of heroes and rascals, as the challenges and opportunities created by scarce supply tend to attract the good, the bad, and the ugly. Yet at its best, this local food frontier has energy, momentum, and direction. It is inspired by wise guides and visionaries. It is informed on the ground by experts in sustainable agricultural practices and aided by an explosion of new techniques for producing and selling food locally.

If we do this right, as Sharon Astyk says, "not only can we cease to do the harm that industrial agriculture does, but we can replace it with something better—a better way of growing and preparing food—and also a democracy of the sort that Thomas Jefferson imagined for his nation, a democracy that is not vulnerable to being stolen or sold, as our present one is."[54]

This will be a revolution!

PART 3

THE FULL EXTENT OF OUR PREDICAMENT

The transition to a fossil-fuel-free food system does not constitute a distant utopian proposal. It is an unavoidable, immediate, and immense challenge that will call for unprecedented levels of creativity at all levels of society.... A hundred years from now, everyone will be eating what we today would define as local organic food, whether or not we act. But what we do now will determine how many will be eating, what state of health will be enjoyed by those future generations, and whether they will live in a ruined cinder of a world, or one that is in the process of being renewed and replenished.

—RICHARD HEINBERG

CHAPTER 10

Peak Everything Revisited

It is far better to grasp the universe as it really is than to persist in delusion, however satisfying and reassuring.

—CARL SAGAN

The world is leaderless as we face the greatest danger that humans have ever faced.

—ALLAN SAVORY

We all find ourselves thrown into a process of profound transition (and it *is* a process). We may not be exactly clear about what we're transitioning *to*, but we're increasingly aware of what we're in the process of transitioning *from*: an unsustainable way of living on this planet, an unsustainable population level, an unsustainable impact on the biosphere, an unsustainable economic system, and, among other things, an unsustainable exploitation of fossil fuels and a host of other nonrenewable "resources." What is unsustainable, we are learning, will not continue for long.

Clearly, we are entering into a period of overwhelming change, an era of unintended consequences. The coming changes will alter not only how we live but even how we conceive of ourselves, how we think about the world, and how we see the future. And not only will we have to cope with severe disruption to our conception of ourselves and the world, but we will also need to forge a new vision of the world that we can live by. Where will that vision come from?

All our communities are in transition—and so are all cultures, all nations, and all institutions. We are in a transition as a species, even as a planet in a larger universe. Of course, the outcome of this great transition is uncertain, unpredictable. But this is what we're preparing for.

We live at a time when the underlying structures of the industrial growth society are beginning to unravel before our eyes, at a time when there is a growing feeling that human civilization is sliding into decline, at a time when ecosystems and species are being ravaged by the early stages of climate change, and at a time when we are learning that human population has likely been, in ecosystem terms, in dangerous "overshoot" for centuries.

We live at a time when we are beginning to wake up to all this and beginning to feel deeply what it all means. And in this uncertain time, evolutionary catalysts are being mysteriously called to an extraordinary level of service in response to humanity's predicament. We bear with us the seeds of an emergent future, a new story that will carry the essence of what it means to be human far beyond this threshold.

One of the requirements for being an evolutionary catalyst is being able to face reality head-on, without fear or preference. "Being with" uncomfortable realities is a vital skill. This part of the work may not be pleasant, but it is necessary.

A caution—what we're exploring here could be taken merely as information to be considered. But if we take it that way, we'll miss much of what's available. My suggestion is to just take all this in and to let it affect you deeply. Set aside for now your opinions, your beliefs, your defenses, your objections—even your agreement. Just take it all in; see where it takes you. If you will, just trust the process. This is a journey, and it's going somewhere.

OUR PREDICAMENT

Our collective predicament on this planet is far more dire and urgent than we allow ourselves to recognize. We face multiple converging crises of global scale that together actually threaten the survival of life on this planet. A few years ago Richard Heinberg began calling it all *Peak*

Everything. Since 2005, James Howard Kunstler has called it the *long emergency*. John Michael Greer prefers the *long descent*. Environmental writer Ellen LaConte calls it *critical mass*.

Here's the brief summary of Peak Everything, just going straight to the bottom line.

Peak Energy

We can expect sharp fluctuations in fossil fuel prices and a decline in fuel availability. This will plunge our economy into chaos, for it is built on false (and unsustainable) premises. We've burned up about half of the world's supply of fossil fuels. From now on, every ounce will be harder and more expensive to get out of the ground. Ultimately (within years or a couple decades), demand will outstrip supply—in spite of the development of tar sands, opening up Alaska, and offshore production. Renewable energy sources will not be available fast enough to maintain our current way of life. There will be a wrenching energy transition that will change how we live, where we live, and even who lives. We cannot prepare our communities with new technology alone or with incremental decreases in energy consumption. We need to live very differently—and we have to hurry.

Peak Climate Stability

First we called it *global warming,* then *climate change,* then *climate destabilization.* And then, as David Orr calls it, *climate collapse.*[55] The collapse of our climate is going to change *everything*—and quickly. The scientific consensus is that human-caused greenhouse-gas emissions are *already* having a devastating impact on the ecosphere, and this will get much worse in the future. It is clear that our governments are simply not going to be able to rise to the occasion in time to mitigate the impacts.

Peak Economic Growth

Economic recession will likely soon accelerate to inevitable collapse. There will be no long-term economic recovery. The underpinnings of the global economy are fundamentally unsustainable, and they are beginning to unravel. It is not possible for economic growth to continue at such scale without destroying life on our planet. The economists and politicians who are predicting recovery are the same ones who were recently predicting that there was virtually zero chance that we could slip into an economic recession—and we now understand that they were saying this at a time when we were already at least a year into recession. In the future, we will most likely experience roller-coaster periods of global recession followed by weak and partial recoveries; this will ultimately give way to grinding, long-term global depression. In the process, many of the institutions on which we have come to rely will surely fail, some of them slowly, some of them suddenly and spectacularly. The next several decades will be chaotic, and the chaos will prevail long after most of us have left this planet.

Peak Industrial Agriculture

> On a global basis, agriculture is the largest threat to biodiversity and ecosystem function of any single human activity.
>
> —WES JACKSON

> We need to stop pretending human agriculture is a given— and especially to stop pretending that we will be able to feed ourselves using the same fragile, annuals-based, fossil-energy-dependent agriculture we now employ. Because we certainly won't. And heck, we might not be able to employ any agriculture at all—at least not as it's now recognized.
>
> —DAN ALLEN, "WHEN AGRICULTURE STOPS WORKING"

The way we're feeding ourselves is devastating the environment. It's also destroying our soils, undermining our health, and eroding local economies. And this food system is beginning to unravel. It will never be able to feed the world.

Peak Soil

Allan Savory reports that the world is losing soil at the rate of ten billion tons per year. Here in the United States, arable land has already reached peak production. All those petroleum-based products that fueled the

Green Revolution—especially pesticides—have turned most American farmland into dead soils.

Peak Water

Worldwide demand for fresh water is expected to exceed supply by 50 percent as soon as 2025. If the droughts continue, that will happen long before 2025, because agriculture is the biggest user of water. The California drought is a useful example. Recently an observer wrote that perhaps it's time to stop thinking of it as a drought, but as *peak water.* In other words, the water situation in California now is likely to be as good as it will ever be. That's true in many other areas as well.

Peak Health

Food-related diseases have reached epidemic proportions, including heart disease, obesity, cancer, type 2 diabetes in children, and an explosion of food allergies. In fact, the Centers for Disease Control said not so long ago that food is the leading cause of death, after tobacco. Human life expectancy is now decreasing. In addition, we can't not talk about mental health. In 2013, *Newsweek* reported that suicide now takes more lives than war, murder, and natural disaster combined. Since 2010, in the developed world, suicide became the leading cause of death for people ages fifteen to forty-nine. In wealthy countries, suicide is the leading cause of death for men in their forties and in the top five causes for men in their fifties. Globally, suicide rates are up 60 percent since World War II.[56]

Peak Population

Perhaps the least discussed aspect of our predicament is that humanity has been in overshoot for some time, perhaps since the time of the American Civil War. Given the earth's resources, a sustainable population level may be no more than one billion people. If we are to sustain a kind of human society we could call *civilized,* two things will be required: a much smaller human population and a means of food production that is not dependent on fossil fuels and that does not destroy our soils. We are accumulating a deep deficit to support our population (all in the form of externalized costs). The debt is quickly coming due. Population collapse is inevitable. We could call it *population decline,* but it is highly unlikely that it will decline quickly enough to avoid collapse. We are heading toward a wall. It is highly likely that food (or the lack of it) will be profoundly involved in this process.

Peak Food

We're facing a looming global food crisis. Michael Klare has said, "At this point, the focus is understandably on the *immediate* consequences of the still ongoing Great Drought: dying crops, shrunken harvests, and rising food prices. But keep an eye out for the social and political effects.... Better than any academic study, these will offer us a hint of what we can expect in the coming decades from a hunger-games world of rising temperatures, persistent droughts, recurring food shortages, and billions of famished, desperate people."[57]

Peak Species

And just for perspective, we're all waking up at the very moment when we're realizing that we're also in the midst of a mass extinction of species on our planet, the most dramatic geological event in the last sixty-six million years, a mass extinction that has been caused by the way humans have been living on this earth. We're adding a total of two hundred thousand new people each day (births minus deaths), and at the same time, up to two hundred species are going extinct, day after day. But we're not just causing this mass extinction, we are also rapidly eliminating the very conditions for the renewal of life.

⌒⌒

Peak Everything is no longer in the future; it is already upon us. It is our predicament. What it all means is that in each of these arenas, going forward, we can expect only decline—and in some cases, collapse.

These are not separate crises; they are deeply interrelated. For instance, our global economy is based on cheap fossil fuels, and burning fossil fuels is dramatically altering our climate and causing mass extinction. Therefore, economic growth cannot and will not continue. The way of life that we have come to consider normal cannot and will not continue. *This is really what we evolutionary catalysts are preparing ourselves and our communities for.*

THE FULL EXTENT

I think it's important to communicate as emphatically as possible— even though people generally don't like it—that the situation is actually far more serious and far more urgent than almost anyone realizes. When, year after year, we see reality exceeding our scientists' worst-case scenarios, we can be sure that something unprecedented and radically unpredictable is unfolding.

It's safe to say now that the future—say, just fifteen to twenty years out—will be so different from the world we live in today that it is simply impossible for us to imagine it. While I don't sense that we'll see the extinction of the human species in that time, it will probably be apparent that we're on the kind of trajectory that James Lovelock speaks of— where we'll wind up with maybe only a few hundred million people on the planet before the end of the century—perhaps long before the end of the century.[58] Some of us here may live to see this unfold. And our children? Well, we certainly need to consider that carefully.

I think we'll see the unprecedented hardship that Bucky Fuller spoke of. Many are experiencing it now, of course, but it will spread like a plague. Frankly, it will be a horrible adjustment. We're heading toward an evolutionary bottleneck, and it's likely that, at best, only a few of us will squeak through. The devastation will be profound, though perhaps not quite total.

We're beginning to understand that it's simply too late to avoid this. We need to recognize—and help others recognize—that we're not going to "solve" climate change and related disasters. Instead, at least some of us will learn to adapt to a radically changed environment as our population is being reduced dramatically. Perhaps we'll even have to live underground.

ABOUT FEAR

I will not attempt to convince you of the impending global disaster and even the possible collapse of human population or the extinction of life on this planet. If you do the homework, you won't need convincing. I'm fascinated by Margaret Wheatley's recent observation that information does not change minds any more.[59] But we will all need to learn to face the deep fear that comes up. Joanna Macy and others are doing very important work around this, such as "The Work That Reconnects."

I've been astonished over the years that almost every time we talk about these things to a new audience, we are admonished by someone saying that we shouldn't be trying to motivate people using fear. This is a strange response, and it has taught us a great deal. Some have accused us of being doom-and-gloomers.

It's true that we have followed the tradition of the relocalization movement, especially as expressed in the Transition movement, with a commitment to continually raise awareness about our collective predicament. We're sometimes criticized for this, and we are hardly alone. The great environmental writer Gus Speth recounts that in *The Death of Environmentalism,* the authors remind us that Martin Luther King Jr. did not proclaim, "I have a *nightmare!*" Here's Speth's reply to them: "King did not *need* to say that—his people were *living* a nightmare. They needed a dream. But we, I fear, are living in a dream. We need to be reminded of the nightmare ahead. Here is the truth as I see it: *we will never do the things that are needed unless we know the full extent of our predicament.*"[60]

As a people, we have been in denial about so much for so long that we are dominated by a profoundly distorted view of reality. Ironically, this may be especially true of those who have access to the most data. And the actions and lives based on such a twisted grasp of reality are likely to produce unintended consequences beyond our capacity to imagine or deal with.

The belief that staring reality in the face is an attempt to use fear to motivate action is itself a fear-based response, though it is disguised as being rational and emotionally mature. *We need not fear reality, but we do need to face it.* Our failure to do so is an act of cowardice. We have the inner resources—the strength and the wisdom—to face all this with equanimity and to respond appropriately.

This is certainly a time of great peril. But it is also a time of great promise. And if we can hold both possibilities in our being, even as we discover that the stakes are far greater and more urgent than we had ever imagined, we will be brought to a moment of decision, of choice, of commitment, and—I would even suggest—a moment of *surrender.*

Here we are finally motivated by deeper values: authenticity, integrity, genuine emergence—even mystery. Such extraordinary moments in history, such evolutionary thresholds, call for an extraordinary response. If we are open and honest, we will find ourselves being called. Here we begin to yield to the angels of evolution, who are calling us to greater service.

And individuals everywhere *are* responding. Often they awaken alone, unrecognized, seemingly unqualified, invisible to the world, without the usual trappings of wealth or power.

One of the great dilemmas of our society is the "silo effect," which essentially amounts to the belief that ours is the only "reality" that matters or is relevant. We are accomplished at this kind of myopia. It is the ultimate form of denial, and it enables a kind of moral relativism. What is being denied is any possibility of an objective reality. There is great fear and confusion underneath this mostly psychological strategy. In its most extreme form, especially in America, it produces severe economic and social disparity, as well as an ever-deeper disconnection from reality.

Thankfully, we are now beginning to awaken to greater realities, which call us to break down the silo walls, to let them dissolve, to not be confined by them (which has often been an unconscious choice).

This does not need to happen violently. As we face bigger and more challenging (and even harsher) realities, we also simultaneously begin to encounter greater possibilities than we have ever allowed ourselves to consider before. Mysteriously—in what many consider to be humanity's darkest hour—collaboration, community, and cocreation are emerging in the human sphere as never before.

The evolutionary impulse here is to bridge the separation gap, to heal, to regenerate, and to evolve. Emergence itself is coming into focus as how evolution unfolds, and it can do so through humans.

In the emerging picture, it is clear that twenty years from now, life on this planet will likely be unrecognizable compared to what it is today. And what life becomes on this planet—if there is to be any life at all—will basically be up to us.

Given that it is now highly unlikely that industrial nations will be able to unite quickly enough to slow the progression of Peak Everything, we who are aware of these trends are then left to grapple with the urgent question of how humanity will survive and even thrive in the face of this unfolding disaster. That's the impossible challenge that has chosen us.

The most potentially devastating of all these, of course, is climate change. In *Requiem for a Species: Why We Resist the Truth about Climate Change,* Clive Hamilton writes, "We will be powerless to stop the jump to a new climate on Earth, one much less sympathetic to life. The kind of climate that has allowed civilization to flourish will be gone and humans will enter a long struggle just to survive."[61] This means a profound shift for human existence, one that we have hardly begun to accept.

The words of poet Drew Dellinger, from "hieroglyphic stairway," are relevant here.

> *It's 3:23 in the morning*
> *and I'm awake*
> *because my great great grandchildren*
> *won't let me sleep*
> *my great great grandchildren*
> *ask me in dreams*
> *what did you do while the Planet was plundered?*
> *what did you do when the Earth was unravelling?*

surely you did something
when the seasons started failing?
as the mammals, reptiles, birds were all dying?

did you fill the streets with protest
when democracy was stolen?
what did you do
once
you
knew?

Here I ask the reader to begin considering this very personal question: In the face of Peak Everything, what is the urgent, overwhelming, impossible mission that is waiting for you to step forward and accept, that only you can do, that all depends on you, whether you're qualified or not, whether you're ready or not?

CHAPTER 11

Climate Collapse:
The Rogue Factor

From a presentation I gave to a Metro State College ethics class, November 2013. While some of the data here may be slightly outdated, the essence of the perspective remains sound. While Guy McPherson's conclusions are highly controversial and provocative, his research appears to be impeccable. In my view, he is perhaps the most prolific reporter and interpreter of climate change research functioning today.

Before we go any farther and get to the real point of all this, I want to go back to the issue of global warming and climate collapse. And here I'm going to draw from an author who has gotten much attention lately, Guy McPherson, a former tenured professor and environmentalist at the University of Arizona who resigned his post there. He recently published a book about his journey, *Walking Away from Empire*,[62] and he writes a blog called "Nature Bats Last."[63] And in fact, Guy was here in Boulder just a couple of weeks ago, where he said unequivocally, "The climate situation is much worse than we've been led to believe and is accelerating far more rapidly than accounted for by models."

McPherson really got my attention when he gave the keynote address at the recent Bluegrass Bioneers conference in Louisville, Kentucky, in 2012—delivering the best summary of the latest climate science I've seen anywhere.[64] McPherson's main story is that global economic collapse is upon us—which is good news, because, as he says, "*if* we stop this omnicidal, suicidal set of living arrangements that we call industrial civilization, then that will actually force us to stop climate chaos."

But what is this climate chaos, this climate collapse? What is happening, really? What is the truth that's being kept from us?

In his presentation, McPherson sequentially lays out the most important scientific studies about climate change, and some of them we hadn't even heard about. Here's the progression:

1. In 2007, the United Nation's Intergovernmental Panel on Climate Change (IPCC), in their fourth assessment, conclude that global warming will produce a 1 degree Celsius temperature increase by 2010. That's already catastrophic news, because a 1 degree global temperature increase, as they said, leads to "rapid, unpredictable, and non-linear responses that could lead to extensive ecosystem damage."

2. A year later, in 2008, the Hadley Center for Meteorological Research—with more computational power and more data—concludes that we're headed to a 2 degree Celsius warmer world by the end of this century. Two degrees is truly catastrophic, we now understand. Because of positive feedbacks, self-reinforcing feedback loops, 2 degrees leads almost immediately and with great certainty to 6 degrees Celsius.

3. Six months later, in mid 2009, the United Nations Environmental Program comes along and says we're headed to a 3.5 degree Celsius warmer world by 2100.

4. Soon after, the Hadley Center, just a year after their first assessment, says, "four is the new two, and it's coming by midcentury." Four degrees Celsius is 7 degrees Fahrenheit. Remember, two leads to six. As McPherson says, "four is the last nail in the coffin of human experience."

5. About the time of the Copenhagen climate change meetings, the Global Carbon Project and Copenhagen Diagnosis come up with 6 and 7 degrees Celsius warming by the end of the century.

6. The day after Thanksgiving in 2010, the International Energy Agency's World Energy Outlook says we're headed to 3.5 degrees Celsius warmer by 2035.

7. In December of 2010, several weeks later, the United Nations Environment Program says we're in for more than 5 degrees Celsius increase by 2050. McPherson reminds us that 5 degrees Celsius kills the oceans—they become so acidified that essentially nothing can live there, including the thermophiles found at incredible depths and at enormous temperatures.

8. Just after Thanksgiving in 2011, only a year after their previous assessment, the International Energy Agency (IEA) says 6 degrees Celsius by 2035. They later retract this, without explanation.

And I'll add a couple more, even more recent than McPherson's lineup.

1. The day before the presidential election, the global accounting group PricewaterhouseCoopers announces a major economic analysis predicting 6 degrees Celsius increase by the end of the century, with the admission that this could occur even sooner. As a result, they tell us, we can expect nothing less than economic devastation. That's a showstopper, as they're one of the most respected and influential financial institutions in the world. Did you read about this in the media? I didn't think so.

2. And on November 6, 2012, in the United Kingdom, Dr. Kevin Anderson, deputy director of the Tyndall Center for Climate Change Research (the United Kingdom's premier climate modeling institution), speaking to a sold-out crowd at Bristol University's Cabot Institute, says that *our future is essentially not possible*. He says we are almost guaranteed to go to 4 degrees Celsius warming and perhaps beyond that by 2050 (4 degrees is "beyond the point at which agriculture, the ecosystem, and industrial civilization can survive"), and that we'll almost certainly hit 6 degrees no later than the end of this century. Four degrees, he says, "would be incompatible with an organized global community"—very nuanced language. The title of his speech was "Real Clothes for the Emperor: Facing the Challenges of Climate Change." Did you read about this? Anderson accuses other scientists and government leaders of knowing all this but refusing to predict anything beyond a 2 degrees Celsius

warming—a blatant cover-up, in other words. You can read all about this online, and hear his speech, at EcoShock Radio.

Just like the studies that McPherson cites, Anderson's analysis doesn't even take into account the effects of positive feedbacks, self-reinforcing feedback loops.

Recently, we've been reading about the new IPCC Fifth Assessment, which will be released next year. Did you read about it? Doesn't sound as bad as we feared, does it?

However, the entire IPCC body of work fails to take into account positive feedbacks. This means that their projections are, to say it politely, ultraconservative. To be a little less polite, they're extremely misleading. If we're making our decisions based on IPCC data, we're simply going in the wrong direction and radically underestimating our predicament. You could even make a pretty good case that the recent IPCC report is a cover-up. We don't really need to go there, but we do need to listen to the scientists who are reporting positive feedbacks, the factors that are increasingly accelerating climate change and sending us toward a tipping point from which there is no return.

What are these positive feedbacks? They are the *results* of global warming—like the increase of water vapor in the atmosphere—that accelerate the *rate* of global warming itself.

McPherson told us in Boulder recently that from the scientific literature, he's identified no fewer than twenty-seven major positive feedbacks, only two of which are reversible (i.e., "at a temporal scale relevant to our species"). He introduced these feedback loops with this caveat: "These feedbacks are not additive, they are multiplicative; they not only reinforce within a feedback, the feedbacks also reinforce among themselves."[65]

1. rapid release of Arctic methane
2. warm Atlantic water defrosting the Arctic as it shoots through Fram Strait
3. Siberian methane vents growing to 1 kilometer across
4. 2010 Amazon drought triggering release of more carbon than in United States

5. peat in boreal forests decomposing

6. invasion of tall shrubs warming soil, destabilizing permafrost

7. Greenland ice darkening

8. Antarctic methane being released; melt rate catching up to Arctic

9. Russian forest and bog fires growing

10. cracking of glaciers accelerating in presence of increased carbon

11. the Beaufort Gyre reversed course

12. exposure to sunlight increasing conversion of exposed soil carbon, accelerating thawing of permafrost

13. microbes in melting permafrost eating carbon and producing more heat

14. summer ice melt in Antarctica is highest level in a thousand years

15. floods in Canada sending silty water into the Beaufort Sea

16. surface meltwater draining through cracks in ice sheets, warming them from the inside

17. Heinrich Event anticipated in Greenland

18. breakdown of thermohaline conveyor belt affecting Antarctic, melting permafrost

19. loss of Arctic sea ice causing the jet stream to slow and meander, producing weather blocks

20. Arctic ice growing darker, hence less reflective

21. extreme weather events exacerbating climate change

22. ocean acidification reducing the release of radiation-shielding dimethyl sulfide by plankton

23. sea-level rise causing slope collapse, tsunamis, and release of methane

24. rising ocean temps reducing plankton (upsetting natural cycles of carbon dioxide, nitrogen, and phosphorus)

25. warming triggering earthquakes, which trigger methane release

26. Arctic drilling fast-tracked by Obama administration

27. supertankers taking advantage of slushy Arctic

The one that we've been paying the most attention to recently comes from a collaboration of scientists who call themselves the Arctic Methane Emergency Group. Just last week they issued a report that starts off powerfully.

> While we go about our day, working, taking care of our family and doing life, a crisis that many are unaware of is unfolding in the Arctic that … will affect every living thing on Earth, including us. As recently as of Monday, October 28, 2013, consistently high levels of methane have been detected through the methane tracker that the Arctic News monitors. Not only will the Arctic soon be ice-free, but something far worse and a symptom of climate change is happening in real-time: This methane, previously stored for millions of years in frozen clathrates deep below the ocean, is starting to be released at a staggering rate in October, alarming scientists and researchers worldwide.[66]

One of the climate scientists in the group, Paul Beckwith, at the University of Ottawa, predicted a year ago that because of positive feedbacks, especially methane release, we could see a 6 degree Celsius temperature increase—nearly 11 degrees Fahrenheit—within the next ten years. That's incredibly fast, and it's quite possible he's right. Actually, we're starting to see a number of predictions clustering around 4 to 6 degrees Celsius in the next decade or so.

There's more.[67] The *Proceedings of the National Academy of Science*, one of the premier science journals in the world, published a paper titled "Climate Change Is Irreversible," finding that the atmospheric level of carbon dioxide concentration today—we recently hit a record four hundred parts per million—will be the *minimum* level we will experience for at least the next thousand years. This is the highest level of carbon in the atmosphere in three million years.

About all this, McPherson said, "350.org is a bad joke. It's disingenuous, or ignorant. There's no way we'll see 350 parts per million carbon dioxide within at least the next thousand years. Promoting that as if we could get there is ridiculous."

We've been setting records with our carbon emissions. According to the United Nation's Environmental Program, during 2008—the most catastrophic year of the Great Recession—carbon emissions rose to their highest level since we fully implemented the Clean Air Act in this country. In 2009, we increased carbon emissions over that record by an additional 6.2 percent. In 2010, we increased carbon emissions 6.5 percent over that, and in 2011, we continued the trend with an increase of 3.4 percent. The results for 2012 will be similar, and they're just starting to come in. Even though we're in an economic Great Recession, our carbon emissions keep going up. No matter what we've been doing to stop this, it's obviously not nearly enough. And almost no one is talking about this.

In February of 2011, scientist Tim Garrett, from the University of Utah, was finally able to publish an important paper in *Climatic Change,* one of the premier journals in the climate sciences, titled "Are There Basic Physical Constraints on Future Anthropogenic Emissions of Carbon Dioxide?"[68] He had submitted this paper in 2007, but it took four years for it to be accepted. His argument is that only economic collapse will prevent runaway global climate change.

Finally, research by the Arctic Methane Emergency Group indicates that in 2010, methane emissions into the atmosphere have gone exponential. We've reached a tipping point.

Malcolm Light, the author of this group's paper, titled "Global Extinction within One Human Lifetime as a Result of Spreading Atmospheric Arctic Methane Heat Wave and Surface Firestorm,"[69] says that this process will "release huge quantities of methane into the atmosphere and lead to the demise of all life on earth before the middle of this century." And he even gets rather specific about this, estimating that life in the Southern Hemisphere will end in 2047. But life in the Northern Hemisphere will end first, in 2031.

Of course, these are just predictions. And as quantum physicist Niels Bohr once famously said, "Predictions are difficult, especially about the future."

But one of the patterns we see here is that year after year, scientists' worst-case scenarios are being exceeded by the data of what's actually happened.

The point that we need to get is that this is the direction in which we are headed. *It's runaway climate change—climate collapse.* And every year, the more data and the better models we have, the worse it looks. This is what the world that we're inheriting looks like.

❧

Now, I'd like you to take a deep breath.

Richard Heinberg once said that almost every book or presentation about these issues ends with what he calls "a mandatory message of hope." But then he tries to get us to focus on the realities by saying, "My mandatory message of hope is there is no hope—for a soft landing or more of the same or business as usual or perpetual growth or normal life, as we've come to know it…. But isn't that good news?"

Well, yes, I think it is. Don't you?

And I'll follow that with something from James Howard Kunstler that has meant a lot to us: "Hope is not a consumer product. You have to generate your own hope. You do that by demonstrating to yourself that you are brave enough to face reality and competent enough to deal with the circumstances it presents. How we will manage to uphold a decent society in the face of extraordinary change will depend on our creativity, our generosity, and our kindness, and I am confident that we can find these resources within our own hearts, and collectively in our communities."[70]

As you may know, Kunstler is hardly a Pollyanna, but he's pointing to something crucial.

❧

Okay, you've just had a concentrated dose of reality, the truth about our predicament. Can you see this? Can you feel this? Didn't you sort of know this already? Are you surprised that you don't hear about all this in the media? Are you surprised that people aren't talking about this everywhere?

I remember hearing a Canadian scientist say a few years ago, "I don't understand you Americans. You say you stand for freedom and justice and what's right in the world. So why aren't you rioting in the streets over all this?"

Here's the thing, as Arundhati Roy wrote in her book *Power Politics,* "The trouble is that once you see it, you can't unsee it. And once you've seen it, keeping quiet, saying nothing, becomes as political an act as speaking out. There's no innocence. Either way, you're accountable."[71]

I'm sorry to say, this all winds up in our lap. Twenty years from now, life on this planet will be unrecognizable compared to what it is today. And what life becomes on this planet—if there is to be any life at all—will basically be up to us. Industrial civilization is already over, dead. We know that in our hearts, don't we? And we also know that whatever civilization comes next—if there is to be any at all—will be up to us.

In *Eaarth,* Bill McKibben writes, "We *may,* with commitment and luck, yet be able to maintain a planet that will sustain *some kind* of civilization, but it won't be the same planet, and hence it can't be the same civilization. The earth that we knew—the only earth that we ever knew—is gone."[72]

ᐒ

This is what we call an *evolutionary threshold.* It's a moment when the old destroys itself and something new comes to birth. As Bioneers founder Kenny Ausubel says, it's a moment of enlightenment.

When I say it's up to us, I don't mean our generation or our tribe or our people. I'm talking about us specifically, the people here in this room.[73]

What if this is actually true? If you knew it all came down to *you,* what would you do? If you knew it all came down to *you,* it wouldn't matter if you felt inadequate, unprepared, or even pissed off or just depressed. If you really knew that it all came down to you, you would do whatever you had to do. Wouldn't you? I believe you would.

That *is* your situation. That's *our* situation, for each of us. It's up to each of us. It's up to you. And it's up to me. It's up to us. Us.

This is why, for instance, Lynette Marie and I are doing everything humanly possible to build the ways to feed our local population in Colorado, all five million of us, because our global food supply chain is just about to collapse and leave a lot of people here very hungry unless we quickly learn to provision ourselves locally.

Localizing the global food supply is the issue that pulled us out of our lives and into a totally unexpected mission—one that seems extremely urgent, overwhelming, and, at times, just downright impossible. But that's the mission that has come to us, even though we have no visible qualifications for doing such a thing. Yes, there are a lot of other people working on this, but it all comes down to us. *And* each of them. And we all *know* it. We know that if we don't do it, if we don't do it together, *it won't happen.* There's no second string to send into the game should we fail. And we very well might fail.

CHAPTER 12

Stories from the Front Lines

Not coincidentally, we have discovered that almost everyone we know in the local food revolution understands Peak Everything, although they rarely speak of it.

In *Grow! Stories from the Urban Food Movement,* Stephen Grace serves up generous helpings of nutrient-dense stories of farmers and farming in the gritty urban tangle of the sprawling Denver metropolis, revealing a hidden revolution with the power to quietly heal lives and communities.[74] Drawn by a common urge to rebuild food security and sovereignty, the unsung pioneers Grace discovers are arising from broken communities to forge a regenerative local economy that is steadily and unexpectedly transforming fractured landscapes. The book emerged from Grace's attempt to find the bounty available in his own backyard ("so many tasty foods, so many fascinating people"). Reading *Grow!* fires our imaginations, inspires hope, and compels us to join the local food revolution and experience the joys of "living deeply" in our cities.

Here's an excerpt from an interview I did with Grace in the summer of 2015.[75]

MICHAEL BROWNLEE: What's been the most surprising thing about this journey for you?

STEPHEN GRACE: There is so much reason for despair in the world, and all the people I met who are involved in this movement are completely cognizant of the magnitude of the world's problems. They understand the gravity of the situation we are facing, whether it's catastrophic climate change, the diminishment of our national resources, social problems, peak oil, peak this, peak that. They are completely aware, very well educated, and very in tune with these things.

The more you know, the harder it becomes to navigate in a day-to-day world. It would be very easy to succumb to despair. The beautiful thing about this movement, and the great surprise of it, is how joyous these people are in their urban food enterprises. Throughout their day-to-day involvement, there is an undercurrent of joy that drives them just as much as a looming apocalyptic scenario of despair out on the horizon. That incredible, irrepressible undercurrent of optimism was a great surprise. They understand the gravity of these problems. Yet they are driven by an optimism, by a determination to create change, however small it is, in a very meaningful way and in a very joyful way.

These events are so much fun. The premise of an event might be: "Here is a problem. Our food system is horrible, it's destroying our health, it's destroying planetary health, and it's destroying our social connections." But there is always an undercurrent of celebration that rises to the surface, a celebration of what remains of our natural environment, what remains of our food system, what remains of our social connections—and rebuilding and healing all those things that are broken. No matter how grim the premise of an event, I'd always leave feeling good, having a great time and in a very meaningful way, connecting with people in a very, very deep way.

MICHAEL BROWNLEE: So would it be fair to say that what you received out of this project is a kind of optimism in the face of apocalypse?

STEPHEN GRACE: I started in a dark place personally, feeling that things were pretty grim on all levels. A lot of people in my life had been taken from me. I had seen incredible trauma—on a personal level, people in my immediate social circles, and planetary problems—and I wasn't feeling very good about the state of things. That was the big surprise and the big takeaway, something that I'll take with me forever. Every single person that I profiled in the book is completely cognizant of the magnitude of the problems, but every one of them has such joy and determination to do good. Being around people like that, I just can't help being affected by it and taking some sense of optimism from that.

That's what I took personally from that journey, and hopefully I have conveyed that in the book.

I can't help feeling that we are going to be all right somehow, some way, against all odds. That's not rational. If you look at it rationally, whether you crunch the numbers or just start listing out the problems that are out on the horizon, it can seem pretty oppressive. But then, I spend time with someone like Carlos—a young person coming from extraordinarily difficult circumstances that I can't even imagine—and his optimism cannot be repressed. It just keeps rising to the surface, and he keeps moving forward, trying to do good in the world. I can't be around people like that and not have that change my outlook and change me in a profound way. I feel like I can continue to move forward in my life with a sense of optimism and hope and determination. If you keep connecting with people, and you keep helping them cultivate what they do, keep cultivating your own motivation to do good in the world, you can't help but be successful.

There's excellent evidence of success in a lot of these initiatives, and some that aren't successful. In urban food, you're constantly experimenting, constantly trying things, and moving forward. You almost have to have that entrepreneurial spirit: "Oh, this didn't work, but we're going to try this over here, and we're going to keep moving toward success." And even when people don't achieve the success that they envisioned, I think there's such incredible dignity in the fact that they're trying. That, to me, is a victory in the face of the looming cataclysmic thinking of dark apocalypse. I mean, they have tried all sorts of things that didn't work, and they moved on to the next. There is optimism, and there's entrepreneurial spirit. That's something that I hope comes through in the book and what I hope people get from the broader movement.

To me, it's bigger than just the food movement. It touches on something deep and meaningful in the human spirit. Maybe it's the urban pioneers, or a new wave of can-do optimism when we are at our best as Americans—the idea that, yes, this is daunting, but we're going to make it work.

෴

What strikes me is that involvement in urban agriculture has been personally revolutionary for the individuals that Grace writes about. The local food revolution is healing lives and communities. The people Grace encounters—the mostly unsung heroes of the local food revolution—are the source of a rich stream of nutrients that nourish our souls. These individuals, motivated by unseen forces, represent the abundant and diverse variety of "edibles" growing mostly quietly in our midst, even mostly hidden. They rise mysteriously from the exhausted soils of community—*recovering* community, we could say, for these fierce local food heroes are lovingly cultivating and rebuilding this troubled soil in ways that fire our imaginations and make our hearts swell with hope, and compel us to join them. They thrive in an emerging ecology of restorative economics that is so radically different from what most of our society has become that, at first, it might seem utterly alien to us. But underneath it all, we can recognize that in this meandering path they are forging, in this process of recovering our food sovereignty, lies home.

PART 4

EMERGENCE: THE
EVOLUTIONARY PERSPECTIVE

Evolution unfolds in a series of quantum leaps, not in a continuous linear process. The movement forward is radical, unexpected, fundamental. Each shift from one stage to the next brings about irrevocable deep change, at the same time providing a new foundation for the unfolding of the future.

—DEEP TRANSITION WORKSHOP

CHAPTER 13

The Problem with
Peak Everything

> Until recently I believed complete collapse of the world's
> industrial economy would prevent runaway greenhouse and
> therefore allow our species to persist for a few more genera-
> tions. But in June 2012, the ocean of evidence on climate
> change overwhelmed me, and I no longer subscribe to the
> notion that habitat for humans will exist on Earth beyond
> the 2030s. We've triggered too many self-reinforcing feed-
> back loops to prevent near-term extinction at our own hand.
>
> —GUY MCPHERSON, *EXTINCTION DIALOGS*

Much of the purpose behind presenting the data about Peak Everything
is to provide the context for the work of an evolutionary catalyst, most
particularly one working in food localization. It's important that we
know why we're compelled to do what we are called to do.

From a certain perspective, it appears that Peak Everything can only
end badly: the sixth mass extinction of species could ultimately include
our own. Guy McPherson certainly makes a compelling, if compassionate, argument for this inevitability.

When we finally face the full extent of our collective predicament,
it does at first seem that all is lost—or perhaps that we're in the fourth
quarter of the game, with three minutes left, and we're down ten points.
Unless something completely unexpected and unpredictable happens,
we will surely lose the game. Or so it seems.

On my recommendation, a friend recently dove into the McPherson material for the first time, and even though I had given him fair warning, he was immediately overwhelmed. After just a brief exposure, he emailed me: "Pretty sobering stuff, which, if believed, makes the food relocalization effort pointless, does it not?"

Never mind, for the moment, that he felt that he actually had a choice whether to believe McPherson or not.[76] On first encounter with McPherson's tough love, this individual was apparently ready to abandon his commitment to local food, to just give it all up as hopeless. *Why?*

What this reveals is that my friend's veneer of hope and positivity was suddenly stripped away, and his underlying fear and hopelessness (previously denied, but lurking beneath the surface) were moved starkly into the foreground. This is not a pleasant experience for anyone, but it is instructive.

The problem with this reaction is that the context is incomplete, as I wrote back to my friend.

> To the contrary, this makes the food-localization effort *urgent* and *essential*. What McPherson does not understand is *emergence*. Revolution is (can be) a manifestation of emergence. The reason McPherson can't see any way through this evolutionary threshold (*impasse,* to him) is he is a scientist who cannot look beyond a certain bandwidth of physical reality, cannot comprehend that there are even larger forces at work that are being expressed through 13.7 billion years of physical evolution and are heading in a particular direction, and that humans are capable of embodying the thrust of evolution itself, even consciously. In other words, he's looking at an artificially limited data set—yet another form of denial. His data set leads to only one conclusion: extinction; but he's not seeing the whole picture (this is the problem with scientism). *And* his data set is extremely valuable to evolutionary catalysts (keeps us honest and outside the realm of ideology).

Well, this exchange perhaps demonstrates that such matters are not best discussed via email.

Part four of this book is an exploration of the broader context in which Peak Everything and the local food revolution are occurring. And here I would slightly paraphrase Gus Speth's admonition: "Unless we comprehend the full *context* of our predicament, we will never do what is necessary."

ॐ

As a people, we do not know where we are or when we are.[77] Thus we do not know *who* we are or who we are becoming or how we should proceed together on this planet. This, too, is part of our predicament, characteristic of our plight.

Nostalgic or indignant as we might be over our myths and creation stories of the past, they are simply no longer relevant. Created for earlier eras and tribal peoples, they can no longer serve us. We must let them go.

In our predicament, we can grasp that somehow we must become one people, the people of earth. Yet we have no shared origin story, no unifying myth, no single context that might make this possible.

A collective context is beginning to appear, however, which we might call the *evolutionary context,* based on a growing understanding of the patterns by which the universe itself has evolved. This perspective has developed only recently in human history, and it changes everything.

- We are beginning to discover that healing and regeneration are natural, inherent, evolutionary responses that are, in fact, emerging nearly everywhere in our midst on this planet, and that we evolutionary catalysts are ourselves instruments of that evolutionary force—and thereby instruments of healing and regeneration. At least we have that opportunity—and potential responsibility.

- Emergence arises out of cataclysm. This is an important realization. This evolutionary drive for healing and regeneration is the only source of hope that has any solid grounding these days. The universe, it turns out, is not only self-organizing but also self-healing.

- As Brian Swimme and Thomas Berry make undeniable in *The Universe Story,* the evolutionary processes that have been unfolding in the universe for the last 13.7 billion years—and for 4.5 billion years on this rarest of planets—are deeply embedded in us as humans, and they are now beginning to become conscious in us.

- It is increasingly clear that our converging global crises have one single cause—our fundamental disconnection from nature, from spirit, from the sacred. Any "solution" that does not address this disconnection will not only fail but will further exacerbate our predicament.

It's been said that the New Cosmology is America's spiritual gift to the human species. And in a way, it is a uniquely American gift to humanity.

ॐ

There are many ways to view the evolution of the universe, of course, and nearly every day our media bring us astonishing glimpses into the ways our cosmos seems to work, often accompanied by flights of unbridled speculation. While these can provide endless fascination, they too lack an overarching context.

Our own rather revolutionary understanding of the evolution of the universe—and of the process of evolution—has come to us through a traceable thread that goes back to Pierre Teilhard de Chardin, a Jesuit paleontologist of the mid-twentieth century, whose writings and teachings on evolution were banned from publication by the church until after he died, in 1955.[78] This awakening has since been amplified by the likes of Jean Gebser, Henri-Louis Bergson, and Sri Aurobindo. In recent decades, Thomas Berry and Brian Swimme forged a seminal breakthrough in our comprehension, which has been carried forward and amplified by Mary Evelyn Tucker at Yale and Sister Miriam Therese MacGillis at Genesis Farm, and many others.

Meanwhile, there have been other voices who have shown us additional syntheses and dimensions of the evolutionary perspective, including Barbara Marx Hubbard, Michael Dowd and Connie Barlow, Ken Wilber, and Andrew Cohen (who even developed an "evolutionary spirituality"). There is something important to be learned from each of these pioneers. A good introduction to all this is a fairly recent book by Carter Phipps, *Evolutionaries: Unlocking the Spiritual and Cultural Potential of Science's Greatest Idea.*[79]

And there are still others, people whose work is far less well known, who have given us an even deeper understanding of how the evolutionary process itself unfolds, and how we can align with it and embody it: for instance, Arthur M. Young, the inventor of the first commercially successful helicopter and the author of *The Reflexive Universe: The Evolution of Consciousness;* David Sibbet, Young's American student, who has given us the whole discipline of graphic facilitation and who broke the code for practical human cocreation; and, perhaps most radically, the visionary architect Christopher Alexander, who, in recent years, has been saying such disruptive things as, "Everything we do is in the service of God" (by which he means the natural creativity in the universe).[80] It is Arthur Young, David Sibbet, and Christopher Alexander, in particular, whom we draw upon heavily and whose work we will build upon in this book.

Part of the promise and the challenge of this book is to begin to understand, align with, and consciously yield to these evolutionary processes—to become conscious agents for emergence or evolutionary catalysts. This turns out to be quite different from being "change agents."

In *Blessed Unrest,* Paul Hawken has spoken eloquently about the rapid emergence of awakening individuals and organizations around the planet and how together they represent the planet's immune system finally beginning to kick in. Well, yes, there are powerful evolutionary forces at work here. We evolutionary catalysts are finding ourselves in the most extraordinary situations, and we need support. We need orientation. We need grounding. We need evolutionarily significant tools and processes, cocreators, and communities of practice. And all that just begins to point to what this book is truly about. The book itself is an emergent process, and we're constantly learning.

ॐ

The evolutionary perspective (especially as expressed in *The Universe Story* by Thomas Berry and Brian Swimme) is having a tremendous impact, which we're just beginning to perceive and integrate. This appears to be but the beginning of an entirely new paradigm, one that will ultimately displace those of the past. It's difficult to see how profound the impact of all this will be, but it's likely to be much more far-reaching than the discovery that the world is not flat or that the world is not the center of the cosmos or that the universe is 13.7 billion years old and comprises billions of galaxies. This perspective embodies the fundamental discovery that the universe is an unfolding, self-organizing process that is *alive* and can find conscious expression in what humans are capable of becoming. This perspective also includes the dawning reality that this universe is likely replete with intelligent life and that we are but a young, naïve, emerging species.

And if we can but hold it, we will also begin to see that the increasingly prevalent suggestion among scientists—that this universe is part of a much more vast multiverse—is part of the same process of our reality or context being radically expanded. (At this point, we can't even imagine what the impact of integrating this aspect of reality could be.)

We need to be quite humble about what we think we know and understand. For instance, on this beautiful island of earth, even the most aware of us are just beginning to grasp the recently discovered reality that we inhabit but one of forty billion worlds that lie within the habitable zones of hundreds of billions of stars in this Milky Way galaxy—which is but one of perhaps a trillion galaxies in the entire universe, which we are now learning could be but one of an infinite number of universes. We simply do not have the mental capacity to hold all this—yet—but there is considerable evidence, rapidly unfolding now, that this approximates reality.

It's useful to remember that merely a hundred years ago, our best scientists believed that our own Milky Way galaxy was all there was to the entire universe. Edwin Hubble shattered that conception ninety years ago, when he was only thirty-five years old, and our view of reality has since continued to expand exponentially.

This process is likely to continue indefinitely. This may seem disorienting, but learning to shift paradigms is a skill that we need to cultivate. After all, we don't want to get stuck in an obsolete reality. We are learning not to convert beliefs—even scientific beliefs—into certainties.

I am reminded of the admonition of the evolutionary ethicist John David Garcia: "To be certain is unethical."[81] All beliefs need to be held tentatively, as hypotheses. We have to learn to not fear abandoning them when they are superseded.

As we will see, where this evolutionary perspective will ultimately have the most impact is in a complete reconsideration of what it means to be human (individually and collectively) in this vast panorama of life, and of what our real purpose is. We are about to discover who we are. Or, perhaps, who we are becoming.

Every great culture has had, at its beginning, a creation story or creation myth. These stories have informed us about our identity and about the world we live in. But there has never been one truly universal creation story that was free of religious dogma, tradition, and beliefs. We may have been the first generation born without a creation myth; this was probably necessary, to free us to receive something entirely new.

CHAPTER 14

Patterns of Emergence:
The Evolutionary Process

The more we learn to use this method, the more we find that
what it does is not so much to teach us processes we did not
know before, but rather opens up a process in us, which was
part of us already.

—CHRISTOPHER ALEXANDER, THE TIMELESS WAY OF BUILDING

In the early 1980s, I had the privilege of working for Apple in media
communications, including helping to introduce to the world the whole
radical concept of "personal computing." In those days, Apple was
bringing in the smartest people they could find—as consultants, as teachers at Apple University, as employees. It must have worked, because it
became the most highly valued company in human history.

One of the early players was David Sibbet, the creator of the discipline of graphic facilitation, who had based his organizational development work on an evolutionary process model that had its origins
with Arthur M. Young, David's teacher.[82] I had an opportunity to study
briefly with David, and it led to a whole new understanding for me of
the role of communication in evolutionary process. One of the first
things he said that got my attention was that you can tell what stage of
development a company is at by observing the kind of *meetings* they
are having.

Arthur Young was the inventor of the first commercial helicopter—
the Bell Model 47, which had its first flight in 1945 and was the whirly-
bird featured in *MASH* (both the movie and later television series)—a

project that took eighteen years to accomplish. From childhood, Young had known in his bones that there was a helicopter that wanted to come into the world, and he understood that he was the vehicle through which it could happen. And he knew that he needed to discover the *process* by which such things could come to pass.

Once he invented the helicopter, he devoted himself to discovering ways for humans to better create together. His great intuition was that the key lay in grasping the process of how the universe itself has evolved—that is, *how the universe creates*. He began studying everything that science could tell him about evolution.

In the early 1950s, Young and his wife established the Foundation for the Study of Consciousness. In 1976, after decades of study, he finally published *The Reflexive Universe: The Evolution of Consciousness*, which laid out his grand theory of process. While this work remains little known today, it is being utilized and applied in many disciplines by extraordinary people.

Brian Swimme and Thomas Berry have beautifully demonstrated that the evolution of the universe can be related as a *story*, "scientific in its data, mythic in its form." Since its publication in 1992, *The Universe Story: From the Primordial Flaring Forth to the Ecozoic Era* has been the primary source of inspiration for many seeking a common universal story. And in recent years, a collaboration between Swimme and Mary Evelyn Tucker (who, with her husband, John Grim, directs the Forum on Religion and Ecology at Yale University) has brought us a highly compressed depiction of this story in a well-produced one-hour film, *Journey of the Universe*.[83]

Being able to describe the unfolding of the universe as a coherent story should be considered a great achievement in human history (a catalytic event), one that could not have been possible before the closing years of the twentieth century. However, when this somewhat linear story is paired with an understanding of the patterns within the process of evolution, derived from an extension of Young's work, we have a powerful tool that allows us to rethink everything we thought we knew and to reorganize our discovery and learning through discerning the patterns of process in *everything*.

What follows is a glimpse of Young's theory of process and an outline of the history of the evolution of the universe itself. It gives us a new window on the essence of the process of emergence that we, as evolutionary catalysts, have been working with and learning with. Please don't take this as pure science, but more as poetic myth—a new creation story, perhaps. Yes, it's based in current scientific understanding, but our so-called science is still primitive. Arthur Young's basic insight remains valid, but it is continually being updated as science itself evolves.

While this story is based in part on a deep understanding of what science has taught us, it goes far beyond that. Mystery is a part of the story, and the Mystery must be honored and respected, even cherished.

To explore this process in a book on food localization may at first seem of little relevance. However, I hope to show that the process not only illuminates the greater context of our human plight, but points to deeply embedded pathways of healing and regeneration that are now being activated in the process of localizing our food supply. The result, if I am successful, will be a map and guide for our way forward as an endangered species.

For now, I ask for your patience....

IN THE BEGINNING...

> Stories of creation are concerned not just with an event in the past, but with "beginningness" in all its manifestations.
>
> —CHARLES M. JOHNSTON, MD

> The story is the one that you and I will construct together in your memory. If the story means anything to you at all, then when you remember it afterward, think of it, not as something I created, but rather as something that we made together.
>
> —ORSON SCOTT CARD

You already know the story, although it could not have been told before our lifetime. The story is in us.

Before the beginning, there was nothing. This is so strange and so difficult for us to hold in our minds that it makes us uncomfortable. We can't conceive of the void, because it is *before conception*. But the nothingness of the void was everything. Nothing existed in it. Nor was the void anywhere; there was only nowhere. It is not really appropriate to say it was "before the beginning," because it existed outside of time. We can't even say it *existed*, because it was nothing. Perhaps the closest thing we can compare it to is deep, dreamless sleep.

Genesis says that the earth (the universe) was void and without form, and darkness was upon the face of the waters. Darkness. Nothingness. Stillness. Silence. Emptiness.

It is not necessary to understand this. The void is beyond all understanding. There is nothing to know, nothing to understand. But this nothingness is the heritage we all share in common.

Yet, apparently this nothing was powerful, for somehow all things sprang from it.

Stage One: Light/Potential

Light emerges out of nothingness.
Suddenly, in the midst of the vast darkness comes an unimaginably brilliant explosion of pure light. Pouring forth in all directions from a single point, light splits the void and shatters the darkness.

This explosion of light is the moment of the dawning of creation, the first order of existence and the principle of *potential*. This is the Initial Flaring Forth, the miraculous appearance of a force so awesome and powerful that it will eventually call forth life itself.

The peculiar thing about this early light is that it is without substance, boundless, completely free. First light does not travel through time and space. Rather, it creates time and space in its wake. Everything derives from light, even the entire universe.

As the explosion of light ripples outward, it leaves behind a seething inferno, a fireball that expands only slightly more slowly than the light that gave it birth.

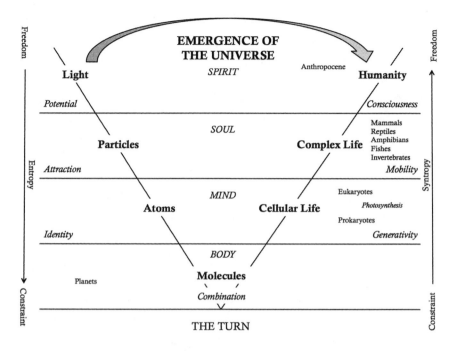

Figure 1: The Emergence of the Universe

Stage Two: Particles/Attraction

Particles emerge from light.

What is this fireball that will become the universe? In the intense heat and energy of the explosion, photons of light are radically changed. They flame out and die, and their energy is condensed into minuscule bundles or particles. This happens almost instantly, leaving behind a superhot, radioactive soup made up of a host of primitive particles of energy— electrons, positrons, quarks, neutrinos, leptons—all wildly careening in a cosmic matrix of free photons. We can think of this cosmic soup as the second order of existence, representing the principle of *attraction*.

These particles,[84] the first descendants of photons of light that have given up their energy, are strange. They are not things or objects so much as they are momentary arrangements of energy, and they are constantly changing. They have no definable location in time and space—a hard concept for us to grasp.

In the cosmic soup, these particles perform a kind of dance with each other. Depending on the energy charge they hold at any particular moment, either positive or negative, they are attracted to each other or repelled. Some of them form brief unions, creating new patterns of relationship, then shift, transform, and leap forward to new encounters, as Swimme and Berry explain, "The first particle interactions were not fixed and determined in the way they are today. There was an element of freedom, of randomness, associated with these interactions. The electrons, positrons, the quarks, the neutrinos had not yet achieved their identity. They enjoyed a chaotic freedom of possibilities they would later be denied. Most likely there were even from the beginning innate biases for certain kinds of intensities to these interactions, but there were also in every interaction degrees of freedom that disappear in later eras."[85]

Lasting only microseconds, the relationships they form are highly unstable, volatile encounters. You could say these encounters are "structures"—and if we could look at them, we would begin to see that certain structures or patterns of relationship are appearing more often than others.

Stage Three: Atoms/Identity

Form and structure emerge, invisibly at first.
One particular pattern or structure eventually begins to dominate the dance. Several electron particles clump together to form what we call a proton, and a single electron circles endlessly around them. This simple pattern of relationship represents the first of a whole new order of existence. We call this now a hydrogen atom, like it is a thing, but it is actually only a relationship of energies.

This hydrogen atom, this simple structure, is the first stable, identifiable substance in the universe. These elementary atoms—tiny clusters of relationship—begin appearing in great numbers, and hydrogen gas begins to spread throughout the rapidly expanding universe. This signals the birth of form and structure, the third order of existence, yielding the principle of *identity*.

Soon, other patterns of relationship emerge, and new types of atoms begin to appear. First are the simplest gases—hydrogen, then helium.

Then come the rest of the noble, inert gases—each new atom slightly more complex than the preceding ones. And here we suddenly see the first clear signs of a larger pattern emerging, a trend toward increasing complexity.

These simple gases are the fallout from the initial explosion of light. Huge clouds of these gases clump together—mostly hydrogen and helium—drawn together by the allure of mass attracting mass, becoming great swirling, superhot clouds, glowing with intense radiation. Gradually, these clouds become galaxies.

Within these infant galaxies, pockets of glowing gases and cosmic dust draw more and more gaseous atoms to themselves, becoming increasingly dense, until at last they ignite as stars, cosmic fusion furnaces where new elements are forged from simpler ancestors.

It is now a violent universe. Through a continual cycle of birth, death, and rebirth, a succession of stars cook atoms in their nuclear furnaces and throw off ever more complex atoms, the stuff of which new stars and other heavenly bodies are made. Thus, the basic material of the universe is recycled and recast, flung out and spun into a fine tapestry of diverse elements.

Stage Four: Molecules/Combination

Planets emerge, the physical foundation for reversing entropy.
Some stars throw off enormous amounts of material into space. In spiral galaxies, these fields of amorphous matter become the breeding grounds of planets—condensations of energy into matter, the unexpected progeny of that first explosion of pure light. According to Swimme and Berry, the primary mechanism for evolution at this stage is supernovas. "Galaxies after supernovas are qualitatively different from galaxies before supernovas. When the stars implode and the neutrinos blast out, base remnants of the stars are sent streaming away at such high velocities that in a relatively short time these new elements are thoroughly mixed into the swirling gases and stars of the galaxy. Stars of second, third, and higher generations arise out of a fundamentally different galactic matter."[86] This process sets the stage for the fourth order of existence, representing the principle of *combination*.

Out of the alchemical crucible of the supernovas, new atoms are cast out. Being heavier and denser than the atoms in their mother stars, these new atoms are attracted to each other and begin to combine in new patterns, creating a completely new and more complex order—molecules. The first molecules are crystals, simple joinings of the same kinds of atoms. But over time, more diverse atoms are united together to form wholly new molecular substances. Molecules begin joining with other molecules, rapidly ascending the ladder of complexity, ultimately building single structures made up of billions upon billions of atoms.

About nine billion years after the Initial Flaring Forth (by the way we reckon time), near the edge of a galactic spiral system we now call the Milky Way, a star is born. This star is rather small and ordinary, by cosmic standards, one of hundreds of billions that populate the galaxy.

Around this newly formed sun, cosmic dust and gas swirls and spins, gradually crystallizing into dense matter. Half a billion years later, planets are formed. The third planet from this star, our own earth, is the clay from which life will be wrought.

Initially, the surface of this infant planet is a tortured, heat-blistered crust of rock and crystal. Beneath burns a tremendous fire. All is molten but the thin surface mantle. In the cauldron below, heavy elements such as iron sink to the center. Lighter elements float upward, combining into granites, basalts, and other igneous rocks that eventually become part of the heaving crust.

Continuous volcanic activity brings up a rich supply of minerals, lifting up chains of mountains, spewing great clouds of sulfurous and carbonic gases into the hellish methane atmosphere that enshrouds the earth.

Gradually, this violent, seething ball begins to cool. And when the atmospheric temperature finally falls below the boiling point of water, the choking clouds give up their precious cargo. Hot acidic rain begins to fall, further reducing the earth's surface heat. Much of this moisture returns to the clouds as steam, falls again as rain, evaporates, and falls again; each new rain is a little cooler.

The endless rain collects in the low places between upraised plains and mountains, forming great seas. The rain slowly dissolves the rocks upon which it falls, turning the oceans into a thin, salty soup.

In pools of primordial ooze, increasingly complex molecular forms begin to coalesce and join with one another, creating new types of molecules of incredibly complex structure. Some of these new molecules develop the peculiar ability to replicate themselves. It is as if inanimate matter is struggling to come to life in a chaotic but extremely fecund cauldron.

Interlude

This is a staggering story, immense, beyond our ability to comprehend. But while it may be interesting, it may not yet seem to have anything to do with *us*. After all, we are talking about things that took place an unimaginably long time ago—beginning nearly fourteen billion years ago. We don't really understand how all this came about—or why. It simply *is*.

But consider this. We are talking about the history of the creation of the universe. This history, which we have only recently begun to discover, is a kind of parable for us, rich with guidance for our lives. Thus, it is not merely history—the story of what happened—but a *pattern* we are learning that is reflected in everything that has emerged in the universe since the so-called big bang. This is the pattern of *creation itself*.

How are we to relate to this story? The story reveals the universe as a *living process—cosmogenesis*. So far, we can see that the process of the evolution of the universe proceeds in distinct stages, each successive stage building in complexity. Each stage is an evolutionary quantum leap, a radical and unpredictable phase shift or transformation from what preceded it, yet embodying everything that came before.

Through the first stages of the process, light—the free energy of creation—is becoming increasingly bound up in matter. Light has been moving from absolute freedom to absolute constraint in physical matter.

At stage four, the process of evolution has reached a pivotal stage, which we call the *Turn*. It appears to scientists that the universe is caught in an inevitable process of entropy, in which the total available energy will eventually be so spread out throughout the universe that it will become completely stabilized. This state of stasis, known as *thermodynamic equilibrium*, is like death, with nothing happening. This is expressed in the second law of thermodynamics. But as Tim Robbins has so presciently said, "The universe doesn't have laws, it has habits. And habits can be broken."[87] As we will see, it is possible to break the universe's habit or tendency to run downhill into oblivion. This has important implications for us all.

At the Turn, light begins its long journey from constraint back to freedom in most unexpected ways, reversing entropy.

Stage Five: Cellular Life/Growth and Generativity

Living beings emerge.[88]

At last, after billions of years of molecular evolution, something entirely unexpected and unpredictable occurs, ushering in the fifth order of existence. We do not know where or when, exactly, and we cannot yet imagine how, but at a definite place and time on this young earth, the first living cell stirs. It is a strange microorganism, vastly complex compared to any molecular structure that has preceded it—a wholly new order of organization of matter and energy. And this single cell, the first living, self-replicating being, becomes the progenitor of all living beings on the fledgling planet, introducing the fifth order of existence and principle of growth, of *generativity.*

Up until this point, the entire universe has been cooling and expanding as the energy from the first order is increasingly converted into matter, dissipating energy and distributing matter toward a featureless steady state, a stasis of equilibrium.[89] But these simple cells, born in a remote region of the expanding universe, introduce a new force, actually beginning to reverse the process of the universe gradually winding down.

First to appear are life forms known as *prokaryotes,* simple single-celled organisms, including bacteria and archaea, which, in time, fill the seas, feeding on the exotic, energy-rich chemistry of the hot early earth. Eventually, some of these early cells, known as *cyanobacteria,* develop the capacity to capture photons of light within their cells and store the energy in the form of chlorophyll—captured sunlight. From this stored energy, growth and reproduction are made possible. Each cell is a manufacturing unit, driven by the process of photosynthesis, absorbing light and hydrogen and giving off oxygen into earth's anoxic atmosphere of methane, carbon dioxide, and nitrogen.[90]

Photosynthesis will have far-reaching consequences. As they multiply, in enormous numbers, these new creatures begin to irrevocably transform the earth's atmosphere, making it more hospitable to other forms of life. Photosynthesis is the crucial factor, the ability to process light. The emergence of photosynthesis is to the emergence of life as the big bang is to the emergence of the universe.

Later, building on this foundation, come *eukaryotes,* a vastly more complex and specialized (and larger) form of single-celled life, characterized by membrane-bound organelles within the cell, especially the nucleus—which contains the genetic material that makes reproduction possible, as well as memory. Eukaryotes incorporate the capacities of prokaryotes, including photosynthesis, and generate new ones—including sexual reproduction. All future species of life will evolve from the eukaryotes, including plants, animals, and fungi.

Stage Six: Complex Life/Mobility

Mobility and agency emerge.
But life is not content to remain limited to single cells. Soon, eukaryotic cells are compelled to join together as they multiply, initiating the phase of complex life. Their bonding reflects the dance of the second order. Eventually, millions of these cells begin adhering together to form specialized tissues. Thus, multicellular life forms are born and begin proliferating in great number and variety throughout the planet, first in the oceans, later on land.

This proliferation of photosynthetic life dramatically increases the oxygenation of the atmosphere. The debris from trillions of cellular life cycles deposits enormous amounts of carbon and other crucial minerals in the silt and dissolved rock that collects on land and in the sea, later to become stone and soil. Life is radically transforming the surface of the planet.

Photosynthetic cells build a foundation upon which all life depends. This includes the oxygenation and cooling of the early atmosphere. Among eukaryotes, life begins to diverge into three primary branches—fungi, plants, and animals—with animals being significantly dependent on the chlorophyll of plants. There is a biosymbiosis here, including an exchange of carbon dioxide and oxygen. From the teeming oceans, plants first make their appearance on land—essentially terraforming, making possible the emergence of land animals.

Little by little, green cells cool the earth and clean the air, creating a fertile spawning ground for new forms of life. Life demonstrates itself as a transforming power. In plants, complex life is rooted, immobile, able to grow only toward the source of light that sustains it—the mother star of this planetary system. But in plants, life cannot go anywhere. Its movement is restricted to the distance that seeds can be carried by wind or moving water.

Yet life has a powerful momentum. Suddenly, in tiny bits of protoplasm, life begins to move. The process reflects the same step-by-step increase in orders of complexity seen in the plant kingdom. First, single-celled organisms appear that are capable of independent movement, introducing the sixth order of existence and the principle of *mobility*. They can seek out food and mates, and they can move away from danger. Curiously, these tiny creatures absorb oxygen in their cells and return carbon dioxide into the atmosphere—a direct reverse of the breathing process of plants, creating a symbiosis of planetary proportions.

In addition, the new order of life consumes the bodies and organic by-products of the previous order. Animals eat plants (and each other), taking advantage of the enormous amount of energy stored in their cells. So it must be, for the new animals require much more energy than plants to support their movement.

As ever more complex animals and plants appear, the earth's environment is increasingly transformed. The planet flourishes with an astonishing variety of evolving life. This process continues for more than a billion years, reaching a peak of perhaps more than a hundred million species of living beings.[91] Life extends into the farthest reaches of the earth's surface, from the highest mountain peaks to the depths of the oceans.

Stage Seven: Humans/Consciousness

Consciousness emerges in complex beings.

Life is not content. Its momentum, so dramatically expressed in the mobility of its most complex animal offspring, restlessly seeks a new form of expression. The next stage in the creation of life brings together all the highest accomplishments of the previous six orders of existence. A wholly new order of life appears, a single species, with a capacity of consciousness. Suddenly, in *Homo sapiens sapiens,* life is aware of itself. Consciousness flames into awareness.

In this new species, life evolves in a totally new direction and at a pace unprecedented since the dramatic entry of light into the nothingness. With a mental capacity unequaled in the animal kingdom; with the ability to make and use tools; with a highly individualized consciousness, possessing conscious memory; with an ability to create language; with an apparently unlimited potential for learning and becoming; and with an existence that ultimately transcends the physical, this new species represents a fundamental breakthrough in the continued creation of the universe—a new and radically different order of existence, representing the seventh order of existence and principle of *consciousness,* of dominion.

Humans have unlimited choice-making capabilities and have the capacity for will. And, incredibly, they exhibit the capacity to create. This goes far beyond the ability to reproduce, which we see in plants and animals.

What's more, humans are now developing the ability to become conscious of the process of evolution itself. That is, in humans, the process of evolution is at last becoming conscious. This has taken approximately fourteen billion years of evolutionary history to accomplish.

At stage seven, there also appears the potential for evolution not only to be conscious but also to become *intentional*—opening the possibility of the transformation of human existence.[92]

This is not to suggest, however, that humanity is the pinnacle of the evolution of the universe. First, it is quite likely that conscious beings have evolved in other parts of the universe as well. Second, humanity is clearly still in the early stages of its evolution. That is, we do not yet know what the potential of human beings really is. Finally, there are indications that humanity itself is an endangered species, at risk of extinction.

PRINCIPLES OF EMERGENCE

It is now necessary to pause in the story and remind ourselves of what we are doing here. In the broadest strokes possible, we are telling the story of who we are, where we came from, why and how we are here, and what our life is about. It is a living story, embedded into our very cells, and it wants to be coaxed into awareness.

While this story of creation is rich and complex, it is also astonishingly simple, a cycle of seven radical transformations that initiate fundamentally new capacities.

1. Light/Potential
2. Particles/Attraction
3. Atoms/Identity
4. Molecules/Combination
5. Cellular Life/Generativity
6. Complex Life/Mobility
7. Humanity/Consciousness

This is the basic sequence of the process of evolution, orders of existence that increase in complexity, each stage built upon the foundation of everything that went before.

It may still seem that this process is remote, abstract, and not relevant to our lives. But consider the possibility that the process of evolution, if we could see it clearly, might allow us to see ourselves in a new way. We are not pursuing a hidden truth that will solve all problems or form the basis for a new religion. This is a *story* that is still unfolding, revealing deep patterns of emergence.

- We can now see that the universe unfolds or emerges in a purposeful process of seven distinct but cumulative stages or phases of evolution.

    * The trajectory of this seven-stage process—with its four levels, with its journey from freedom to constraint and back to freedom again, and with the recursive seven substages at each stage[93]—constitutes the fundamental pattern by

which the universe evolves, through an irreversible emergent process.

* The universe does not merely evolve. The universe is a living process of emergence, which moves progressively through patterns of radical self-transformation that are mirrored at all levels of existence, from the macro to the micro.

* Evolution unfolds through a process of emergence. The universe emerges in stages. Within each stage, radically new capacities and structures arise that, while unpredictable, reflect the patterns of emergence of the universe itself.

* The universe is self-organizing, self-transforming, and self-healing. It is progressive and directional ("evolution's arrow"),[94] reflecting a greater force or organizing principle that is being expressed through its unfolding. In other words, it is not the universe that is evolving. The universe is a *being*, through which something larger and more fundamental is being expressed.

- Emergence is the fundamental process moving through the evolution of the universe and everything within it.[95] Through emergence, evolution itself evolves. It is not some supernatural creator, but the natural creativity of the universe, the awesome creativity that surrounds us.

- Evolution possesses a clear direction; the organizing purpose of each stage is fulfilled in the next.

  * Light organizes the fundamental energy of creation.

  * Particles organize the energy of light into electrical charge.

  * Atoms organize the frenzy of particles into form—identifiable patterns of mass and energy that neutralize charge.

  * Molecules organize atoms into combinations of physical matter.

  * Cells organize molecules into living form, thus reversing the law of entropy through reproduction and self-replication.

  * Multicellular life organizes living tissues into mobile units of life, introducing will or volition in the form of instinct and agency.

* Finally, humans organize living matter and energy into self-conscious awareness, capable of unlimited choice—including self-evolution.

- The evolution of the universe reveals a pattern of emergence that we can apprehend and find repeated in every process within the universe.

  * As theoretical biologist Stuart Kauffman has said,[96] the becoming of the universe cannot be sufficiently described by natural laws, but is radically creative and open. Thus, not only do we not know what will happen, but we also do not even know what *can* happen. Reason is therefore an insufficient guide in charting our path forward. The future is unimaginable.

- It is possible for evolutionary catalysts to consciously align with the direction and process of emergence, to become a vehicle through which it unfolds.
- The universe is a vast field of existence—one among a potentially infinite number in an unimaginable multiverse—where a great drama is being played out.

Remember, evolution itself was completely invisible to us until recently, and it remains invisible to those who refuse to look. If you do not look, you cannot see; if you cannot see, you cannot understand; and if you cannot understand, you cannot know. We're just beginning to discover the patterns by which evolution or emergence happens. We're all becoming students of emergence. Becoming aware of these patterns turns out not only to be essential but also fun. And it makes our work a lot easier and more joyful.

Food localization is also, fundamentally, a process of emergence. In this regard, it is impossible to force it to happen; it's impossible to control it. We can be in service to it, align with it, support it, and even (to an extent) learn to catalyze it. But it is emerging of its own accord. It is a creative, evolutionary process. And this process can express itself through us, if we choose. That is, we can choose to allow this process to manifest in us and through us.

THE REST OF THE STORY

In a few human beings, after only about six thousand years of recorded history, the process of evolution begins to become conscious of itself.

In the final moments of the second millennium, after the brief life of one of the most remarkable representatives of the human species, others begin awakening to revolutionary insights: the evolution of the universe is a living process, and it is far from complete;[97] the evolution of humanity is also an unfinished process.

In this extraordinary time in human history, a small number of human beings are faced with the startling realization that they can consciously and directly participate in the unfolding of this process—in themselves and in the world around them. They glimpse that this process even has the potential to fundamentally reverse the seemingly inevitable entropy of the universe.

Suddenly, even more momentous realizations begin to take hold on the planet, in a multitude of ways. To those who are looking, it seems evident that the fundamental design of the universe calls forth a species of cocreators who will inherit the task of completing that design and will come to accept responsibility for its ultimate implementation. This is perhaps the destiny of humanity—to be the vehicle through which the fourteen-billion-year process of evolution becomes not only conscious but also limitless, *as if God is at last awakening in the human species.*

At first, such breakthroughs in conscious evolution occur to only a few individuals. The rest of humanity, still mired in the struggle for survival, gives almost no credence or attention to these startling developments. But simultaneously, as if it was part of a masterful strategy, comes the widely inescapable realization that the struggle for survival itself has produced a global crisis that threatens the existence of life on this small and fragile planet.

While a sense of resigned, helpless panic still grips most of the human race, evolutionary pioneers rise up throughout the world. They proclaim that the major challenge in human evolution is shifting from behaving like an animal struggling to survive to behaving like an unlimited being choosing to evolve. This proclamation is the first clear expression of the evolutionary imperative, a clarion call for human beings to learn to make the necessary shift to conscious, intentional evolution.

This, then, is our story—the story that we are living today. And in the telling of the story, we can begin to live it consciously. But we now ask, *how can humanity choose to evolve?* It is with this question that our part in the story truly begins.

SOME REFLECTIONS ON EMERGENCE

That there is no God or Creator mentioned in the story should be of no concern. The story simply does not address that particular issue. But you may choose to. The story does not suggest how human beings were created (or when or why). In fact, it says nothing at all about how or why anything was created. It just gives us the story of what has happened and what continues to happen.

The story is also not a theory, to be proven or disproven. It is a myth, an epic story in which we can perhaps see ourselves. It does not purport to be based on scientific understanding, though what is considered to be scientific knowledge is used to weave the story. The story is told here in broad strokes; it's just a sketch. This is just the beginning. Listen for the story beyond the words here. You may wish to learn and tell parts of the story yourself. Any portion of the story can be amplified greatly. And each portion of the story will contain the whole. This is a great mystery.

THE FREEDOM JOURNEY

We are not working in the realm of explanation here. We are not attempting to explain how anything happens, or why. Instead, we are simply looking at the patterns that emerge from the story.

There is much to be learned from the sequence of the universe's unfolding. For instance, we can see that the first four stages of the process deal with the emergence of matter, while the last three stages involve the emergence of life.

It is rather odd that in the evolution of matter the process begins with light—unbounded energy, distinctly nonmaterial. In a sense, light has to be "stepped down" (literally reduced in frequency) in order to be transformed into physical substance. At first, this does not seem an evolutionary advance. We could even call it *involution* rather than *evolution*. In this part of the process, free energy—in the form of photons—descends into the bounds of matter.

At the dawn of creation, in stage one, the energy of light is unlimited by time and space. In fact, light seems to literally create time and space. Light is an order of existence that is almost incomprehensible. Albert Einstein and his intellectual successors have helped us to understand that light does not exist in a universe of time and space. That is, for light, time and space do not exist. Even the so-called speed of light, long held to be a fundamental constant, appears to be not a limitation of light itself but a boundary condition of matter. Or as Arthur Young says, "not a boundary to space, but a boundary to the combination of time, i.e., velocity."

It is important to remember that in exploring the evolutionary process, we are not charting the evolution or unfolding of light itself, but that of which light is an expression or emanation. Light is not the Creator or monad, but the first means through which the Self is expressed.

The initial freedom of light is progressively diminished—literally "bound up"—as it descends into matter. First, the original energy of photons is condensed into mass to form charged particles, which still exhibit some freedom, in that their location and identity are always in a state of probability or potential (that is, they are not anywhere in particular at any given moment in time, and their fleeting identity is dependent on the relationship that occurs in the subnuclear dance).

Next, particles of opposite charge lock into a fixed pattern of relationship to form neutrally charged *atoms,* thus giving up their freedom. With the appearance of atoms and their joining together to form molecules, space (location), time, and identity all become possible for the first time, constricting the original energy into recognizable matter.

Finally, the free molecules are compacted together to form dense, inert objects—with no self-motion, bound by the exacting universal laws of matter.

The original energy of the beginning of the evolutionary process has become trapped in matter. We can consider this descent into matter a "fall," a loss of freedom, an increase of constraint. With each stage, the constraint becomes greater, until we reach the seeming determinism of lifeless physical matter.

This involution or fall also moves toward increasing entropy. From an examination of the physical laws of the universe, many scientists have concluded that the universe must be "a gradually subsiding agitation of lifeless objects."[98] Entropy is the tendency of the energy and matter of the universe to become more uniformly distributed, so that the destiny of the system will be a steady state in which the total energy is averaged out and therefore unavailable—a perfect description of death. This view conjures up the image of a universe that is gradually winding down and will likely collapse. Indeed, based on the evidence that science can currently examine, this is the logical conclusion, as T. S. Eliot said, that the world will end not with a bang, but with a whimper.

Thus, in the usual view of science, the fall is not only inevitable but also, ultimately, fatal. This belief has pervaded scientifically based cultures, most particularly our own. But the fall is only half the story. This story of entropy does not take into account the other half, the story of the emergence of life.

THE TURNING POINT

Life turns out to be as enigmatic, as fundamental, and as impossible to describe as light is. It could be said that the evolution of the universe really begins with the appearance of life. It is not the fate of the universe to end in entropic stasis.

But before considering the mystery of life, we must turn our attention to the evolutionary development of molecular matter, where we can see the appearance of life being presaged. At a point that is precisely mid-stage in the increasing complexity of naturally occurring molecular structures, certain types of molecules begin to build up energy and move against entropy. The first to exhibit this unusual characteristic are the chain molecules known as polymers—found in substances like cellulose and rubber.

Polymer molecules are not living, in the usual sense of the word, even though they do possess the seeming ability to grow and replicate themselves. Chemically inert, they consist of chains of hundreds of thousands of units, each unit being made up of a dozen or more atoms. These long chains not only build themselves but are also endothermic (unlike their predecessors, crystals); they are able to store energy and cool the environment around them.

It is at this point, midway into stage four, that the monad or Self—after its long descent into the constraints of time, space, and physical laws—at last begins to exert itself and climb out of the abyss. We call this reversal of the fall (involution) the *Turn*. This reversal has all the appearances of a voluntary act, an expression of volition, while everything that preceded seemed to be automatic and involuntary.

The appearance of growing, self-replicating molecules is an evolutionary about-face; it marks the beginning of the evolution of life in the universe. This may be said to be the most important point of the whole evolutionary process, when the monad begins to break free of the constraints into which it had fallen.

RETURN TO FREEDOM

The Self began its journey in the total freedom of light and gradually descended into the crushing restraints of physical reality. From the point of the Turn, the Self begins a return to freedom.

In the realm of the cells, the unfolding Self is imbued with the spark of life—that mysterious quality that is a wholly new order of existence in the universe. In cellular life, the Self gains the freedom of growth and self-replication, the ability to generate new and ever more complex forms of life.

In the development of multicellular organisms, the Self acquires mobility. And with this freedom to move within the bounds of time and space comes the freedom to make choices—about where to go, what to eat, when to act, and with whom to mate.

This freedom of choice is elevated to a potentially infinite level in human beings. Here, the Self can make choices that go far beyond the strictures of space, time, and physicality. It can now choose to transcend the realm of the finite for the possibilities of the infinite. This is a return to the initial freedom of the universe of light, where the Self moved without restriction, at will. In this final stage, the Self now possesses consciousness, a capacity for awareness and learning that is apparently unlimited. And, most importantly, in human beings, the Self achieves the unfettered ability to create, thus completing the shift from being a creation to being a creator.

It may seem that the subject here is the evolution of the universe, but that is only part of it. The unfolding of the universe reveals that it is the vehicle through which the Self is emerging. In a sense, we can perhaps say that it is the Self that is being manifested in and through the evolving universe. This is a subtle but powerful concept.

We have seen that the process of evolution forms an *arc,* represented graphically by a *V.* The left side of the *V* depicts the Fall, the descent into matter. At the bottom, at the point of the *V,* is the Turn. This is where volition appears to be manifested for the first time. Thus, an act of will reverses the fall, initiating the Return to freedom. Of course, this is not a return to the beginning, but a return to the realm of freedom (we could say *Spirit*). The Self returns to freedom completely transformed, having acquired powers previously nonexistent and totally unimaginable.

CHAPTER 15

Human Evolution at the Turn

We are the unfinished product of an accelerating cosmic evolutionary process characterized by collaboration, complexification, and convergence, and the self-reflective agents of our future evolution.

—John Hands, Cosmosapiens:
Human Evolution from the Origin of the Universe

HOW WE GOT HERE

There is much more to be learned from the patterns of emergence in the evolution of the universe, but that is beyond the scope of this book. The previous chapter was but an introduction. I can only hope that some readers will be sufficiently intrigued to engage in a much deeper exploration. For now, I must trust these patterns have catalyzed deeper insights.

Equipped with a broad evolutionary context that reveals these patterns of emergence, we can now begin to better understand how we have arrived at Peak Everything and to grasp the larger dynamics at work. This exploration will allow us to understand our evolutionary risks and opportunities, and later, it will give us the ability to uncover the deeper meaning of the local food revolution. Along the way, we will hopefully gain experience in using the process of emergence as a practical tool for learning and intentional evolution.

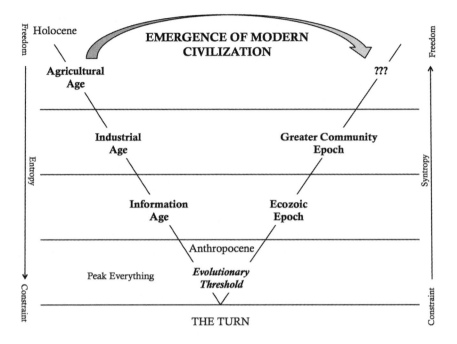

Figure 2: The Emergence of Modern Civilization

We're still establishing context. We began with the context of the evolution of the universe in the last chapter, and we can now narrow our gaze to the historical evolution of modern human civilization. We won't analyze the entire evolution of the human species but will focus on recent millennia, beginning with the birth of organized agriculture some twelve thousand years ago. This period represents but a fraction of a moment in the 4.5-billion-year evolution of this planet.

Humans had existed in some form for perhaps as much as two or three million years before the agricultural age—although it's hard to know when consciousness as we know it appeared or when *Homo sapiens sapiens* first emerged as a distinct species (the oldest known fossils date to around two hundred thousand years ago).

It all began with the initiation of the Holocene epoch 11,700 years ago, following the last major glacial age. Humans were still recovering from a devastating supervolcanic eruption (the Toba event, about seventy-five thousand years ago, possibly the largest volcanic eruption in the last twenty-five million years), which, by some accounts, reduced our ancestors' numbers to perhaps fewer than ten thousand (a genetic bottleneck) and ushered in a global winter.

Stage One: The Agricultural Age

The retreat of the glaciers and the warming of the climate at the beginning of the Holocene made it possible for us to shift from living as small nomadic groups dependent on hunting and gathering to living in small settlements that produced their own food by domesticating animals and plants. This age of agriculture began around 10,000 BCE.

Before the age of agriculture, humans did not have mathematics or written language or cities. Written language only evolved after the so-called agricultural revolution, first in the form of numbers. In fact, agriculture birthed economics and finances—the language of numbers— long before language of expression came into being.

Daniel Quinn's perspective is useful here, as related in "The Little Engine That Couldn't: How We're Preparing Ourselves and Our Children for Extinction."

It has been the work of my life to pin down and demolish the lie that is at the root of this mythology in our culture. It's to be found in the way we tell the human story itself in our culture. You can see it perpetuated in textbook after textbook, and if you keep your eyes open, you'll see it repeated weekly somewhere—in a newspaper or magazine article, in a television documentary. Here it is, the human story as it's told in our culture, day in and day out, stripped to its essentials. "Humans appeared in the living community about three million years ago. When they appeared, they were foragers, just like their primate ancestors. Over the millennia, these foragers added hunting to their repertoire and so became hunter-gatherers. Humans lived as hunter-gatherers until about ten thousand years ago, when they abandoned this life for the agricultural life, settling down into villages and beginning to build the civilization that encircles the world today." That's the story as our children learn it, and it has just this one little problem, that it didn't happen that way at all. Ten thousand years ago, it was not HUMANITY that traded in the foraging life for the agricultural life and began to build civilization, it was a single culture. One culture out of ten thousand cultures did this, and the other nine thousand nine hundred and ninety-nine went on exactly as before. Over the millennia that followed, this one culture, born in the Middle East, overran neighboring cultures in all directions, finally arriving in the New World about five hundred years ago. At which point it began to overrun the native cultures of THIS part of the world as well. It is a truism that the conqueror gets to write the history books, and the history our children learn is history as WE tell it. And the central lie of this history is that HUMANITY ITSELF did what WE did.[99]

In evolutionary terms, the main point is that the advent of organized agriculture marked the beginning of something, a journey that has taken us to where we are today. This is not to suggest, as some do, that agriculture is the culprit, or that we should endeavor to go back to the time before agriculture. Evolution is irreversible. The purpose of this exercise is to offer some context for our current situation, to see how evolution is unfolding and where it might be taking us. We are looking for patterns.

While it might be possible to identify the substages of the evolution of agriculture—and that would be a valuable and interesting exercise—that's not our task. We're only attempting to see the shape of evolution in one slice of human history, during the emergence of modern civilization.

Stage Two: The Industrial Age

Agriculture remained the primary organizing principle of human civilization for some twelve thousand years—until the 1700s, when a revolution in economic and social organization brought about the age of industry.

We easily forget how recently the industrial age began. It wasn't just the invention of the steam engine, but a shift from relying on human muscle power to the awesome power of machines—which rely on fossil fuels (ancient sunlight, from the Carboniferous period, 360–286 million years ago). Coal was the first and most abundant accessible fossil fuel, but since the 1950s, industry has been dominated by a mix of petroleum products and natural gas.

The industrial age has given rise to what Joanna Macy and others have called the *industrial growth society,* based on the premise of unlimited economic growth—which has a propensity to externalize real costs. People like *Yes!* magazine cofounder David Korten and Richard Heinberg say that this has now reached the point where continued economic growth of the extract-and-consume variety cannot and will not continue for much longer.

Today, despite rust belts, the industrial age is not over, any more than the agricultural age is over. Both are very much in play. In fact, agriculture itself has largely been industrialized and globalized.

Stage Three: The Information Age

Birthed during the late stages of World War II, the emergence of digital technology ushered in the information age. Both agriculture and industry have been greatly enhanced by the technology of the information age.

Today, the majority of global economic activity is concentrated in information technology. From bitcoins to derivatives, the primary fuel of the world's economic engines is digital data. To emphasize this, Slow Money founder Woody Tasch startled his readers in 2014 when he wrote about the appointment of an algorithm to the board of directors of a venture capital fund.[100]

> Deep Knowledge Ventures [DKV], a firm that focuses on age-related disease drugs and regenerative medicine projects, says the program, called VITAL, can make investment recommendations about life sciences firms by poring over large amounts of data.
>
> Just like other members of the board, the algorithm gets to vote on whether the firm makes an investment in a specific company or not. The program will be the sixth member of DKV's board....
>
> VITAL makes its decisions by scanning prospective companies' financing, clinical trials, intellectual property and previous funding rounds.

In the story, an official of the company, Charles Groom, remarks, "It's not what you call AI [artificial intelligence] at this stage, but that is the long-term goal."

~

These first three stages of the emergence of modern civilization are cumulative, building on each other, and they overlap. All three are in full bloom today, each presumably in one of its seven substages. There is nothing linear about this process. There are feedback loops between the stages and between substages. But what is harder to see is that the entire process is moving *in a direction,* and with increasing complexity.

It's also worth noting that through these three stages, the evolution of human civilization seems to be greatly accelerating, even to the point that it's highly likely we're already being swept into stage four, the Turn. This is worth thinking about and learning from. I can't say this acceleration is always characteristic of the progression of the first four stages, but it's certainly a prominent feature of human evolution.

Stage Four: The Anthropocene Era: The Turn

> Humans are now squarely in the Anthropocene Era, where we are having Deep Time impact of geological scale.
>
> —DEEP REVOLUTION WORKSHOP

Cumulatively, the developments of the first three stages of the evolution of modern society have brought us to Peak Everything, to the brink of global disaster and apparently irreversible entropy. They have also delivered us into the belly of an evolutionary threshold or bottleneck.[101]

Humanity's impact is now so vast that we have entered a new geological era, the Anthropocene. While we're not the first species to have a planet-scale influence—cyanobacteria oxygenated the earth two billion years ago and radically disrupted all life—but we're the first to do so and become aware of it, so it's ironically appropriate that this geologic era is named after us.

In its early stages, evolution moves from freedom to constraint, with increasing entropy. In stage four, constraint and entropy become extreme. We understand this dynamic at the first half of the Turn as Peak Everything, a time of crisis and chaos, seemingly inevitable endings, and descent into irreversible entropy. At this point, from a global perspective, we must consider the very real possibility of collapse—economic collapse, ecosystem collapse, population collapse, and climate collapse.

We're facing a mass extinction of species,[102] which we ourselves have caused, and in which the survival of humanity itself is threatened. Human population will likely be significantly reduced, perhaps to pre-industrial levels (one billion) or even fewer. Economic growth will cease, and agriculture will go through a radical transformation.[103] During this time, a united humanity will initiate a global project to ensure our future evolution. Wars and national conflicts will be set aside as it becomes evident that mere survival will require all of our resources and energies.

Since the publication of Jared Diamond's *Collapse: How Societies Choose to Fail or Succeed*,[104] the potential for global-scale collapse has increasingly become a topic of great concern and debate. We are learning that collapse, like extinction, can be sudden or gradual, and it can occur in steps.

Extinction events—or at least near-extinction events—are inevitable in evolution. We humans are learning to anticipate them, recover from them, and perhaps even prevent them altogether. (For further reading on the subject of collapse, please see the appendix.)

Going Supernova

A few years ago, Lynette Marie and I persuaded a handful of the leaders in the fledgling Transition movement in this country to assemble at the beautiful Genesis Farm near the Delaware Water Gap in New Jersey to enter into dialogue and contemplation together and to consider how we should be responding to the human predicament. This seemed to me a reasonable way to spend three days, and I was surprised to find the board of directors of Transition United States—of which I was a founding member—resisting the meeting. They were concerned, I was told, that some conclusion or decision would come out of this gathering that they might not agree with, that might take them into some unknown territory. Out of deference, we even invited every one of the board members to join us, but not one of them accepted. In fact, they did their very best to talk us out of even convening.

But convene we did, and while we clearly didn't have all of the right people there, there were some moments of discovery that came close to what I had hoped for. One came when an irrepressible question arose out of nowhere: "Are we a species attempting to commit suicide?" I knew immediately this was a question to hold in the forefront, and even though some in the group wanted to avoid it, it would not go away. Of course, there is a lot of evidence to suggest that this is so, and—if we allow it—the question brings us face to face with much that we'd rather not look at. For me, if the best outcome of those three days was just holding this question, together, that would be an accomplishment. I can't say that actually happened for everyone there, but it surely did for me. I felt it was leading us somewhere.

What if it *were* so? What if we are attempting to commit suicide? What would it mean for those of us who are working in our communities to bring resilience and self-reliance and justice and healing and restoration and regeneration and some semblance of sanity? What does one say to someone hell-bent on suicide? Should we be on a societal suicide watch while we try to figure out what to do? This is a tough, juicy question, one that keeps you awake in the middle of the night.

During those days we were deeply studying Brian Swimme's *Powers of the Universe* video series, a rich and moving masterpiece.[105] Here was a mathematical cosmologist speaking in the most evocative and spiritual language I had ever heard. Each segment stunned me into greater respect for the Mystery that was becoming visible through his eyes.

But the truly unexpected gift of this video series came as he was describing the supernova of an ancient star that created our own sun and our solar system. Swimme and Thomas Berry named this star Tiamat, after the primordial goddess of salt water of ancient Mesopotamia. "When we reflect on the fact that such a supernova explosion of the star Tiamat gave birth to our own existence, to our stellar system, that most of the atoms in our body were created by Tiamat and sent to us from its supernova explosion, we begin to recognize that beauty, elegance, and destruction are all layered into our ancestral origin. *Our birth required drastic and vehement destruction of well-ordered communities of beings.*"[106] The supernova event, they say, "is simultaneously a profound destruction and yet an exuberant creativity."

As I understand it, in a supernova, a maturing star essentially *sacrifices itself* in the most magnificent manner imaginable, thereby creating atoms more complex than those that had existed before—atoms necessary to make possible whole new expressions of evolutionary creativity. Life itself could not exist without the gifts of supernovas.

From this story, an uncomfortable thought began to grip me: could it be that our Peak Everything—or long emergency or long descent—is not our species' attempting to commit suicide but is preparation for humanity's going supernova? And if we're going supernova, what would that mean for the role of the evolutionary catalyst?

This is to suggest that the natural creativity of the universe likely has some profound surprises in store for us and that we'd best not hold on too tightly to our ideas or expectations. Perhaps, on a larger scale, it's just cataclysm followed by emergence, followed by cataclysm, followed by emergence, over and over again. That's how evolution works, and as evolutionary catalysts, we're intimately involved in the process—so we might as well relax and enjoy the journey.

Here's the point: *the evolutionary catalyst is not focused on bringing about change.* Food localization is about preparing ourselves and our communities for the changes that are coming.

Stage Five: Ecozoic Era

After the Anthropocene, comes what Thomas Berry and Brian Swimme have called the Ecozoic epoch, an entirely new phase, in which humanity not only devotes itself to repairing the destruction it has inflicted upon the world but also engages in a new relationship with nature and with life itself. Here, with the partnership between humanity and the community of life, the biosphere gradually becomes self-renewing and ecologically sustainable.

Stage Six: Greater Community Era

If we can attain a significant level of equilibrium in the Ecozoic epoch, we may then emerge into a realm of life that goes far beyond our planetary sphere, perhaps engaging in a greater community of intelligent life.

Stage Seven

Our ultimate destiny (our design) is unknown and unknowable at this point. But clearly it will go beyond (and yet still include) the physical universe.

PATTERNS OF MASS EXTINCTION

> The nature of this earth is change. The nature of this earth is endings. The nature of this earth is extinction. Simply being human at this time in history—and particularly being a middle-class human in one of the world's richer nations—makes you, and me, agents of extinction.
>
> —PAUL KINGSNORTH

> Extinctions destroy life, but they also reset the conditions for life's evolution.
>
> —LISA RANDALL, *DARK MATTER AND THE DINOSAURS*

> Emergence happens far from equilibrium.
>
> —BRIAN SWIMME, *POWERS OF THE UNIVERSE*

> Radical change is the biggest consequence of a mass extinction.
>
> —FRANK LANDIS, *HOT EARTH DREAMS*

The Holocene epoch comes to an end with a mass extinction event, one caused primarily by the way humans have been living on the planet. This is often called the *sixth mass extinction,* the most recent of those geological events (which are defined by at least 75 percent of the earth's current living species vanishing within a geologically brief two million years).[107]

The first mass extinction, ironically, isn't included on the list of the six mass extinctions, because it gradually unfolded over a period of two billion years rather than the two-million-year length of the later extinctions. It occurred some 2.3 billion years ago, in the late Precambrian era. Among prokaryotic cyanobacteria—blue-green algae—the capacity for photosynthesis emerges, converting photons into chemical energy and allowing these cells to process hydrogen from water molecules into life-giving fuel in the form of simple sugars. The principal metabolic by-product of this process is oxygen. At this time, most forms of early life breathe methane and thrive in a hothouse carbon-dominated atmosphere that is hostile to more complex forms of life.

Cyanobacteria unleash the photosynthetic revolution—an innovation, even an evolutionary breakthrough ("one of the greatest acts of creativity in the four billion years of the living Earth," say Swimme and Berry)—which will ultimately form the chemical and geological foundation for complex life. But first it destroys nearly all living forms on the planet, in a massive extinction event that unfolds over perhaps two billion years.

It's a dramatic story, one that scientists are still piecing together. It appears that the oxygen liberated from water by cyanobacteria is first absorbed into the rocks of the churning lithosphere, changing the chemical nature of the land. When land and rock can absorb no more, oxygen begins accumulating rapidly in the atmosphere, suffocating those anaerobic cellular beings for whom oxygen is poisonous.

Eventually, in a struggle to adapt to radically changing conditions, other organisms begin to emerge that can assimilate carbon dioxide into their cells. With the diminishing of carbon dioxide and the radical increase of oxygen in the atmosphere (going from 0.5 percent to 21 percent oxygen), the global atmospheric hothouse quickly becomes an icehouse, plunging the planet into the first and most significant ice age, known as Snowball Earth, a frozen world locked in limbo (or wildly fluctuating in cycles of icehouse and hothouse conditions) for 1.5 billion years. Most anaerobic species become extinct, unable to adapt.

For life, this becomes an era of chaos and great uncertainty—"the time between when the biosphere learned to make atmospheric oxygen and the time when everybody else learned to breathe it and use it," as California Institute of Technology geologist Joe Kirschvink puts it.[108]

Thus, the first mass extinction event is the greatest of all. Life barely survives. American journalist Annalee Newitz says, "Today we worry that cow farts are destroying the environment with methane; back in the Proterozoic, it's certain that algae farts ruined it with oxygen."

Eventually, as Snowball Earth begins to thaw (likely due to volcanic outgassing and a recurring abundance of atmospheric carbon dioxide), a new kind of cell appears in the oceans, cells that learn to thrive on oxygen. These are the eukaryotes, which emerged about 2.1 to 1.6 billion years ago and made possible the evolution of all species of multicellular life. The end of Snowball Earth marks the beginning of the period known as the Cambrian explosion of life on the planet.

Major Extinction Events

For quick perspective, here is a rundown of the six mass extinctions and their possible causes.[109]

1. *Ordovician-Silurian,* 450–440 MYA (million years ago); global cooling and a drop of the sea level, nearby supernova

2. *Late Devonian,* 375–360 MYA, mainly affecting marine life; multiple causes, including changes in sea level, widespread ocean anoxia, global cooling

3. *Permian-Triassic,* 252 MYA (also called the Great Dying); multiple causes, including continental drift, methane eruptions ("clathrate gun"), hydrogen sulfide emissions, bolide impacts

4. *Triassic-Jurassic,* 201.3 MYA; climate change, volcanism, asteroid impact

5. *Cretaceous-Paleogene,* 66 MYA; Chicxulub asteroid impact

6. *Anthropocene,* ongoing; humans

Lessons of Extinction

Scientists conclude that mass extinctions are usually precipitated by short-term shocks to systems that have been under long-term stress.[110] From the history of mass extinctions, we can see that as a living planet evolves, there will inevitably be globally significant incidents that deeply threaten the survivability of life, whether caused by geologic or cosmic cataclysm, or by the way certain forms of life themselves have evolved at a certain point.

In the previous five extinctions, life has been able to rise from the ashes and evolve into new forms, adapting to the new conditions. After each extinction, there is a period of recovery (sometimes lasting tens to hundreds of millions of years) before life can fully flourish again. Some mass extinctions have actually accelerated the evolution of life, because the elimination of the previously dominant life forms made way for new ones (e.g., the disappearance of the dinosaurs opened up new ecological niches in which mammals could evolve).

From the Great Oxygenation Event of the Proterozoic eon to the current human-caused extinction, we can see that for evolution to continue, life must learn to recover from crises and bottlenecks. But this has changed, for now we must learn how to anticipate and prepare for them as well, and perhaps, ultimately, we might learn to prevent such disasters. As Elizabeth Kolbert suggests, it seems that this will become a necessary capacity to ensure the long-term viability of life. "Right now, in the amazing moment that to us counts as the present, we are deciding, without quite meaning to, which evolutionary pathways will remain open and which will forever be closed. No other creature has ever managed this, and it will, unfortunately, be our most enduring legacy. The Sixth Extinction will continue to determine the course of life long after everything people have written and painted and built has been ground into dust and giant rats have—or have not—inherited the earth."[111]

✑

It's worth considering that not only did the early cells invent photosynthesis but they also invented cellular memory, which could pass on fundamental experiences to succeeding generations. As Swimme and Berry write, "The aim of the cells is to remember such effective creativity. The sum total of all such significant historical events cannot be contained by any particular bacterium. The DNA of each is not long enough to contain all memories that might some day be valuable. Instead, the memories are dealt freely among the living bacteria so that the irreplaceable learning is held by the community as a whole. It is thus the entire community that probes, creates, discovers, learns, develops, and remembers."[112]

Paul Kingsnorth makes the point that 98 percent of all organisms that have ever existed on this planet are now extinct.[113] Extinction is common in the evolution of life, perhaps even necessary. Extinction events—or at least near-extinction events—are inevitable in evolution. It is possible that life is learning how to recover from them and that recovery is happening more quickly.

Near-Term Human Extinction?

There is much discussion these days of near-term human extinction (NTHE). Given the devastating damage that our industrial growth society has unleashed upon this world, we now must take seriously the claim by Guy McPherson and a growing number of others that the human species may become extinct by as early as 2030.

We started hearing about Guy a few years ago, after he gave the keynote at the Bluegrass Bioneers conference in Louisville, Kentucky. He subsequently spoke here in Boulder and left a number of people quite rattled, some really upset—some of them our friends.

In late 2014, along with Carolyn Baker (a longtime friend of ours in Boulder), Guy wrote *Extinction Dialogs: How to Live with Death in Mind*. It's a story that few have dared to explore, and only a handful are speaking about it. But I think we all need to contemplate this perspective at a deep level.

> We're on track to cause our own extinction, probably within a matter of two decades because of ongoing climate change. The only legitimate hope to prevent our near-term extinction, and that of the thousands of species we're taking with us into the abyss, is completion of the ongoing collapse of the industrial economy. Even that may not suffice.... The omnicidal culture we know as Western civilization is about to reach its overdue end. Time is not on our side. It's long past time to let go of a system that enslaves us all while destroying all life and therefore all that matters. And it's not merely time to let go, but to terminate this increasingly

violent system that values the property of the rich more than the lives of the poor.[114]

This small book will save you years of research. McPherson's opening chapter, "Abrupt Climate Change: Giving New Meaning to 'Hard' Science," may be the best survey of climate change literature currently in print.[115] Here McPherson provides a succinct, updated analysis of what science is telling us about the realities of the future we're facing, and I highly recommend it. You won't read about this in the media, and you can't find a college course about it anywhere. But given who we are and where we are, we need to come to grips with this.

What this book makes obvious is that we've come to the end of a phase of evolution on our planet, and there are no answers that our society or civilization can offer. We've simply come to the end. Every institution of human civilization has failed. Only an evolutionary breakthrough (a miracle?) will make possible a transformation that will create any future for humanity and for this planet.

∾

At the beginning of the recent (unfinished) documentary *Apocalypse, Man,* Michael Ruppert asks, if you were the last person on earth, *how would you know?* Well, you wouldn't, he says. You would just *be* it.[116] I find that strangely unsettling.

As a people, we have thought about our legacy at least throughout recorded history. But near-term extinction—or even near-term *near* extinction—gives us a different perspective on legacy. Usually, we think about our legacy when we are facing death, sometimes a long time before our death. What shall we leave behind? Who do we intend to receive it? Perhaps we should convene groups to consider developing a last will and testament for humanity, just in case.

Even in the event of a sudden global cataclysm—a massive asteroid strike, for instance—there would probably be at least a few survivors. What if you survived near-term human extinction? What if you knew you were the last person on earth or were among a small group of the last? What would you devote your life to?

A few years ago, in thinking about the unfolding disaster that we so glibly call *climate change,* I began seeing one possibility that is almost never discussed: that climate change (or climate collapse) will give humanity a near-death experience. What strikes me about a near-death experience is that it gives one an entirely new outlook on life. People often come to see their previous life as empty and self-centered, and they devote the rest of their days to service. So the near-death experience is another kind of initiation. A big part of the realization that comes with this, much like what usually comes with any major psychospiritual experience, is that death is never the end.

Frequently accompanying the near-death experience is an even more shocking realization: there is someone on the other side who knows us very well. *Who is there? Why do they know us?* Our understanding of reality is limited and is dominated by our human and physical existence on earth. Indigenous people seem to have a radically different perspective, one that recognizes that there is a thin and porous membrane between physical life and the realm of spirit. Modern Western society is disconnected from spirit and the sacred, and this profoundly distorts how we think, how we see, how we live, and how we relate with each other. It also cuts us off from a realm of being that is likely far more vast than the entire physical universe.

Is it too much to say that it's now fairly obvious that one's life does not end with the death of the body? Those who have survived a near-death experience certainly confirm this. Perhaps it's even possible that a *species* does not end with physical extinction.

We know little about such things—so little that we tend to ignore them or live in denial of them. Consequently, we live little lives, stuck in the temporal—a strange and sad fate for beings who may well be immortal and timeless. We do not yet know who we are, where we came from, who sent us, or what we came here to do. The process of remembering is slow, yet possible. However, remembering does not seem to be essential for doing this work. All that seems truly essential is surrendering to that deep evolutionary force longing to unfold within us, through us. That's the discipline of emergence we're learning, the practice of being an evolutionary catalyst.

My own sense is that Peak Everything will turn out to be a near-death experience for humanity—or near-term near extinction, if you prefer—but it will probably be a very close call.

If you know that you're suffering from a potentially terminal illness (and collectively we surely are), it's a good idea to prepare for the worst—to get your affairs in order, as they say. And in the case of humanity, preparing for the worst might not necessarily mean preparing for the end of everything. It might mean preparing for the next phase of evolution.

CATACLYSM AND EMERGENCE

> There have been five great die-offs in history. This time, the cataclysm is us.
>
> —Elizabeth Kolbert

One of the key principles of emergence is that it is often preceded by cataclysm. We can see this most starkly in the supernova process that makes complex atoms possible—a mature star essentially sacrifices itself so that life can eventually spring forth from the destruction. Without such cataclysms, emergence would be impossible, and life would not exist.

With the impending cataclysm of Peak Everything, it would be reasonable to assume that there's no hope, that we are a species heading toward suicide, going over the cliff. For the evolutionary catalyst, however, this is not where we focus our energies. We are well aware of the forces of cataclysm, but we recognize in ourselves the forces of emergence, the underlying thrust of evolution itself. These forces of cataclysm and emergence are present in each one of us and are reflected everywhere we choose to look. But what we give ourselves to is emergence. This represents the fundamental direction of evolution itself, the long arc of evolution.

Emergence is the most important framework for the evolutionary catalyst, for we are not seeking to create change. We are becoming the vehicles through which emergence unfolds. We are, in effect, manifesting the fundamental evolutionary force. We serve not our own will, but that of emergence. Thus, as evolutionary catalysts, our learning and skill development—and practice—should be to support this. We see the same dynamic in the mass extinctions of species that have occurred in the past. Such events have not resulted in the elimination of life, for life is more resilient than that.

In our lives, we will likely witness collapse, perhaps experience it, and perhaps in multiple forms. The modern way of life on this planet is clearly destined for collapse. But at the Turn, in our darkest hour, we can already begin to see the emergence of something entirely new. There comes a moment when we can step out of the entropic thrust (which is based on the perceived need to make something happen) and surrender to the evolutionary force that seeks expression through us. This is the moment of revolution.

It's entirely possible, even likely, that such efforts will fail at first. Evolution has seen countless failures and dead ends, but it is nevertheless relentless, unstoppable. It is going somewhere, and it will ultimately find its expression. The question is whether we will allow it to be expressed through us. At the Turn, extraordinary and completely unexpected things can begin to emerge that will radically alter our reality.

The poet Rainer Maria Rilke said, "If I don't manage to fly, someone else will. The spirit wants only that there be flying. As for who happens to do it, in that he has only a passing interest." This, it seems to me, is a decent basis for faith.

It also needs to be said that a core emerging understanding is that humans are, above all, vehicles for communication and transmission. Part of what sets us apart from other beings, sentient or not, is that we have the capacity for yielding to this mission intentionally, consciously— aligning with the evolutionary thrust of the universe, actually becoming a vehicle through which it can move and be expressed.

ॐ

If humanity is in the process of going supernova, or soon will be, perhaps we could consider ourselves a transitional species. What could our collective demise give birth to? What do we know about being human that we would want to see survive in our successor species? What is the cosmic legacy we would like to leave behind? What is the legacy that we *must* leave behind? Surely we have something to give those who will come after. What would we want to bequeath to them? What is our gift? What have we learned that we can pass on? What wisdom do we have to impart?

To put it another way, given everything we know, if it were possible for us to send a message to an intelligent species on a planet far away that was approaching the advent of agriculture in its evolution, what would we say to them? If we could send a message to a distant species that was approaching its Industrial Revolution, what would we say? Or if we could send seeds to another world, what seeds would we send? What seeds would we cultivate here on earth in order to have seeds worthy of being sent to a distant world?

If it were possible for us to send a message to a distant intelligent species that was approaching the tipping point of climate collapse, what would we say to them? What seeds would we send?

Perhaps some among us have been through all this before. Perhaps, because of our previous experience, we were sent to this planet, at this crucial moment in human evolution, bearing deep inside us messages and seeds and gifts that are needed here on this planet right now.

And if we allow ourselves to contemplate deeply and freely, it will perhaps become apparent that the current situation on this exceptional planet is far from exceptional in the larger scheme of things. Perhaps the evolutionary threshold that humanity faces is even rather typical of planetary civilizations that reach a certain level of technological and economic development and thereby fall into population overshoot, resource depletion, and catastrophic environmental destruction. Perhaps the stakes on this particular planet are far higher than we have considered before.

Meanwhile, we have much work to do to prepare for what is coming.

CHAPTER 16

Message to Students

In early 2015, I was asked to speak to a group of college students studying writing and rhetoric who had been exploring some of the issues concerning the industrial food system and the local food movement. This is how I began the presentation.

My primary interest in being here today is to talk with you about what you're facing—what we're all facing—and how we might respond.

It's certainly not fair, but if you do your homework, you will discover (if you haven't already) that you have been born into a world that is now experiencing its worst crisis in sixty-six million years. By some estimates, up to two hundred species of life are going extinct every single day, and humanity itself is on the endangered list. No kidding. Extinction has become a very real possibility for the human species.

Human-caused climate change is rapidly transforming into an inevitable global climate disaster, and almost no one is willing to even discuss this, let alone address it. Even the environmental and climate movements (and scientists) are reluctant to admit just how bad it's going to get—perhaps 4 to 10 degrees Celsius warmer in the next few decades. The coming devastation is almost unimaginable, and everyone will be affected—much sooner than is being talked about publicly.

If you haven't already realized these things, you will in the next couple of years. It's unavoidable.

Like it or not, this planetary crisis is what *your* life is about. This is what you were *born* for, to respond to. This is the situation that calls forth what you have to give. The sooner you realize this and commit to giving yourself to this, the less you will suffer. There is no escaping or denying this reality. This is the nature of life on this planet in the early twenty-first century.

The kind of future that we have all wanted—and that many of us have worked toward for years—is simply not going to happen. Our future will be radically different from what we all expected and wanted—for the world has reached a turning point, and there is no going back.

You might protest that I'm just being negative, but actually I'm just being realistic and candid. We all need to become realistic.

In this situation, there are some things that you will absolutely need—some perspectives and some skills that you will need to develop—in order to survive and thrive in such a future. I'll mention just six of these, for starters. These constitute the best advice I or anyone else can give you.

- Learn to face the truth of our collective predicament; learn to see and feel the depth and urgency of this planetary crisis, this evolutionary threshold.
- Seek and discover the meaning and purpose of your life, the gift that you have come here to contribute in this time of profound crisis. This must become your highest priority, and it will take a long time. This requires preparation and discipline.
- Learn how to decolonize your mind and your behaviors. Stop being a consumer. Encourage others to do the same.
- Discover why real freedom is almost nonexistent on this planet.
- Learn to see and feel (and become part of) what is attempting to emerge here on this planet—and in you and through you.
- Discover what is truly sacred, and bring that into the center of your life.

∾

We're clearly heading toward an evolutionary bottleneck or pinch point, and it's likely that, at best, only a few of us will squeak through. The devastation will be profound, but perhaps not quite total.

Of course, it's simply too late to avoid all this. We need to recognize—and help others recognize—that we're not going to "solve" climate change and related disasters. Instead, at least some of us will learn to adapt to a radically changed environment as our population is reduced dramatically.

In a report leaked in late 2013, the United Nations' ultraconservative Intergovernmental Panel on Climate Change estimated that climate change will reduce global food production by 2 percent per decade for the rest of the century ... at a time when population-driven demand for food will increase by 14 percent per decade. Just using these extremely conservative numbers, we can see a global food calamity looming on the horizon unlike anything the world has ever seen before. The global industrial food system is headed for catastrophic collapse, and we must begin to prepare for that now.

While there is great uncertainty ahead—and near-certain global climate calamity—there is one arena where we can make an extraordinary contribution toward ensuring human survival beyond this evolutionary crisis: we can learn how to feed ourselves again, as locally as possible, localizing our food supply, and thereby regain some semblance of freedom and sovereignty. In fact, this may be the only arena of human activity where we can do this now. It's a great place for us to make a stand.

Humanity faces a near-term and prolonged global food crisis, driven by converging forces of climate change, soil and water depletion, environmental destruction, species extinction, and economic decline. The profoundly unsustainable and already-failing global food system will not be able to adequately support our growing human population, leaving billions of people at risk—even many in the United States. To avert disaster and to successfully make the transition into a world of declining resources, the global food supply chain must be localized to the greatest extent possible, beginning in local communities and regional foodsheds. *This is the most urgent and most important social cause of our time.*

CHAPTER 17

Radicalization

I've quoted Tim DeChristopher already, and perhaps it's appropriate to share here why I think his perspective is so important and useful. I wrote the following words in early 2013, for a Deep Transition workshop at the College of Holy Names, in Oakland, CA, so it's a bit dated, but it represents the intersection of the lives and stories of evolutionary catalysts who have had a profound impact on our understanding.

In mid-February 2013, a provocative essay by Wen Stephenson appeared in the *Phoenix* in Boston, under the banner "Global Warming Is the Great Moral Crisis of Our Time: Why the Climate-Justice Movement Must Embrace Its Radicalism to Fight It." What Stephenson writes about is very relevant to us here, and very timely.[117]

Stephenson reveals one of the most interesting evolutionary catalysts we have learned about in the last couple of years: Tim DeChristopher, who in 2008 disrupted a Bureau of Land Management auction of oil and gas leases by managing to win bids worth $1.8 million for some twenty-two thousand acres of public land near Canyonlands National Park—bids he had no intention of paying for (and no means). Stephenson writes, "He had acted spontaneously, on his conscience, engaging in nonviolent resistance to the heedless new extraction of fossil fuels that are catastrophically heating the planet and threatening innumerable innocent lives."

It took a long time, but DeChristopher was finally sentenced to two years in prison, plus a $10,000 fine. At his sentencing, he stood quietly defiant before the judge and said, "This is not going away. At this point of unimaginable threats on the horizon, this is what hope looks like. In these times of a morally bankrupt government that has sold out its principles, this is what patriotism looks like. With countless lives on the line, this is what love looks like, and it will only grow. The choice you are making today is what side are you on."

His long and eloquent statement at his sentencing helped to galvanize a growing climate-justice movement. About a month after DeChristopher spoke those words, one of the largest civil-disobedience actions in a generation began as fifteen thousand people surrounded the White House, and 1,253 climate activists were arrested, protesting the Keystone XL pipeline, the project that is slated to tap the second-largest carbon deposit on earth. President Obama apparently listened and temporarily delayed the tar-sands pipeline.

But the story continues. Last Sunday, February 17, some forty to fifty thousand people converged on Washington to demand that Barack Obama reject the pipeline once and for all. Bill McKibben was, of course, one of those arrested in front of the White House. Again.

I remember when he came to Boulder last year, a very tired McKibben reported that he had just gotten a call from his wife, who had said, "Do you realize that in the last year you have spent more nights in jail than you have at home?" I was deeply touched by this, and it made me question my willingness to put my own body on the line the way that Bill has.

The climate crisis has a particularly unforgiving time limit, poignantly summarized in McKibben's statement: "If we don't solve it very quickly, we won't solve it."[118] That's why McKibben has been flying all over the planet in search of a way to slow the juggernaut. He says about all this travel, "I have the worst carbon footprint on the planet. So wherever I go, I need to make what I do there really count." Clearly, Bill McKibben is an evolutionary catalyst, and he is about as radical as they come.

What Stephenson points to in his essay is that those who are fighting against global warming, if they are to have any significant impact, are going to have to significantly *ramp up their radicalism*. They must become as radical, he suggests, as those heroic abolitionists who brought slavery to an end in the nineteenth century. It's a powerful thought, and it's not something that Stephenson came to lightly.

In the many months between DeChristopher's conviction and his sentencing, he was interviewed by the British socialist magazine *Red Pepper*. "We are at a time in our movement," he said, "where we need to be honest"—that it's "too late to stop a climate crisis," and that averting unthinkable catastrophe will now require deep, urgent, transformative changes. "We should not try and hide our vision about what we want to change, of the healthy, just world that we wish to create. *We are not looking for small shifts: we want a radical overhaul of our economy and society.*"[119]

Stephenson was personally very disturbed by this. He thought, "No! What are you doing? You can't say that stuff. This sort of talk, if it goes too far, has consequences. People are listening to you now. If the movement radicalizes, we'll alienate people, we'll be marginalized, we'll never get anything from Congress—we'll sacrifice genuine, if incremental, progress for the sake of some kind of moral, or ideological, purity. And we don't have time for that. We have to take whatever progress we can get."

By his own admission, Stephenson was still trying to fit his ideas of what needed to be done inside the suffocatingly cramped quarters of the "politically possible" at that moment. He had yet to fully face the facts of the situation in front of us. He wasn't as far along as DeChristopher.

And then, toward the end of 2012, came the flood of new perspective on global warming, essentially what I shared with you last night, and it was heartbreaking. The impact on Stephenson was profound, and by late December, he hit bottom—in despair for the planet and his children's future. I think a lot of other people hit bottom around the same time—people who were paying attention. That period of time was a very difficult moment for many of us.

At about that same time, in the darkness of the winter solstice, Stephenson read an interview with DeChristopher in *Orion* magazine, by Terry Tempest Williams. As Stephenson tells it, "What happened, quite simply, is this: *DeChristopher, a convict, convicted me.*"

In that interview, DeChristopher tells of the "shattering" moment in March 2008 when he met climate scientist Terry Root, a lead IPCC scientist, at a symposium at the University of Utah.

> She presented all the IPCC data, and I went up to her afterward and said, "That graph that you showed, with the possible emission scenarios in the twenty-first century? It looked like the best case was that carbon peaked around 2030 and started coming back down." She said, "Yeah, that's right." And I said, "But didn't the report that you guys just put out say that if we didn't peak by 2015 and then start coming back down that we were pretty much all screwed, and we wouldn't even recognize the planet?" And she said, "Yeah, that's right." And I said: "So, what am I missing? It seems like you guys are saying there's no way we can make it." And she said, "You're not missing anything. There are things we could have done in the 1980s, there are some things we could have done in the 1990s—but it's probably too late to avoid any of the worst-case scenarios that we're talking about." And she literally put her hand on my shoulder and said, "I'm sorry my generation failed yours."
>
> That was shattering to me. And I said, "You just gave a speech to four hundred people and you didn't say anything like that. Why aren't you telling people this?" And she said, "Oh, I don't want to scare people into paralysis. I feel like if I told people the truth, people would just give up."
>
> And I talked to her a couple years later, and she's still not telling people the truth.
>
> But with me, it did the exact opposite. Once I realized that there was no hope in any sort of normal future, there's no hope for me to have anything my parents or grandparents would have considered a normal future—of a career and a retirement and all that stuff—*I realized that I have absolutely nothing to lose by fighting back. Because it was all going to be lost anyway.*

For evolutionary catalysts like ourselves, these are very important words to hear and to take in.

Actually, DeChristopher does allow *some* hope, as we saw in chapter three. He says, "I have a lot of hope in my generation's ability to build a better world in the ashes of this one." In response to these stirring words, Stephenson writes, "DeChristopher expresses here what I had been repressing. He knows that building the sort of movement that can 'fight back'—and create the conditions in which we can build that better world—will require something of us beyond the ordinary conduct of politics. The climate crisis, he says, justifies 'the strongest possible tactics in response,' by which DeChristopher means 'nonviolent resistance.' *That doesn't mean everyone has to go to jail, he says, but 'the willingness for that is what's necessary. That willingness to not hold back, to not be safe.'*"

The willingness to not be safe.

Let me just read from the conclusion of Stephenson's powerful essay, where he really puts it on the line. This is Stephenson awakening as an evolutionary catalyst.

Tim DeChristopher is an *abolitionist*.

I know that DeChristopher can be a little scary. He scared the shit out of me.

But here's the rub: today, in our present crisis, one can easily argue that those who will have the "blood" on their hands, will not only be the denialists and the obstructionists on the right, but the moderates, the cautious pragmatists—the reasonable, serious, center-left types—who fail to acknowledge the true scale, urgency, and gravity of the climate crisis, and so fail to address it in any meaningful way.

People like that (and I was one of them) will say that people like DeChristopher have no "plan," no "workable solutions." But as any number of seasoned activists will tell you, it's not Tim DeChristopher's or the climate movement's job to offer detailed policy prescriptions that fit within the confines of our current politics. The movement's job is to tell the truth, however extreme—and to force those in power to recognize that even the outer limit of what our current politics will allow (a modest carbon tax, for example) is utterly inadequate to the crisis. Its job is to force that reckoning. To confront—and be prepared to sacrifice.

Yes, radicalism still carries risks, as it always has. But today those risks are mainly political, in the near-term. And at a moment when political possibility is closed off, we have to ask, are we actually risking anything meaningful at all? You might say I'm understating the risks of radicalization, that there may be other real consequences, from the personal to the social: that friendships, marriages, families may be torn apart; jobs lost, careers ruined, life options foreclosed; that there will be economic hardship, that social unrest, even violence, could erupt (just ask anyone over 55). Yes, I understand.

Meanwhile, the risks of moderation, of accepting and working within our current political constraints, are infinitely more grave. The risks of moderation are a matter of life, death, and suffering for untold millions of human beings, alive today and yet to be born. If we can't radically alter our politics—radically expand the limits of what's politically thinkable, as the abolitionists did in Lincoln's day—then we might as well not even talk about "climate action."

We might as well change the channel, and drift back to sleep.

Just to bring this back to our own calling as evolutionary catalysts here, I'd like to read the conclusion of DeChristopher's interview in *Orion*.

TERRY TEMPEST WILLIAMS: How has this experience—these past two years—changed you?

TIM DECHRISTOPHER, *sighing:* It's made me worry less.

TERRY TEMPEST WILLIAMS: Why?

TIM DECHRISTOPHER: It's somewhat comforting knowing that things are going to fall apart, because it does give us that opportunity to drastically change things.

TERRY TEMPEST WILLIAMS: I've watched you, you know, from afar. And when we were at the Glen Canyon Institute's David Brower celebration in 2010, I looked at you, and I was so happy because it was like there was a lightness about you. Before, I felt like you were carrying the weight of the world on your shoulders—and you have broad shoulders—but there was something in your eyes, there was a light in your eyes I had not seen before. And I remember saying, "Something's different." And you were saying that rather than being the one who was inspiring, *you were being inspired.* And rather than being the one who was carrying this cause, it was carrying you. Can you talk about that? Because I think that's instructive for all of us.

TIM DeCHRISTOPHER: I think letting go of that burden had a lot to do with embracing *how good this whole thing has felt.* It's been so liberating and empowering.

TERRY TEMPEST WILLIAMS: To you, personally?

TIM DeCHRISTOPHER: Yeah. I went into this thinking, *It's worth sacrificing my freedom for this.*

TERRY TEMPEST WILLIAMS: And you did it alone. It's not like you had a movement behind you, or the support group that you have now.

TIM DeCHRISTOPHER: Right. But I feel like I did the opposite. I thought I was sacrificing my freedom, but instead I was grabbing onto my freedom and refusing to let go of it for the first time, you know? Finally accepting that I wasn't this helpless victim of society, and couldn't do anything to shape my own future, you know, that I didn't have that freedom to steer the course of my life. Finally I said, *"I have the freedom to change this situation. I'm that powerful."* And that's been a wonderful feeling that I've held onto since then.

And so it often is for an evolutionary catalyst. We, too, are that powerful, if we allow ourselves to be. That is, we can allow the power of the forces of evolution to move in us and through us.

There's a postscript to all this, and it comes from Naomi Klein, author of *The Shock Doctrine,* who is now working on a book and a film about global warming[120] and who actually has been working closely with Bill McKibben and 350.org. Wen Stephenson also interviewed and wrote about her in the *Phoenix.*[121]

According to Stephenson, the message that McKibben and Klein are carrying to the environmental and Occupy movements goes like this: "Look, this is it: science tells us that time is running out, and everything you've ever fought for is on the line. Climate change has the ability to undo your historic victories and crush your present struggles. So it's time to come together, for real, and fight to preserve and extend what you care most about—which means engaging in the climate fight, really engaging, as if your life and your life's work, even life itself, depended on it. Because they do."

Klein told Stephenson of her challenge in persuading the leftists of the Occupy movement in New York to take on global warming. "For a really long time," Klein told him, "lefties thought climate was the one issue they didn't have to worry about, because big, rich green groups had it covered. And now it's like, actually, they really don't. That was a dangerous assumption to make."

She related her encounters with Yotam Marom, one of the key leaders of Occupy Wall Street, who had been quite resistant to integrating climate into his worldview. But Hurricane Sandy had changed him, as it did so many others. "He said something so insightful," said Klein. "When he thinks about why he was resistant, he realized that if he accepted the reality of climate change, truly accepted it into his body, his soul, then he would have to drop everything he was doing. And he doesn't want to drop everything he's doing."

But what Klein is trying to say to those like Marom is that they don't have to drop everything. "In fact," she says, "you need to do it even more."

And here's the point, as Naomi Klein puts it: "Climate change lends urgency to our fights for social justice, like nothing else before. We have to win these battles against free trade, we have to win these battles to re-localize our economies. *This isn't just some little hobby.* So it's not about abandoning all of those fights, it's actually about *supercharging* those fights and weaving them all into a common narrative. That's the story we need to tell."

Naomi Klein is, of course, an evolutionary catalyst.

And so are all of us here.

PART 5

TOWARD DEEP REVOLUTION

Let us give thanks for this extraordinary period of human history we lived through. Let us recognize that we are moving into a new phase of history. Let's be brave and wise about it, and prepare to move on.

—JAMES HOWARD KUNSTLER, *THE LONG EMERGENCY*

CHAPTER 18

A Truly Revolutionary Revolution

Dark and difficult times lay ahead. Soon we must all face the choice between what is right and what is easy.

—DUMBLEDORE, TO HARRY POTTER

For several years I've been compelled to speak of a local food *revolution* without fully comprehending what I was pointing to. I have felt the revolutionary nature of what's happening around local food—that this is not just a social movement, but an expression of something much deeper emerging in our world.

Being able to see that the evolution of modern human civilization has brought us to an evolutionary threshold is useful, especially in the larger context of the evolution of the universe. Without this perspective, it would be reasonable (but shortsighted) to conclude that humanity's trajectory can end only in the tragedy of irreversible entropy.

But, as we have seen, with the broader evolutionary perspective—and understanding something of the dynamics of cataclysm and emergence[122]—we can anticipate that the Turn in human evolution is naturally a time of extreme chaos and confusion, as patterns and structures held to be fundamental are radically transformed or even destroyed. Many individuals sense these things, of course, but have no adequate conceptual framework in which to hold them, let alone a pathway to follow.

I have great empathy for the individual who feels or sees all this and feels called to some greater level of participation, that of being an evolutionary catalyst (consciously or not). It is not within the scope of this book to explore the reasons why someone may feel called, as this is a matter of destiny and purpose, which each individual must ultimately pursue for himself or herself. I can, however, offer heartfelt confirmation that these feelings and intuitions are real and meaningful, are intimations of what seeks to emerge in our troubled world, and are indicators that one has a potential role at this crucial moment in human evolution.

∾

For the last year or so, I've struggled to grasp the connection between revolution and evolution. The long history of revolution is dominated by bitter and often violent conflict. For instance, "A Brief History of Revolution," a 2010 Adbusters essay, characterizes *revolution* as "the ultimate social leap—a period when the gradual accumulation of mass bitterness and anger of the exploited and oppressed coalesces and bursts forth into a mass movement to overturn existing social relations and replace them with new ones."[123] This is clearly the riot, revolt, resistance, rebellion, and insurrection of which Chris Hedges writes so eloquently in *Wages of Rebellion*,[124] and which we have become accustomed to seeing played out in the daily news.

This view has been troubling, for I have somehow known that the revolution I was seeing and feeling was not at all like this. While I could not articulate it, I sensed that the inevitable revolution Robert Kennedy alluded to in the 1960s could not have been mere revolt.[125] To me, it seemed to point to much more of a step toward Teilhard de Chardin's Omega Point and the arrival of something new and generative on the planet, not a mere uprising against the evils of the world.

The kind of rebellion or revolt of which Hedges writes can lead only to further entropy. But what the local food revolution embodies is a *reversal* of entropy. Here we witness the emergence of an entirely new human capacity, of aligning with evolution's arrow rather than making our own way. This is not a subtle distinction; it is fundamental.

Thus, the revolution manifesting around local food can occur only at the moment of the death of a civilization, at the Turn, in the same way that the supernova process is possible only with the death of a star. At the Turn, our challenge is quite simply whether we humans will choose to continue on our path of at least the last twelve thousand years, on which we seek control and manipulation of the resources around us, or whether we will yield to the evolutionary force seeking to emerge within us.

In the process of evolution, we know there are spontaneous and radical phase shifts that can occur and, along the way, moments that open up the space for the shift from one phase to the next. These are revolutionary moments.

Because the word *revolution* has been largely associated with confrontation and violent conflict, I have felt uncomfortable in using it (and I've certainly observed the discomfort of those who've heard me speak about it)—and yet there has seemed to be no viable substitute. There was no getting around the reality that most revolutions have historically ended in failure or have, at least, devolved into a repeating cycle of conflict. I now see that this is because previous revolutions have derived exclusively from the first three or four stages of the evolution of modern human civilization.

What we are calling *deep revolution* is profoundly distinct, radically expanding our collective context, and drawing all of humanity toward a higher level of evolution and engagement. Deep revolution is emergent and cannot be created by force of will. It is an invitation the universe offers us in times of evolutionary crisis to align with the fundamental flow of unfolding evolution, even in the face of apparent cataclysm. As evolutionary catalysts, we can declare that we join this deep revolution, a greater force for good, now beginning to take hold, invisibly, everywhere on our planet.

This deep revolution appears to be guided and inspired by the angels of evolution (past and present, visible and invisible) who gently and often silently assist us as they serve a Higher Order seeking to emerge and manifest here, expressing itself through nearly fourteen billion years of evolution's unfolding in this universe. We are the servants of this deep revolution, the willing and sometimes unconscious vehicles through which it is moving. While this is beyond our current ability to fully comprehend, it is not beyond our ability to purposefully and gladly join.

In searching my memory banks for historical examples, it began to occur to me that the Buddha, Jesus, and Muhammad—and the resulting movements of Buddhism, Christianity, and Islam[126]—perhaps represent the essence of early deep revolution, clearly catalyzing historical moments of evolutionary emergence. In this context, the evolutionary perspective pioneered by Teilhard de Chardin and his spiritual and intellectual descendants similarly represents the emergence of deep revolution.

Deep revolution must be ignited by a higher purpose, aligned with evolution's own purpose. Whether humanity as we know it will survive its current phase shift is, for now, unknowable. But we can now see that the evolutionary thrust of deep revolution is to usher in the Ecozoic era.

The local food revolution offers a doorway to all this—certainly not the only doorway, but perhaps one of the most inviting and open these days—and heralds the deep revolution that is soon upon us. The local food revolution is a powerful emergent center of aliveness in the midst of a dying civilization.

I cannot really explain any of this, nor am I convinced it is remotely explainable. Perhaps it can only be known in the core of one's being. For now, I find myself unable to construct a manifesto for deep revolution or even to define explicitly what it means. It may be that I can only point. But I sense that this deep revolution is the evolutionary opposite of "the one truly revolutionary revolution" of which Wendell Berry writes, by which he means the Industrial Revolution and its accumulating excesses, "which has proceeded from the beginning with only two purposes: to replace human workers with machines, and to market its products, regardless of their usefulness or their effects, to generate the highest possible profit—and so to concentrate wealth into ever fewer hands."[127]

❧

It's significant that the local food revolution finds its emerging center in the American landscape.

In the American Revolution of the eighteenth century—and in the French Revolution that followed—we can perhaps perceive that what was attempting to emerge in those fertile times, rich with potential, did not come to full fruition. A profound course correction was possible at that time, but it did not completely manifest. As a result, our troubles have grown to encompass the entire planet.

In evolutionary terms, however, perhaps enough was accomplished in those days to lay the foundations for such a needed course correction now, when the conditions for deep revolution are present once again. Today, we face our global emergency just at the moment when many among us are awakening to who we are, where we are, and what our purpose is as humans, signifying that the conditions conducive to a *global* deep revolution have at last arrived.

Time does not appear to be on our side, however, for the accumulating effects of the last twelve thousand years of humanity's descent into stage four are just now becoming obvious—and they are increasing at a fearsome pace, far beyond worst-case scenarios. Now, in this extreme situation, we will either respond decisively or our emergency will become a global cataclysm.

There seem to be few visible signs that the kind of deep revolution needed is actually emerging or even *could* emerge any time soon. After all, part of our collective condition is a tendency toward self-deprecation, depression, and despair. But I submit that deep revolution is emerging with great vigor and creativity in what we have called the local food revolution. If we nurture this center of aliveness, there is great potential for the underlying values and commitments and purpose of the local food revolution to become highly contagious, to go viral, and to ignite other emerging centers of aliveness, creating a truly revolutionary deep revolution.

The time has come on this planet when a deep revolution is necessary. It is stirring in many individuals and in many places among us, but it seems to be most visible and most robust in the local food revolution, which we can now see as the emerging edge of a breakthrough in human evolution.

CHAPTER 19

Deep Revolution and the Evolutionary Catalyst

There is nothing rational about revolution. In the face of insurmountable odds, revolution is an act of faith, without which the revolutionary is doomed. This faith is intrinsic to the revolutionary the way caution and prudence are intrinsic to those who seek to fit into existing power structures. The revolutionary, possessed by inner demons and angels, is driven by a vision. I do not know if the new revolutionary wave and the revolutionaries produced by it will succeed. But I do know that without these revolutionaries, we are doomed.

—CHRIS HEDGES, *WAGES OF REBELLION* (SLIGHTLY PARAPHRASED)

The job is to make wholeness. We have the knowledge in our hearts to do just what is needed, and not push beyond our abilities, to experiment and learn gradually, depending on the results in the work itself as our teacher. The teacher is the feedback you gain with experience.

—CHRISTOPHER ALEXANDER,
*THE BATTLE FOR THE LIFE AND BEAUTY OF THE EARTH:
A STRUGGLE BETWEEN TWO WORLD SYSTEMS*

This chapter is a preliminary and evocative map of the process by which an individual emerges and develops as an evolutionary catalyst. This

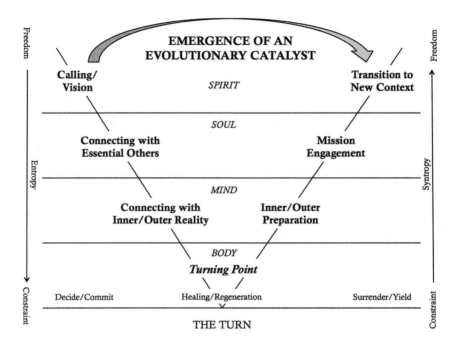

Figure 3: The Emergence of an Evolutionary Catalyst

material will be explored in greater depth in chapter twenty-four and in subsequent deep revolution workshops.

STAGE ONE: CALLING OR VISION

> Sometimes when you're in a dark place you think you've been buried, but actually you've been planted.
>
> —Christine Caine, *Heart Centered Rebalancing*

> There is more to us than some of us suppose.
>
> —Wendell Berry

> Not so much driven towards a vision, but possessed by it.
>
> —James Baldwin

During a time of evolutionary emergency, there comes a point in our lives when it is undeniable that we are here on this planet for a purpose. Even if that purpose is not completely clear, we are drawn. We are called. This usually comes as a profound shock, and it is often precipitated by or followed by a life crisis.

At this point, we may think that we have a choice. We may do our best to live a normal life, suppressing or ignoring the calling, but this detour will ultimately fail. We may attempt to obliterate this uncomfortable urge by devoting ourselves to extreme distractions such as alcohol or drugs, work, entertainment, or relationships (even family). This strategy can have disastrous consequences, and it often ends in premature death or, at best, an unfulfilled life, a life of quiet suffering.

The calling comes when the world's great need and our deep inner longing finally intersect. The evolutionary catalyst will not resist the calling for long.

The process often begins at a particular moment when we are inescapably confronted with realities that shatter our worldview and our view of ourselves. For many, this occurs when it finally sinks into us that global warming is an undeniable and devastating reality, that Peak Everything is upon us, that the collapse of human civilization as we have known it is likely imminent, or that the risk of human extinction is all too real, even in the near-term. Such realizations are momentous and deeply disruptive, and some of us struggle mightily when we face them. Fortunately, they are usually accompanied by the unshakable sense that there is something we must do in this situation, something we might be able to contribute (even if we feel completely unqualified to do so). We find ourselves inexplicably drawn to a particular issue, problem, or cause. Here, mercifully, we are given a glimpse of what is possible—a vision, although it may be quite hazy at first.

This inner stirring represents the evolutionary force seeking to manifest in us and through us, and it firmly sets us on an irreversible path. Often this experience plunges us into chaos and confusion. Life for us will never be the same.

STAGE TWO: CONNECTING WITH ESSENTIAL OTHERS

> Alone I can do nothing.
>
> —*STEPS TO KNOWLEDGE: THE BOOK OF INNER KNOWING*

At first, we seem to find ourselves completely alone in our awakening. But we are not alone. We have the force of 13.7 billion years of evolution supporting us. We have the inheritance of the lives of our ancestors, countless individuals in history who have made it possible for us to arrive at our time and place. There are also those in the invisible realms who apparently rely upon us increasingly, themselves evolutionary catalysts dedicated to the much larger project of the evolution of life in the universe and the ending of separation. We could think of them as angels of evolution or angels of emergence.

The remedy to our aloneness is to begin seeking and attracting those who are similarly called in this world, by giving voice to what we have seen and felt in our awakening. We recognize each other at deep levels of resonance and perhaps find ways to align our lives sufficiently to take this journey together, at least part of the way. It may take a long time, however, to find our true companions.

STAGE THREE: CONNECTING WITH INNER AND OUTER REALITY

The disastrous economic and political experiment that attempted to organize human behavior around the dictates of the global marketplace has failed. The promised prosperity that was to have raised the living standards of workers through trickle-down economics has been exposed as a lie. A tiny global oligarchy has amassed obscene wealth, while the engine of unfettered corporate capitalism plunders resources; exploits cheap, unorganized labor; and creates pliable, corrupt governments that abandon the common good to serve corporate profit. The relentless drive by the fossil fuel industry for profits is destroying the ecosystem, threatening the viability of the human species. And no mechanisms to institute genuine reform or halt the corporate assault are left within the structures of power, which have surrendered to corporate control. The citizen has become irrelevant. He or she can participate in heavily choreographed elections, but the demands of corporations and banks are paramount.

—CHRIS HEDGES, *WAGES OF REBELLION*

The converging crises of our time all arise from a common root that we might call Separation. Taking many forms—the human/nature split, the disintegration of community, the division of reality into material and spiritual realms—Separation is woven into every aspect of our civilization. It is also unsustainable: it generates great and growing crises that are propelling us into a new era, an Age of Reunion. Separation is not an ultimate reality.

—CHARLES EISENSTEIN, *SACRED ECONOMICS*

The work now requires a deeper understanding of the realities we face and how they came about. We must grasp the larger context of our human predicament and our particular arena of calling, and we must begin to come to terms with why *we* are being called. We learn the principles of emergence in evolution and how evolution unfolds in humanity. In other words, we come to terms with who we are. Preconceptions fall away. We leave behind our culturally based identity.

The revolutionary work of an evolutionary catalyst cannot be truly effective—or even moral and ethical—unless it first takes reality into account, no matter how bleak. Our reality is that we live in a revolutionary moment, a time of evolutionary bottleneck, a time of great peril and great promise.

STAGE FOUR: TURNING POINT

Radical transformation cannot happen without a spiritual initiation, and what makes the transformation radical is the downsizing of the human ego and rational mind and the limitless expansion of the Sacred Self.

—Carolyn Baker, "Turning to the Dark Side"

In order to evolve and fulfill our purpose, we must intentionally shift the patterns of our life in order to build a stable foundation. This is revolution beginning from the internal level, and it will require a course correction, healing, and letting go of our past. Here we go beyond mere commitment. We choose to surrender our personal preferences and ambitions and to begin to yield to the evolutionary force that is moving within us. We choose this because we have no other choice.

STAGE FIVE: INNER AND OUTER PREPARATION

The sole purpose of human existence is to kindle a light in the darkness of mere being.

—Carl Jung

Here we are not yet ready to fulfill our calling, not yet ready to fully contribute. First, we must enter a period of self-transformative preparation. Through inner and outer discipline, we hone a balanced vehicle for communication and transmission. We rigorously build our capacities. This cannot be done without proper guidance and instruction, which we must somehow locate and integrate.

STAGE SIX: MISSION ENGAGEMENT

Never forget: We are alive within mysteries.

—Wendell Berry

Finally, we enter our work in the world, our arena of calling. We may discover along the way that what we assumed was our calling had obscured our underlying mission. This stage is a long period of exploration, experimentation, trial, and setback, which will cause us to frequently reassess everything. Here we are learning to align our very being with the arrow of evolution and to join with others who have chosen such a life of total service.

STAGE SEVEN: TRANSITION TO NEXT CONTEXT

> The quality without a name cannot be made, but only generated by a process. It can flow from your actions; it can flow with the greatest ease; but it cannot be made. It cannot be contrived, thought out, designed. It happens when it flows out from the process of creation of its own accord.
>
> —CHRISTOPHER ALEXANDER, *THE TIMELESS WAY OF BUILDING*

There is little one can say about this stage, for few have arrived here. Perhaps we can say that the work at this stage gradually moves beyond the sphere of this planet, perhaps even beyond the physical world. Here we are engaging directly and consciously with a Higher Order, entering our next larger context of life.

PART 6

FIELD NOTES FOR THE EMERGENCE OF A FOODSHED

Recognition of one's residence within a foodshed can confer a sense of connection and responsibility to a particular locality. The foodshed can provide a place for us to ground ourselves in the biological and social realities of living on the land and from the land in a place that we can call home, a place to which we are or can become native.

—JACK KLOPPENBURG JR., "COMING IN TO THE FOODSHED"

CHAPTER 20

How the Local Food Revolution
Can Unfold

Since the U.S. food supply is currently fed by a global foodshed and almost totally dominated by an industrialized system, in the near future, virtually every region in the country will need to undergo a process of localizing its food supply to the greatest extent possible. Local food supply chains will need to help consumers make healthful, informed choices. The emerging local food industry will need to increase efficiency and improve market connections. Eaters will need to learn more about the human connections to food. Farmers will need to produce food for local consumption. Numerous entrepreneurs and organizations are already working on these challenges—or aspects of them—but the process is often chaotic and disorganized.

Food localization can result in a stronger community economy, ecological sustainability, better nutrition and health, and more civic engagement. But the transition to a localized system means that nearly every aspect of the way we feed ourselves must be redesigned and rebuilt. Getting there will require the involvement of entrepreneurs, farmers, chefs, restaurateurs, retailers, distributors, and others. Local government will need to be involved too, but at the right time. And the general public of eaters—all of us—needs to be involved as well. How can all this happen?

❧

When our organization formally began working on this in Boulder County, we naively proposed a goal of 25 percent food localization over a ten-year period. We saw it as a man-on-the-moon project that our community could embrace together. It seemed doable, but nine years later, I can't say that we have moved very far in the direction of local food, either in Boulder County or in the state of Colorado. We're currently still somewhere between 1 and 2 percent local food (no definitive data is available).

We worked for years before we seemed to have much impact locally. On the surface, it appeared that there was a great deal of activity, because the movement was already gaining momentum on its own—there was an explosion of interest in permaculture and reskilling. But eventually we realized that we were facing deep structural problems—the demand for local food, which we had helped to increase, was far outstripping the local production capacity.

We found that we were confronting at least four major overlapping challenges. We had to

- increase and support demand for local food, especially among commercial buyers, wholesalers, and retailers;
- increase production capacity;
- rebuild the infrastructure (aggregation, processing, storage, distribution, and marketing); and
- scale the entire localization effort.

Just being able to identify these four arenas was a breakthrough in our understanding. Suddenly, they were obvious. When we spoke of these four areas to others, it became obvious to them as well. We soon realized that we were developing a common language that might make it possible for us all to see and think together about food localization. We even found a suitable name for the process, *thinking like a foodshed.*[128]

The challenge we saw running through all four of these arenas—especially rebuilding infrastructure and taking the whole effort to scale—was the need for an enormous amount of capital. We understood from Michael Shuman's study that approximately $1.8 billion in capital investments would be needed to get to 25 percent localization in Colorado. And while we also knew that 25 percent localization could ultimately produce massive economic development for the entire state, we had no idea where that investment capital could come from.

The scope and complexity is intimidating, far beyond the capacities of any organization or coalition or government. It looks as daunting as trying to fix climate change or trying to overcome poverty and hunger in the world. Food localization is what's known as a *wicked problem,* and the solutions seem well beyond our reach. Once we begin to comprehend the institutional, governmental, economic, and social structures that hold this problem in place—and their tendency to powerfully resist our efforts toward localization—we can feel completely overwhelmed, that this is just too hard.

Well, it *is* hard. It's almost impossible. But it needs to happen.

We need to remember the context for our predicament. Our society is held in the grip of a global food system that controls something like 98 percent of our food supply. This system is controlled by the Unholy Alliance of Big Ag, Big Food, and Big Pharma, and is powerfully supported by Big Banking and Big Government. The Unholy Alliance doesn't want us to localize our food supply, because it runs counter to their values and their plans. In fact, food localization runs counter to our entire export-oriented economy.

But the Unholy Alliance—and the economic system of which it is a huge part, as the largest industry in the world—has grown to the point that it is now the single largest contributor to global warming. It is a primary factor in precipitating the sixth mass extinction of life on this planet. Together, the global industrial food system and the global industrial economy are a disaster in terms of their impact on human health and well-being, on the environment, on our local economies, and on our communities. And now they are heading straight toward their own cataclysmic disaster.

It may be that the most significant result coming out of the 2015 climate talks in Paris is that for the first time, the nations of the world (195 of them) agreed that we must end our dependence on fossil fuels as quickly as possible. I don't think we can take to the streets in celebration just yet, because this is not news that the Unholy Alliance or Wall Street will take lying down, for they are deeply dependent on fossil fuels. Nevertheless, the agreement in Paris—even though it doesn't have much in the way of teeth yet—may be the closest thing we've seen to a global declaration of war.

In any case, the global economy and its food system do not have a happy future ahead. We've known for quite a while that they are profoundly unsustainable; but now they are increasingly unstable, heading toward steep decline or even collapse. It will be a bumpy ride down for them, and they are not likely to go quietly into that dark night.

Localizing our food supply is revolutionary, and for those of us who are involved, it is a formidable challenge that will not be made any easier by the turmoil and chaos that the Unholy Alliance and Wall Street will be going through in the coming years. And it will not be made any easier by the growing realization that the need for localizing our food supply is becoming urgent.

Not only do we need to build regional food systems almost completely from scratch, which is hard enough, but we must simultaneously begin the process of reversing the damage caused by Wall Street and the global food system. We need to heal and rebuild our soils, our souls, and our communities. If we do not tend to this deeper task, if we do not recover our connection with the sacred and with all of life, then whatever we might create together will only add to the massive destruction that modern civilization has wrought upon this planet and upon our hearts and minds and bodies.

This will require a revolution—a *deep revolution.*

ೲ

This work is far bigger than merely building our own regional food system here in Colorado. We should allow ourselves to remember that this has never been done before anywhere in the world—at least not in a region with an already established (and growing) population. So let's agree that we're doing this not just for ourselves but also for emerging foodsheds everywhere.

We should also remember that nowhere in the United States has the process of food localization gone very far. Vermont consistently leads the Locavore Index and is considered the mecca of local food (Colorado was ranked twenty-sixth in 2015).[129] But even after fifteen years of concerted and well-organized effort, Vermont today is at no more than 7 percent local food.[130]

It's possible that the pace of emergence of regional foodsheds could greatly accelerate as the effects of Peak Everything—especially climate collapse—become more painfully obvious. It's possible that whole nations (or even alliances of nations) will take up the challenge, when they realize they must, much as Cuba was forced to do when it lost its primary source of fossil fuels (after the collapse of the Soviet Union) and quickly shifted to organic agriculture to prevent mass starvation.

It's equally possible that the Unholy Alliance will, at some point, perceive food localization as a threat and seek to retaliate. We could see the breakout of what we might call "food wars." Since most governments are driven primarily by economics, and since the Unholy Alliance is a pillar of the economic system, we would then likely see governments react strongly against food localization. The efforts by Congress to block country-of-origin labeling and GMO labeling are early indicators of this reaction.

This will be a difficult struggle. But as foodshed catalysts, evolutionary catalysts, or even as revolutionaries, it is important to remember that we are not responsible for ultimate outcomes (although we are deeply implicated). That is, we will likely never see the full fruits of our labors or even learn whether this effort ultimately succeeds or fails. Our responsibility, meanwhile, is to be faithful to the underlying evolutionary impulse that called us to food localization in the first place.

Many of us are giving our lives to this, our all. We are like the abolitionists dedicated to the freedom and equality of all people at a time when slavery was the dominant economic paradigm. The struggle of the abolitionists lasted for centuries; ours may as well. In fact, in some ways, we've inherited their struggle. It is in the local food revolution that we perhaps have an opportunity to fulfill the underlying evolutionary impulse that inspired the abolitionists in the first place. At the heart of the local food revolution is nothing less than the reclaiming of human freedom and dignity.

CHAPTER 21

Toward a Pattern Language
for Food Localization

We find out that we already know how to make buildings
live, but that the power has been frozen in us: that we have
it, but are afraid to use it: that we are crippled by our fears;
and crippled by the methods and the images which we use
to overcome these fears. And what happens finally, is that
we learn to overcome our fears, and reach that portion of
our selves which knows exactly how to make a building
live, instinctively. But we learn too, that this capacity in us is
not accessible, until we first go through the discipline which
teaches us to let go of our fears.

—CHRISTOPHER ALEXANDER, *THE TIMELESS WAY OF BUILDING*

If we study the patterns that characterize the industrial food system,
we see that they are fundamentally rooted in violence, disharmony,
exploitation, and privilege for the few—but mostly violence, in a great
variety of forms.

These are not the patterns of relationship that we find in nature,
and they are not the patterns through which evolution can move. They
are not the patterns of emergence, but of force. Oddly, almost no one
speaks of this, though many of us are aware of how deeply destructive
the system is.

But there is a part of us that remembers the patterns of life that
are characteristic of a truly local food system. This is an ancient memory that goes back long before the advent of the age of totalitarian

agriculture. This memory is embedded in our very genetic code (which, it could be said, agrochemical companies now seek to alter).

Somewhere along the way, we became disconnected from our food roots. We became disconnected from the soil, disconnected from the land, disconnected from the cycles of the seasons and moon and stars, and disconnected from each other. This disconnection is now visible as a huge and festering wound in our culture, but for the most part, we choose not to look at it. When we do allow ourselves to look, it is shockingly apparent, and it is horrifying.

It's good to look, now and then, just to remind ourselves that we're standing on the edge of a fearsome cliff, and that there are forces that seem to be pushing us with all their might into that yawning chasm, toward oblivion. There is, after all, much momentum behind these forces, growing exponentially, as they have been, since the industrial revolution and reaching their zenith in our lifetime.

We can and must rediscover and reconnect with those fundamental patterns of life that are characteristic of a regional foodshed. Indeed, the heart of this book represents some of the first halting steps toward a pattern language for food localization, for the awakening or emergence of a foodshed.

I can point to all this only in the briefest way here, but let me share with you a few thoughts from Christopher Alexander himself (in *The Timeless Way of Building*), which give us an entry into this rich understanding. Alexander speaks of patterns in buildings, gardens, or cities, but his words are equally true for foodsheds. Just let this wash over you, like poetry, as he speaks of "the quality without a name."

> The specific patterns out of which a building or a town is made may be alive or dead. To the extent they are alive, they let our inner forces loose, and set us free; but when they are dead, they keep us locked in inner conflict.
>
> The more living patterns there are in a place—a room, a building, or a town—the more it comes to life as an entirety, the more it glows, the more it has that self-maintaining fire which is the quality without a name.

And when a building has this fire, then it becomes a part of nature. Like ocean waves, or blades of grass, its parts are governed by the endless play of repetition and variety, created in the presence of the fact that all things pass. This is the quality itself.[131]

To reach this timeless quality without a name requires building "a living pattern language as a gate."

To work our way toward a shared and living language once again, we must first learn how to discover patterns which are deep, and capable of generating life.

We may then gradually improve these patterns which we share, by testing them against experience: we can determine, very simply, whether these patterns make our surroundings live, or not, by recognizing how they make us *feel*.[132]

Emerging patterns eventually interconnect to form a living whole.

No pattern is an isolated entity. Each pattern can exist in the world, only to the extent that is supported by other patterns: the larger patterns in which it is embedded, the patterns of the same size that surround it, and the smaller patterns which are embedded in it.

This is a fundamental view of the world. It says that when you build a thing you cannot merely build that thing in isolation, but must also repair the world around it, and within it, so that the larger world at that one place becomes more coherent, and more whole; and the thing which you make takes its place in the web of nature, as you make it.[133]

With Alexander's insight, we can see that a pattern language for food localization could be about discovering the inherent patterns that bring aliveness, wholeness, and healing to our foodsheds—and our communities. This is an extremely potent development. I would suggest that this is the same impulse underlying permaculture.

It's been hard to find the ways to speak about this. But we're discovering just how extraordinary Alexander's contribution really is.

> Let us consider what kind of process might be needed to let a community become gradually whole.
>
> In nature, the inner laws which make a growing whole are, of course, profound and intricate....
>
> What happens in the city, happens to us. If the process fails to produce wholeness, we suffer right away. So, somehow, we must overcome our ignorance, and learn to understand the city as a product of a huge network of processes, and learn just what features might make the cooperation of these processes produce a whole.
>
> We must therefore learn to understand the laws which produce wholeness in the city....
>
> The process is a single process because it has only one aim: quite simply, to produce wholeness, everywhere....[134]

Now, all this may seem rather mystical, even spiritual. Well, actually, it is, for what Alexander is pointing to is that wholeness, connectedness, aliveness, and sacredness are part of one seamless evolutionary process. As Alexander says, this is "a process which brings order out of nothing but ourselves; it cannot be attained, but it will happen of its own accord, if we will only let it.... The more we learn to use this method, the more we find that what it does is not so much to teach us processes we did not know before, but rather opens up a process in us, which was part of us already.... It is not an external method, which can be imposed on things. It is instead a process which lies deep in us: and only needs to be released."[135]

I remember Christopher Alexander saying that aliveness and wholeness begin with something small. If it's authentic, truly alive, it spreads or unfolds—often in mysterious ways. It's eerily contagious, and it's uncontrollable. This is not something to be "organized." Instead, it grows. It emerges. This is as true for a foodshed as it is for a complex organism.

The challenge for those of us involved in food localization is to be able to see such pockets of aliveness and wholeness in our emerging foodshed and in our communities and to protect them, to lovingly shine the light of day on them, to cultivate them, to catalyze their replication—and then to see what's possible and needed next. This is how foodsheds and communities are healed and ultimately made whole. We're learning that we cannot make food localization happen. But we can surely be a catalyst for this emergence. All it takes is seeing what is possible—and beginning right where we are. It is difficult, but necessary. Who among us holds this vision of a localized foodshed?

People will ask, "But if you don't make things happen, how do you *accomplish* these things?" They want recipes, programs, and policies. Often they just want someone to tell them what to do. The truth is (if we're following the path of the evolutionary catalyst) that we don't do these things. We are simply the vehicles—consciously, willingly—through which the foodshed emerges.

Farmers don't really grow their plants or animals; they love their crops and animals into harmonious, productive existence. They don't give them life, for they already have life. They nurture the life that already exists in them. They cultivate the conditions that are conducive to life. This is the key. Farmers provide, as needed, nutrients, water, access to sunlight, protection from weather, and so forth. They live in service to their plants and animals, to the soil (which is an entire ecology of living beings), and to the land. They also live in service to those who rely on them to supply the freshest, most nutritious, and most sustainably produced local food available.

No one can tell us how to localize a foodshed. But we can, as a matter of service, intentionally be a part of the process. And if we have this intention and follow the process, ultimately we will understand how to do it, because we will have already done it—somehow. We will have lived it. As Alexander suggests, "It will happen of its own accord, if we will only let it."

There is something much deeper at work in all this than our will. This is challenging for those of us who are good at identifying problems or seeing what is in the way of, say, the emergence of a unified foodshed.

We want to *change* these things, to make them better, or to remove obstacles or difficult people. But that's not how a foodshed emerges.

The patterns identified here in the process are signs or indicators of emergence, confluences of forces through which evolution unfolds. We can recognize them, intend them, support them, align with them, and celebrate them. But we don't make them happen.

Unfortunately, *making* things happen seems to always have the disturbing result of deepening the patterns of dysfunction and destruction (and often violence) that have so firmly gripped our society and our food system.

Catalyzing the local food shift is subversive. Localizing a region's food supply is to participate in a profound and much larger shift that is unfolding on our planet, the emergence of our species into a vastly greater community of life.

❧

Because the local food infrastructure has been destroyed by industrial agriculture, it's not enough to motivate eaters. Nearly everyone will have to be reeducated about food and our local situation. Everyone needs to understand that our food supply is almost completely controlled by agribusiness—and that it's destroying our health, our local economies, and our environment.

Food is one of the primary ways we connect with life, with nature, with the land, and even with the human community. And when we understand that our food comes from thousands of miles away, is highly processed, is contaminated with chemicals and pesticides and herbicides and antibiotics, and is genetically modified to the point that our bodies have difficulty recognizing it as food, then we can see that such food plays a crucial role in daily disconnecting us from life, from nature, from the land, and from our brothers and sisters.

Food—dare we say it?—is *sacred*. And for those of us who are involved in localizing our food supply, we must place this realization right at the center of our work—or we ourselves, no matter how lofty our intentions, will only contribute to the commoditization of food and our disconnection from life.

❦

Localization is not merely the earth's immune system kicking in. It is not merely a response to converging global crises. It is a process of emergence by which evolution itself is unfolding. This is why those we call *evolutionary catalysts* are attracted to various aspects of localization. This is an evolutionary front line. We are servants of what it is that wants to emerge in ourselves and in our communities. Localization is the evolution of the universe—on a local level.

The local food revolution, as we're articulating it, is not *ideological* (as in *localism*); it's practical and pragmatic. What's more, it's also a powerful gateway to meaningfully addressing other ecological and social issues that otherwise appear intractable, including global warming.

Food localization is not necessarily a mystical experience, per se, but simply the evolution of the universe itself at work in us and through us. I would suggest that the awakening of a foodshed is an evolutionary event of great historical and planetary significance. I can think of no arena of life in these troubled times where the potential for human evolution—and restoration and regeneration—is more timely or holds more meaning and potential. In one sense, it's a battleground, a matter of survival. But in another sense, it's an opportunity for the human community to rise to an occasion that can only be considered an evolutionary crossroads.

❦

The essence of all the patterns presented here is relationship, relationships of a particular quality. What is emerging is a web of relationships that forms the underlying structure of an emerging foodshed. Everything that happens toward the building of the local foodshed is in service of these relationships. The structure of everything that is created along the way catalyzes and facilitates and nurtures these relationships. This is how community is rewoven in a society where it has been absent for so long that we have forgotten what it is and can scarcely recognize it.

We're really looking at *patterns of relationships*.

Perhaps the reason that local food work is so attractive and engaging—and so satisfying—is that it is really about recovering our very humanity and all else that has been lost with the rise of industrial civilization.

$$\infty$$

Now, if you know that localizing your food supply is going to be essential for your community—your local population, however you define it—*what do you do?* There are some things about the process that are going to be similar anywhere we try it. Food localization is a *process*— and it's learnable, replicable, flexible, adaptable, and systemic—and hopefully even contagious.

The process of localizing a regional food supply unfolds in identifiable stages—the gradual shift from a region's reliance on the global food system to the establishment (and even dominance) of a fully integrated regional foodshed. This is a process of building, in the sense of Christopher Alexander's *Timeless Way of Building*. It is an emergent process, and it cannot be made to happen. We can only take the journey.

Perhaps it's good to frame it in terms of a journey, recognizing fully where we are at the beginning and recognizing that we cannot predict how long it might take, what it might cost, and what will be required of us along the way. It will likely be a process spanning generations.

We are the initiators and early adopters of this process. We are evolutionary catalysts, foodshed catalysts.

CHAPTER 22

Deadwood: A Parable

Deadwood was a television show that aired for three seasons on HBO, beginning in 2004.[136] The show was set in the 1870s in Deadwood, South Dakota, one of the wildest mining camps in the American West. Today, the town has a population of just over a thousand people.

In the course of the series, we see the town of Deadwood morphing from a primitive gold-panning camp composed of crude tents into a rather substantial town, eventually focused on industrial mining. In the process of this development, rugged individualism and authentic entrepreneurialism are undone, driven out, and replaced by corporate capitalism, bigger government, and inevitable corruption.

The intent of the show, according to its director, David Milch, was to study the way that civilization comes together from chaos—by organizing itself around symbols. In Deadwood, the main symbol, of course, was gold.

What we're observing in the emergence of a foodshed is something new emerging from chaos by organizing itself around an unlikely symbol: *local food*. It's a new gold rush and a new frontier. We find ourselves living in the frontier days, just before the railroads and the big bankers from back East come in, smelling opportunity.

It's kind of wild and wooly out on the frontier. There's a great deal of drama, hundreds of amazing stories, and no shortage of great characters—from heroes to rascals, some of them matching archetypes illustrated in *Deadwood*.

In this gold rush, some people are just seeking a way to make a reliable living, even a subsistence living—like the farmers we know who are working full-time jobs in order to afford to farm and give their families the experience of connection to the land. Others are devoted to creating the infrastructure that could make a local food system work, and others are working on the policy barriers that tend to hold all of this back.

Still others are a bit more ambitious, seeking power and influence and—naturally—wealth. We know of one local food entrepreneur who proudly proclaimed a few years ago that he was building a $100 million distribution company in just a few years. A year and a half later, he announced that he'd revised his thinking and was now creating a $1 billion company. Two years later, he closed his doors—out of business.

One of the characteristics of a gold rush is that demand far outstrips supply. And that is certainly the situation we face with local food. There's currently almost no way to connect small and midsize producers with larger commercial buyers. The infrastructure for aggregation, processing, and distribution doesn't exist any more. That infrastructure once existed, but it was wiped out after World War II and replaced by industrial agriculture. So there's no reliable way to meet the demand for local food, demand that's continuing to grow dramatically.

Many of our smaller producers have been focused on direct-to-consumer marketing: farmers markets, CSAs, and farm stands. This is where it's been most profitable for them, where—without a middleman—they can get the highest margins. But it's an inefficient system. And it won't last.

The only way many of these farmers can grow their operations significantly is to reach new markets. And that means retailers, schools, and institutions. But they can't get to these larger commercial markets without infrastructure—and without moving up to a certain level of significantly increased scale and efficiency.

CHAPTER 23

Overview of the Process

This chapter provides an evocative introduction to the process by which a foodshed emerges, the seven stages that transform dependence on a global food system into a living regional foodshed. In the next chapter, we will briefly explore what is occurring for us, the evolutionary catalysts, through each stage of this process. And then in chapter twenty-five, we will explore specific patterns of relationship and activity that are characteristic of each stage.

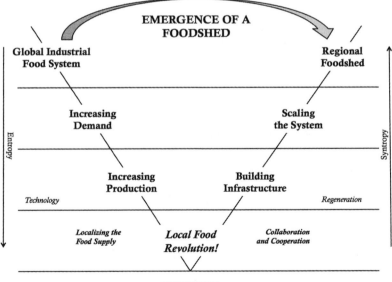

Figure 4: The Emergence of a Foodshed

STAGE ONE:
GLOBAL INDUSTRIAL FOOD SYSTEM

The process begins, of course, within the context of the global industrial food system and the far-reaching control it has established over the food supply in a particular region. Here the foodshed effectively stretches around the globe and seductively provides access to almost any kind of food at any time of year (especially for those people not particularly concerned about quality and nutritional value).

Almost none of the food that people in this region consume is produced locally, even though the surrounding lands are clearly capable of such production. The farmers and ranchers in the area are instead devoted to anonymously producing industrial-scale commodity crops for Big Ag and Big Food, often for export. This is a food system that has been built primarily since World War II, now dominating the entire industrial world (and much of the developing world as well). There is great power and momentum in this system, but it has become virtually invisible to the public eye. Its existence relies on its lack of visibility, its anonymity, and its lack of transparency.

There are, however, a handful of small farmers and ranchers in the region who, at least to some degree, exist outside this system and who are quietly pursuing their passion for growing food for people. These are usually small farmers and ranchers who have found ways to offer what they produce to friends and neighbors. These smallholders may be remnants of the preindustrial food system—the progeny of more traditional farmers—or they may be new to farming, but virtually none of them produce food in order to make a living. *They are simply called.* Many of them work away from the farm to earn their livelihood—to be able to afford to pursue their passion. These smallholders and their customers, along with those who dream of joining them, are the seeds of the emerging foodshed. They may seem to lie dormant for many years before they become locally visible, but to those who have come to depend on them, they are a lifeline of connection and nutrition.

STAGE TWO: INCREASING DEMAND

There is a growing hunger for food and connection that only local producers can provide with authenticity, integrity, and sufficient quality. We learn about local food and connection from friends, websites, webinars and conferences, and the torrent of books and documentary films that have come into our awareness.

We learn from people like Barbara Kingsolver, Joel Salatin, Michael Pollan, Alice Waters, and a host of others who have taken on the task of educating themselves—along with their readers and viewers—about the realities of the global food system and the joys and benefits of local food.

We discover our growing hunger, and as we begin to experience what can satisfy it (through farm visits, eating well-prepared local food, shopping at a farmers market, participating in an all-local potluck gathering, or joining a CSA), we develop an insatiable appetite for that which has been absent in our lives and has largely disappeared from our society.

There is no way to measure this growing hunger, but it is immense.

STAGE THREE: INCREASING PRODUCTION

Before long, producers and eaters and buyers begin to discover that the hunger for wholesome local food far exceeds supply. There is simply not enough local food available to meet the demand.

Realizing that there is more desire for what they produce than they previously believed possible, some producers begin expanding their operations to accommodate more customers and to enter new markets. Their first strategies for expansion are to put more of their available land into crop production, to use more intensive and efficient production methods, and to find ways to market directly—through CSAs, farmers markets, buying clubs, and farm stands.

Eventually, these smallholders reach limits to growth that are difficult to overcome. They cannot afford to lease or buy additional land. They do not have access to sufficient water. And if they can prevail over these obstacles, they usually find there is not enough labor available to support such expansion.

Meanwhile, more and more people want access to local food. Therefore, more commercial food buyers—retailers, restaurants, value-added food entrepreneurs, and institutional food-service providers—want to respond to their customers' demands for local food. But there is woefully inadequate supply to support significantly increased buying. Population growth and increasing urbanization add new pressures on the emerging local foodshed. Farmland is being gobbled up by development.

Other problems surface at this stage. Even with increased production, few farmers are able to make a living producing local food. Moving harvested crops to delivery locations is time consuming and costly. There is no infrastructure to help producers reach their markets. Inefficiencies eat up profits. Weather patterns are increasingly erratic. Government policies and health and safety regulations—generally designed for commercial-scale operations—severely restrict the potential revenue streams of small farms. Few farmers have the skills to successfully manage expanded operations. Even those who do can rarely find the capital required for such expansion.

STAGE FOUR: LOCAL FOOD REVOLUTION

During stage four, those involved in the emerging regional foodshed begin to recognize that the local food movement cannot evolve into a viable industry in the region without radical, systemic change on a much bigger scale. Various factions vie for control or leadership of this effort.

During this increasingly chaotic stage of development, multiple food-policy councils form—either formally mandated by government or organized as informal coalitions. Nonprofits and activist groups proliferate, often with conflicting agendas—dealing with food justice, food waste, food deserts, nutritional education, gardening instruction, food policy, and access to capital and land—and they compete with each other for a shrinking pool of funds.

Other alliances form—around hyperlocal foodsheds (such as small towns), industry segments (vegetable production, grass-fed animal production), economic development (economic "clusters"), city and county planning, food services (restaurants and institutions), and tourism. These efforts are often chaotic, poorly organized, overlapping, underfunded, and temporary.

Local food efforts at this stage tend to be isolated from each other. Regionalism and cross-fertilization are resisted. Attempts at collaboration are difficult, and they often end in frustration or failure. Mismatches abound in motivations, values, goals, and favored methodologies.

An army of experts and consultants attempt to come to the rescue. Government grant funds are offered up, essentially throwing money at the problems. Foundations explore how they can deploy funds to help. Investors begin to investigate new pathways to promising returns. Opportunistic carpetbaggers and scalawags arrive on the scene. It's Deadwood!

ᴄᴡ

At some point, it becomes clear to producers, commercial food buyers, food entrepreneurs, and eaters alike that while there are certainly opportunities in this situation, the shortage of *local* food is precipitating a *regional* crisis. Problems abound, including the sudden failure of many promising farms, ranches, grocers, and businesses (including distributors, food hubs, and value-added producers).

At the same time, the forces of the industrial food system—alarmed by the rapid growth of the local and organic segments—are mobilizing to sabotage, disrupt, and undermine this emerging industry and those who support it. Huge amounts of money are pumped into front-line states and communities to halt efforts to prohibit the use of GMOs or implement more explicit food labeling (e.g., country of origin).[137] Conventional producers, backed by agribusiness interests, organize to oppose, thwart, or co-opt food-localization policies, along with activist individuals and organizations. Public-relations machines are pressed into service to promote the advantages of agrotechnology. Land-grant universities mobilize to seize their biggest opportunity in decades. Repeated everywhere is the mandate "We must feed the world."

As local supplies tighten, competition increases. Large retail chains, traditional food distributors, and commercial food-service providers seek to capture eaters with cheaper and more convenient food alternatives, often using marketing that claims that their anonymously grown products, too, are "local"—a method known as *localwashing*. They cultivate regional producers to grow in scale and efficiency in order to meet volume demands as cheaply as possible, using the monoculture patterns of conventional agriculture.

Some analysts begin to fear that unless scalable, systemic solutions are developed, demand for local food will diminish, people will revert to their previous eating habits—and producers will succumb to conventional commodity-crop production. Others suggest that the local food movement was just a fad after all and that it is passing. Still others declare the local food movement a complete failure.

Ϛ

This is precisely where we find ourselves in Colorado, at the beginning of a local food crisis. Just when we thought everything was going relatively well in the local food movement, we are beginning to realize that the entire effort is in danger of collapse, that this is going to be harder than we thought. It will take longer, require more capital resources—and it all may fail. Meanwhile, the Unholy Alliance is relentless in its drive to control 100 percent of our food supply and is marshaling its financial and organizational resources to advance its agenda on the local level.

For all the local food efforts throughout Colorado, there is no unifying goal or mission. We have been lulled into pursuing our separate agendas while the Unholy Alliance has been consolidating its power.

Despite our efforts and best intentions over the last several years, it now appears that local food perhaps is not scalable after all—or at least that we cannot possibly get it done before climate-withered global food production collapses and a cataclysmic economic downturn forces us into food localization. We do not know if it is possible to build a regional foodshed within our lifetime—or even within generations—but we know that it must happen and that we must give ourselves to this monumental project however we can.[138]

Catalyzing the Local Food Revolution

Food localization in a particular emerging foodshed will not happen unless the process becomes conscious, deliberate, and highly energized.

Galvanizing the effort into an authentic revolution is the only viable and responsible way forward (just as with climate change). Otherwise, the forces of entropy and evil will prevail right through to total system collapse.

While focused decisions and commitments will be necessary at this point, great care must be taken to not attempt to *make things happen,* which will only repeat and deepen the predicament. The fundamental shift is to be in service to what is emerging. Emergence is the primary discipline to learn here—which is little different from farming!

What ignites a revolution?

Micah White, the cofounder of the Occupy movement, has been exploring this question recently.[139] Confronting the reality that the largest protest movement in human history ended in failure and achieved virtually none of its goals, he has come to understand that nothing short of revolution is needed if humanity is to have any hope of freedom or even survival.

White's historical analysis first reveals three familiar types of revolution. The first, *voluntarism,* comes about because people organize together to bring about significant change. In the second type, *structuralism,* outside forces—especially economic crises like a rapid increase in food prices—cause people to rise up, to revolt and rebel. The Arab Spring is a powerful example of this kind of revolution. The third type is radically different, caused primarily as a process within the individual. This is *subjectivism,* and while it may lead to collective action, it often functions primarily internally, precipitating radical change in an individual's life.

But White is now seeing something unexpected, a level of revolution that has never been discussed before, one that is actually inspired by what he considers a supernatural process, in effect, a *divine intervention.* He calls it *theurgism,* a term adapted from *theurgy,* which is from ancient Greek words meaning "god" and "work." It's too early to know where White will take this insight or how others may attempt to apply it, but I see it as an expression of a deep revolutionary impulse. We are likely to see more of this kind of revolution, manifested in unique and surprising ways, in the coming years.

We've learned from permaculture that life is richest and most creative at the margins, at the edges. It's where the action is. Many of us involved in local food have experienced this creativity, and it has drawn us in ever more deeply. It is at the edges that we will most likely find the signs of revolution—such as a vibrant CSA farm or a group of young people organizing a distribution network. These are centers of aliveness, an aliveness that is contagious. Whether they intend to or not, they activate other emerging centers of aliveness. They move us. They are evolutionary catalysts, having an impact far beyond what could ever be projected in a business plan.

And when such catalysts begin connecting with each other, we see just how profound and potentially far-reaching this revolution really is. At such a time, our personal impact can be much more significant (and long term) than we usually allow ourselves to consider.

We are all capable of sensing—*feeling,* really—where the centers of aliveness are in an emerging foodshed—those places and people where forces are powerfully converging that are the heart of this revolution. I doubt that many of our farmers think of themselves as revolutionaries, but if they're working to feed their community, they are certainly engaged in truly revolutionary activities. They are creating centers of aliveness—and we can *feel* this.

Here in Colorado, we can feel it in the Arkansas Valley Organic Growers food hub, a farmer-owned cooperative. We can feel it in the extraordinary work that Brook and Rose LeVan are doing at Sustainable Settings near Carbondale, and the groundbreaking work Jerome Osentowski is doing at Central Rocky Mountain Permaculture Institute. We can feel it in the Rocky Mountain Farmers Union, helping to galvanize a gangly network of some sixteen food hubs in the region. We can feel it in the awesome work of ReVision and their emerging Westwood Community Food Co-op, right in the heart of perhaps the worst food desert in Colorado. We can feel it in the Poudre Valley Community Farm project in Ft. Collins, where a community-owned cooperative is buying conventional farmland, converting it to organic production, and leasing it to local farmers. And we can feel it in Denver, where citizens and government are looking for ways to meet that city's official goal of 20 percent local food by 2020.

They are *foodshed catalysts,* having an impact far beyond what could ever be planned or projected in a business strategy. They are the heart of the story and are demonstrating that local food is not a lifestyle choice, but a choice for life itself—a life-giving, life-restoring, life-generating choice. This is truly revolutionary, the beginning of the reversal of the devastation we have unleashed on this planet, the reversal of our desecration of life, our desacralization of what is sacred and fundamental.

❧

At stage four, it becomes painfully obvious that there are two primary barriers to the growth of a foodshed. First, the local food industry cannot grow to any significant scale without a robust infrastructure to connect producers with larger commercial markets, to facilitate efficient supply-chain distribution, and to provide processing services and storage facilities. And second, the production capacity of farmers is restricted by insufficient land, water, and labor.

These two challenges—limited production capacity and lack of infrastructure—could spark an explosion of business and economic development. It's not difficult to imagine that in this gold rush, there will be numerous competing interests. In early 2015, Colorado State University announced that, with its partnership with state government and industry, Colorado is well positioned to become the "Silicon Valley of agribusiness." Others, less inclined toward industrial-scale agriculture, see similar opportunities emerging around local and organic food.

We can observe two divergent trends throughout this stage. The first is most familiar to us: the economic and financial opportunities that the local food industry might provide. While some of the resulting entrepreneurial ventures may appear beneficial, the reality is that the underlying orientation is often primarily about profits. We should be able to identify this as a version of the overreach that is producing the sixth mass extinction of species on the planet. We can expect to see such early adopters attempt to establish positions that they believe could net considerable fortunes. This trend, which will dominate the scene at first, is but another form of "making it happen," more of the entropic drive to exploit and control.

Within this trend, but far less obvious, are emerging *social* entrepreneurs, who see business (whether nonprofit or for-profit) as a vehicle for achieving social goals such as eliminating urban food deserts or providing disadvantaged populations with access to fresh local food.

Meanwhile, a second trend begins to quietly unfold, usually driven by evolutionary catalysts who are responding to a greater context and are called to a mission that they do not fully comprehend: an effort to unite disparate elements within the local foodshed around a single purpose— *localizing the food supply.* They consciously choose to do this as a collaborative, cooperative effort. In this trend we see the possibility of the fulfillment of the kind of democracy that Thomas Jefferson envisioned.

Land could be considered part of the needed infrastructure. It is needed to increase production capacity. Cities like Boulder have avoided urban sprawl by forcing growth to go vertical—in the form of multistory buildings. In much the same way, entrepreneurial producers are now experimenting with high-density and vertical food production, through controlled-environment or indoor agriculture.

❧

If there is one central requirement for a regional foodshed to pass beyond this tumultuous stage, it is this: a significant number of participants in the effort must *agree by consensus* that the overriding project is the localization of the region's food supply—to the greatest extent and in the shortest time possible. Arriving at this consensus represents the ignition of the local food revolution.

STAGE FIVE: BUILDING INFRASTRUCTURE

At some point, it becomes essential to consciously develop the local food supply chain, the heart of the regional foodshed. The goal at this stage is to catalyze an integrated, collaborative, values-based system to connect producers and food entrepreneurs with their larger commercial markets. This means rebuilding the infrastructure of aggregation, storage, processing, distribution, and marketing—in the form of a network of enterprises. This is the only way that food localization can begin to compete with the global food system and begin to achieve efficiency. This infrastructure begins to bring the regional foodshed into form.

STAGE SIX: SCALING THE SYSTEM

The primary challenge in stage six is to expand the regional food system to ensure the long-term resilience of the foodshed. If a local food system is to feed a significant portion of its population, reaching levels of 25 percent food localization or more, it will be necessary to achieve a level of scale and efficiency far beyond what we're seeing almost anywhere in the United States today. This stage is unknown territory. Nobody in the local food movement has gone there before, and it may be decades away. However, there are lessons to be learned from the development of the industrial food system, and some of that experience can be carefully adapted for more sustainable and equitable purposes. This will require wisdom and courage.

STAGE SEVEN: REGIONAL FOODSHED

If we do all this well, we will have catalyzed a regional foodshed that is economically robust, environmentally sustainable, resilient and self-reliant. It will ensure food security and sovereignty and justice for all, contribute to the health and happiness of our citizens, and revitalize our local economies. This foodshed is a living being, regenerative, itself capable of proliferating similar living beings—spawning other foodsheds. This is what the local food revolution is all about. This collective effort, taking place in regions across the continent and around the world, ushers in the next phase of human evolution, the Ecozoic era.

CHAPTER 24

The Evolutionary Catalyst and the Emerging Foodshed

> Rebels share much in common with religious mystics. They hold fast to a vision often they alone can see. They view rebellion as a moral imperative, even as they concede the hope of success is slim, at times impossible.
>
> —CHRIS HEDGES, *WAGES OF REBELLION*

This chapter outlines the development of an evolutionary catalyst as he or she moves through the seven stages of the emergence of a regional foodshed.

STAGE ONE: GLOBAL INDUSTRIAL FOOD SYSTEM— CALLING OR VISION

We start, of course, in the context of the industrial food system—the current foodshed is global, not regional. As evolutionary catalysts, our initial role is primarily to observe—to watch, to listen, to feel, to understand, and above all, to see. This is essentially the same way a permaculturist approaches a new site, and it is a discipline that we will continue to cultivate throughout the entire process.

During this time, we discover that we ourselves are seeds of the emerging foodshed—not only are we called to this, but we can also begin to see what might be possible. And if we are attentive, we will find others in whom the foodshed is stirring, others who are mysteriously called.

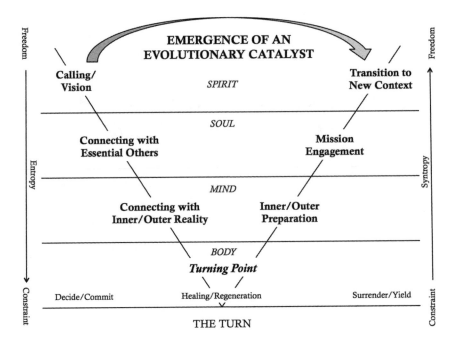

Figure 5: The Emergence of an Evolutionary Catalyst

STAGE TWO: INCREASING DEMAND—
CONNECTING WITH ESSENTIAL OTHERS

The hunger for local food grows in the community, and as evolutionary catalysts, we recognize this same hunger within ourselves. We develop connections in our own area—with local farmers and ranchers, with others who are involved in local food—and we listen. We further our essential education (see the appendix and bibliography for suggestions). We seek to experience centers of aliveness in our foodshed and look for others who may be evolutionary catalysts themselves. And to the extent we can (if we haven't already), we begin to grow some of our own food—and perhaps even learn to preserve a bit of what we grow.

STAGE THREE: INCREASING PRODUCTION— CONNECTING WITH INNER AND OUTER REALITY

With increased demand, growers increase production; CSAs and farm stands pop up; farmers markets flourish. But efforts are inhibited in many ways, such as a lack of infrastructure, the cost of land, and many inefficiencies. As evolutionary catalysts, we seek to feel and understand the dynamics of this stage at a deep level. We become increasingly engaged in the issues of our emerging food system and engaged with those on the front lines of the local food movement. What we are learning here is who we are in all this, what we are truly being called to.

STAGE FOUR: LOCAL FOOD REVOLUTION—TURNING POINT

Stage four of the emerging foodshed is chaotic, with many people and groups working on various aspects of local food, but often at cross-purposes. It is at this point in the process that evolutionary catalysts are called to something radically different, a deeper revolution, more internal than external. Unshakable realizations begin to sink into our being. We find ourselves becoming radicalized, and we begin communicating more directly with others who may be similarly called, sharing what we are discovering.

- Localizing the food supply to the greatest extent possible, as quickly as possible, must explicitly be our unifying goal and mission. How we respond to this calling will determine our evolutionary future for a long time to come.
- We must build our own regional food system, rapidly learning to feed ourselves as locally as possible. This will require us to work together in deep collaboration, which will necessitate learning many new skills. We must be united in this effort.
- Together we must declare our independence from the global industrial food system and actively withdraw from it. We must cease purchasing its products and relying on its infrastructure, and we must resist all overtures for co-optation.

- We all must become food producers, not merely consumers.
- We must bring the sacred to the center of our labors, realizing that we serve something far greater than ourselves.
- We must hold this work of food localization itself as sacred, as an expression of what is seeking to emerge in our troubled world at this time—the beginning of healing, restoration, and regeneration of life on this planet.
- It's not possible for us to make food localization happen. It's part of something much deeper, more important, and more organic and natural than we had realized. The stakes are also much higher than we had previously allowed ourselves to see.
- If we are to serve effectively in this situation, we must commit to our own healing and regeneration.

These are not merely hard-won insights. They are urgings from the force of evolution itself. We can consider them as evolutionary memes and choose to be part of the process of their transmission and proliferation into our society.

Here we also find ourselves at a turning point in our own lives, of course. There is great temptation here to become an activist, an organizer, a planner, a leader. Any of these may indeed be appropriate roles for us, but it is far too soon to know or to commit to them.

A PERSONAL REMINDER

As an evolutionary catalyst, I am at a formative stage and cannot yet understand what my mission is in this work. My true mission and role will be revealed over time and will unfold gradually. My primary responsibility at this stage is to surrender my own ambitions and wants and to yield to the evolutionary force that is emerging within me. While the issue of food localization is what has activated me initially, I am mysteriously being drawn to something much larger and more fundamental. There is more to all this than I had realized. While I certainly have work to do in my emerging foodshed now and in the months and years to come—the situation is urgent, after all—what is most important is not what I accomplish, but who I am becoming. I see that becoming an evolutionary catalyst is a spiritual path and that I am at the point where I must choose to take that path. In truth, I see that I really have no choice in the matter, no alternative. I can delay embarking on this path, but not for long.

In spite of the chaos and conflict evident during this stage, the evolutionary catalyst quietly seeks to infuse moral and ethical values—and even the sacred—into the mix, with the understanding that building a solid foundation for long-term healing and regeneration are the highest priorities in the food-localization effort.

STAGE FIVE: BUILDING INFRASTRUCTURE— INNER AND OUTER PREPARATION

In the emerging foodshed, stage five is practical: rebuilding facilities for storage, distribution, and so forth. For the evolutionary catalyst, engagement at this stage provides an opportunity to deepen one's commitment to the spiritual path that began to open up during the chaos of stage four. We realize that we are still in the early phases of our own development, that we are just beginning to learn what it means to be an agent of evolution. As we engage, however we can, in building the local food infrastructure, we are, most importantly, preparing ourselves on a deep inner level for world-work that we will ultimately do on an external level. This is a long process of learning (which will move through seven substages), and we will have ample opportunity to learn from mistakes along the way.

Here we must also remember that we have not fully completed our own healing process, and to the extent that we still suffer from living in a world of separation, we will be limited in what we will be able to contribute.

Gradually we become aware of our mission, the role that we must play, and begin forming the crucial relationships that will eventually enable us to fulfill it.

STAGE SIX:
SCALING THE SYSTEM—MISSION ENGAGEMENT

Scale and efficiency must increase dramatically for there to be a working regional foodshed. In terms of our own development, this stage overlaps significantly with the work of stage five. We are always preparing and deepening along the way, but little by little, we become engaged in our fundamental life purpose. It's possible that this could eventually take us outside the realm of food localization, which may itself be seen, in hindsight, as preparation for something larger. We begin to see the continuity of our life and can perhaps glimpse where it is taking us. Meanwhile, we are fully engaged in catalyzing the emergence of a new future on this earth.

STAGE SEVEN:
REGIONAL FOODSHED—TRANSITION TO A NEW CONTEXT

> Let us plant dates, even though those who plant them will never eat them.... We must live by the love of what we will never see. This is the secret discipline. It is a refusal to let the creative act be dissolved away in immediate sense experience, and a stubborn commitment to the future of our grandchildren. Such disciplined love is what has given prophets, revolutionaries, and saints the courage to die for the future they envisaged. They make their own bodies the seed of their highest hope.
>
> —RUBEM ALVES, "TOMORROW'S CHILD"

Just as humans are essentially a transitional species, we evolutionary catalysts forever find ourselves plowing new ground, planting new seeds. Here the pathway steadily delivers us into new and unexpected territory, into a broader context or arena of life. We will clearly see that the work of food localization has prepared us well for the next stage of our journey.

CHAPTER 25

Patterns of Emergence in an Awakening Foodshed

While the last two chapters provided an overview of the stages for both the foodshed and the evolutionary catalyst, this chapter explores in far more detail the patterns of relationship and activity that are characteristic of the major stages (starting with stage two).

STAGE TWO: INCREASING DEMAND

The process begins invisibly. Ancient seeds within the hearts and minds of growers and eaters alike begin to sprout and take root. As a people, we begin to become aware of what we have lost and what we truly want (which is not different from what we actually need). As a result, we seek to nourish ourselves and our families—and our neighbors—with truly healthy food. We reorient our lives as locally as possible,[140] as we discover that it is only in the local that we find the authenticity, integrity, and connection we yearn for.

What others mostly see, if they are observant, is an increasing demand for local food, but what is really happening is that we, as a people, are awakening. A revolution is being unleashed inside ourselves, and we don't always know why, especially in the early stages. For many of us, this personal revolution begins with food. This is about our increasing awareness, our process of education—which never ends.

Our education—through books, websites, documentaries, workshops, and community events—shapes our growing understanding, but its primary effect is to kindle our desire for the local food experience.

All the intellectual arguments fade once we begin discovering local food as a doorway into a realm of direct experience that has nearly been forgotten in our society, an experience of aliveness, rooted in the natural order. This is difficult to describe, but not difficult to experience. And the experience, if we open to it honestly and without fear, can be life changing, truly transforming.

What is emerging here is *a community of eaters,* people who are enlivened by the experience of local food and all that it represents. This community includes producers—farmers, ranchers, value-added producers, and other food entrepreneurs, as well as food-service providers. We are all eaters, first and foremost, and what we share together is the (usually unspoken) reality that food is our connection with life and with each other. For those outside this community, this experience is invisible, even unfathomable—until they begin to taste it for themselves.

During this stage, foodshed catalysts must nurture this awareness arising within people and encourage more of the local food experience. They should resist the temptation to direct or control this process through the kinds of activism and community organizing that have become so familiar in social causes in recent decades. Food localization is not a problem to be solved, but a revolution to be nurtured. At this stage, our work is much more about watering the seeds that have already been planted and making sure there is a sufficient flow of nutrients. This is a matter of love.

It's also important for us to remember that increasing demand and consumption is a process that will continue to grow and evolve for a long time, until we find ourselves living together in a truly localized regional foodshed. This will likely take decades, perhaps generations.

Let us remember that *demand* for local food is an expression of a deep inner hunger that drives a fundamental course correction in our society. And let us consider that *consumption* of local food is a practice that increasingly connects us with the sacred that is unfolding and manifesting in our world today. This perspective gives us a larger context for the news that, since 2012, eaters have begun to prefer local over organic or natural foods. This is significant, for while demand for organic and natural foods has been built by traditional marketing methods, demand for local food is spontaneous, coming from the grassroots. This is a revolutionary development. The traditional marketers don't quite know what to make of it. *They can't control it.* Our deep hunger is being unleashed, and will precipitate seismic changes in the way humanity feeds itself—if we will only let it.

Stage Two Patterns

1. Understanding and communicating the context
2. Learning from local food pioneers
3. Developing a public campaign for awareness and education
4. Building essential food skills
5. Defining the foodshed
6. Conducting a baseline food assessment
7. Shifting to economic development
8. Setting a food-localization goal
9. Promoting local food consumption
10. Promoting personal production
11. Cultivating "thinking like a foodshed"
12. Restoring connections
13. Building community spirit
14. Cultivating a local food culture
15. Cultivating community seed saving

1. Understanding and Communicating the Context

Problem: Our food system has become largely invisible to us, and as a people, we have become complacent and unconscious about our food supply and unaware of our deep hunger. As a result we have surrendered our agency—our capacity to act, to choose, especially in a moral or ethical sense—and sovereignty in how we feed ourselves.

Therefore: We learn about our current food system (global and local), its history, and its role in human health and well-being, environment, economy, and democracy. Naturally, we share what we are learning with others in our community, as we are in this predicament together. We also seek to understand how our current food system might be impacted by global warming and how we might prepare for such eventualities.

∾

This learning process will unfold over many years. We seek to understand how to heal our bodies and support our health with food, and what kinds of food will be needed.

For catalysts, it's essential to clearly understand the reasons for food localization—and the urgency. We'll need a solid understanding of our global food situation, the context and meaning of localization, and a vision of both what's needed and what's possible in our community. Fortunately, it's not necessary to persuade people that food localization is our most urgent priority. A far more effective strategy is to work quietly with those who are already beginning to understand this.

(The appendix has a list of recommended reading, under the heading The Global Food Situation. Other sections of the appendix list books on other topics of special interest that you and your team will also want to study. And, of course, there is a host of documentary films that you would do well to watch together.)

2. Learning from Local Food Pioneers

Problem: As individuals and communities, we have much to learn in terms of how to shift our relationship with food and to cultivate a regional foodshed. Our culture has left us ill prepared for this.

Therefore: We study the lessons others have learned and allow ourselves to be inspired as well as informed by their examples. And we note that the process of shared learning is fundamental to the process of food localization, fundamental to the process of the healing and regeneration of our society.

∾

In taking on food localization, we are making a commitment to become lifelong learners, to connect with the best thinking and experience available, and to share what we learn with others.

3. Developing a Public Campaign for Awareness and Education

> Americans today spend less on food, as a percentage of disposable income, than any other industrialized nation, and probably less than any people in the history of the world.
>
> —MICHAEL POLLAN

Problem: We acknowledge that food issues are not merely personal, but impact our entire community. Isolated efforts are unlikely to reach the systemic level. Localizing our food supply is something that can occur only if we are doing this together, as a community. Regionally, this can happen only as a community of communities.

Therefore: We first seek to engage our families, friends, and neighbors in becoming aware and educated about our food predicament and its larger context, and then seek to share this process with an ever-widening circle of stakeholders.

❧

As we've learned from the Transition movement, a fundamental part of any localization effort is educating everyone in the food supply chain, raising awareness of the situation. You don't have to have a lot of answers or understand perfectly how food localization can happen to be able to begin this process. Just start—become a catalyst for food localization. This particular job will never be completed.

4. Building Essential Food Skills

Problem: From the garden to the kitchen to the table, to a great extent, we have lost our ability to grow and prepare our food and have abandoned the joys of sharing together the living process of food.

Therefore: In order to bring living food back into our lives, we will redevelop certain skills that have nearly been lost in the last seventy-five years. These will include sourcing food locally (both shopping and foraging for wild edibles), cooking from scratch, home and community gardening, and canning and preserving.

❧

A key part of any localization effort is for citizens to learn essential life skills so they can take responsibility for some of their own needs. Reskilling programs help people learn new or forgotten skills, because shifting to lower-carbon, mixed-farming organic systems that are less dependent on oil and chemicals will require a lot more people with the right skills working on the land again. Along with gardening, cooking, canning, and storing food, we will need people who can keep bees, raise chickens and goats, produce compost, tend orchards and berry bushes, and on and on.

5. Defining the Foodshed

Problem: We do not know the land or what will be required to feed our local population. And as a people, we suffer from a lack of connection to place and community. We cannot know who we are without understanding where we live. Our current foodshed stretches around the globe. We seek to gradually shrink our foodshed closer to home, so that our food supply is part of nature itself, not some fabricated industrial system.

Therefore: We first begin to explore how we might define ourselves as a population, as a community. Then we seek to understand what accessible land could support our food needs, taking into account the overlapping needs of nearby communities.

❧

Food localization is the process of turning an upside-down food supply right side up. Instead of exporting virtually all the food produced in a region in order to feed the world—and then importing most of what we eat—we're moving toward feeding our local population first and then exporting the surplus.

So we must know what our local population is—the people we're trying to feed—and the geographic area and what it can grow. This is our local foodshed.

In our efforts in Colorado, we were initially concerned with feeding people in Boulder County. But as we began working with the local food movement in Denver, we realized that they faced a severe shortage of available land from which to feed their local population. We often heard people say, "We'll just import food from Boulder County," but we knew for certain that we didn't have enough local production to feed folks in Boulder County, let alone the people of Denver! This led us to begin thinking more broadly.

So we focused on the Front Range Urban Corridor, where 85 percent of Colorado's population lives—4.3 million people—and where there are some nine million acres of farm and ranch land. We came to consider this the Front Range Foodshed. Defining a local foodshed this way is very useful.

With more than nine million acres of farm and ranch land available in the Front Range—even if most of it is currently devoted to animal pasturing, hay, and commodity-crop production for export—there is (at least in *theory*) great potential for sufficient food production to feed the entire local population. A goal of 25 percent food localization in the Front Range could be achievable. Since then, we have conceptually expanded our regional foodshed to include all of Colorado (with "leaky borders"), partly because many of our cherished fruits—especially peaches—come from the state's Western Slope.

6. Conducting a Baseline Food Assessment

Problem: We do not know what local food production or consumption is currently taking place in our region. We do not know what our food needs are or what of these needs our surrounding lands could actually support.

Therefore: We will come to know the existing foodways of our locale—the current patterns of production and consumption (both those that are local and those that depend on the industrial food system) and the historic and cultural context. We will come to know our lands, how they are being utilized and the role they might play as our foodshed gradually becomes localized.[141] We seek to understand what portion of our food consumption is from locally produced food. Our drive here is to understand the realities and possibilities of our emerging foodshed. We take into account the potential for significant upcoming changes in population growth, weather patterns, and water supply.

ॐ

At some point we're going to need to learn everything we can about the current reality of our foodshed—food consumption patterns, current food production (as well as potential food production), and the current (and potential) demand for local food. What exists in our current food system? What's missing, and why? What's working? What's not? Who are the movers and shakers? What can our soils handle? What are people's attitudes about all these things? The answers to these questions, compiled in a community food assessment, will help shape any plan that we might come up with.

Conducting a community food assessment gets people's attention, sometimes even the right people, who can help focus the whole conversation and effort around local food. Keep in mind, however, that performing such an assessment pushes us into the limelight. People will want to know what we're planning to do about what we've learned. Other people will be critical of the information we've gathered or the apparent implications of what we've discovered. Don't expect everyone to be excited about a community food assessment. But be assured that it will stir the pot in the community.

7. Shifting to Economic Development

Problem: Local food is often seen as a lifestyle choice available to the privileged few. The process of globalization of the food supply has stripped the local economy of much of its natural activity. The domination by commodity-crop agriculture has significantly reduced jobs in the area and increased economic leakage, causing a lack of local economic resilience.

Therefore: We seek to understand and communicate the economic benefits of food localization for our communities and region.

∾

Local food's reputation as a healthy but optional lifestyle has motivated quite a few people. But we found a bit more traction when we began shifting the conversation to food localization as economic development, a strategy that was first modeled by Woodbury County in Iowa, which shifted their agriculture practices from commodity crops to organic production because of the economic opportunities. As described earlier, economist Michael Shuman studied the impact of 25 percent food localization in the state of Colorado and reported that it could produce over thirty-one thousand new jobs and add over $2 billion a year to state GDP. That's a level of impact far beyond almost all other kinds of economic development proposals.

8. Setting a Food-Localization Goal

Problem: The process of food localization, if it has indeed begun at all, is largely invisible to our larger community. We lack a sense of unified purpose around our food supply, which renders marshaling resources problematic.

Therefore: As a community, we seek to establish a common goal for localizing our food supply to a certain percentage by a certain time. We recognize that this goal is aspirational and need not necessarily be supported by detailed metrics.

∾

We all should think carefully about what degree of food localization might be possible in our own foodshed. What we've done in Colorado is to set an interim and somewhat arbitrary goal of 25 percent food localization over the next decade or so. In some ways, this might seem a rather modest goal, but it will require fundamental changes in the local food system. The city of Denver has done a similar economic impact study with Shuman, and the mayor of Denver, Michael Hancock, has set an official goal of 20 percent food localization by 2020.

Here's a cautionary note: at this point, no matter how good an idea food localization is, we don't know to what degree it's possible. We'd like to think that 25 percent is possible in the Colorado Front Range. Maybe someday we'll get to 50 percent. But here's what keeps us up at night. When we look at food localization across the country—and around the world—we see community after community hoping to localize their food supply to a certain extent, with the assumption that they'll import the balance. But where will that balance come from? The kind of imbalance we have here in Colorado, where we are currently growing a tiny amount of our essential food supply locally, holds true almost everywhere. This points to a serious challenge—a symptom of a species in population overshoot—to which the answer is that we simply must localize our food supply to the maximum extent possible (even though this is almost impossible to directly measure), and this must be done everywhere possible.

9. Promoting Local Food Consumption

Problem: A large portion of our local population depends almost exclusively on the global system for their food needs and pleasures. Some of this is due to economic disparity, and some is due to a lack of awareness of the benefits of food localization.

Therefore: We inspire all members of the community to eat (and drink) from local sources whenever possible, and we encourage food buyers and food-service providers to increasingly source locally whenever possible.

❧

At the moment, demand for local food is far ahead of supply. But as we expand production capacity, we must also support local purchasing and consumption. Everybody can help with this. This is why we've put so much effort into the 10% Local Food Shift Challenge and Pledge, focusing on retailers and restaurants—the businesses in the best position to influence large numbers of eaters.

10. Promoting Personal Production

Problem: As colonized consumers, we have been taught to be passive in meeting our food needs—to the point that, to a considerable extent, we have actually lost the skills required to feed ourselves to any significant degree. This has disconnected us not only from foodways but also from a host of natural lifeways.

Therefore: As we disengage from the industrial food system, we seek to grow more of our own food—in home and community gardens, in kitchen window boxes, and in attached and freestanding greenhouses. We work to recover the knowledge to do this successfully. And we inspire and encourage our family, friends, and neighbors to join this process.

∾

In the new local food economy, none of us will be able to be mere consumers. Increasingly, we will need to be food producers ourselves. We can all learn to grow at least some of our own food. Something magical happens when we do. Besides, as Ellen LaConte says, "Garden as if your life depended on it, because it will." Given the storm that's brewing over the horizon, she makes good sense. "Take up spade, rake and hoe," she says. "Make compost and raise good soil and garden beds *with a vengeance,* starting this spring—and with an eye toward forever."

It's instructive to realize that during World War II, many American citizens became food producers. We recently learned that there were some fifty thousand victory gardens in the city of Denver alone.

11. Cultivating "Thinking Like a Foodshed"

> There is such a great need here for a regional local food system. There are so many people involved in various aspects

of local food these days, but so few who are thinking systemically. Many are involved in creating wonderful projects, companies, and organizations, and many more are working on their individual or family or neighborhood food situations, but who is truly moving toward collaborating to build our regional foodshed as a functioning integrated food supply chain? Who is consciously working toward building the local food economy, a living foodshed? No organization or company or institution can do this alone. The only way an integrated regional foodshed system can emerge is if we are consciously building it together. And yet, this can't be made to happen. It must be cultivated and nurtured. The seeds have surely already been planted.

—MICHAEL BROWNLEE, PRESENTATION AT
COLORADO SPRINGS LOCAL FOOD WEEK, 2014

༄

Problem: In our society, we have grown accustomed to living largely isolated from each other. Even when we start thinking about local food resources and needs, we generally tend to think only in terms of our immediate neighborhood, community, or county. This creates a fragmented food system.

Therefore: We seek to cultivate a systemic or bioregional view of our emerging foodshed, including how our local foodshed might beneficially interact with and support other adjoining foodsheds. We learn to adopt a holistic view, understanding how all the elements of our local foodshed are interconnected into one living whole.

12. Restoring Connections

Problem: By being so reliant on industrial food, we have lost our connection with what is primary and sacred in life. In many ways, we have lost touch with life itself; our industrialized food system is a sad reflection of this fact.

Therefore: By becoming engaged with our emerging foodshed, we connect with the land, with those who grow our food, with the natural processes and cycles of life that are fundamental to all life, and we begin connecting with each other. We experience a level of aliveness and connectedness that has almost disappeared in our society.

13. Building Community Spirit

Problem: In our society, we have mostly lost any real sense of community. What we generally call *communities* are not the organic, naturally arising living beings that have characterized the most meaningful collective experiences of our ancestors, but are instead simulacrums and substitutes that leave us empty, distracted, isolated, and profoundly lonely. We do not belong anywhere or to anyone.

Therefore: A new sense of community emerges from our shared experience with local food. This may be the most important and most unexpected benefit of food localization. Lives are transformed and communities are enlivened as a regional foodshed awakens to consciousness and begins functioning as a true ecosystem, of which we are an essential part.

14. Cultivating a Local Food Culture

Problem: Having become accustomed to feasting on a cornucopia of dishes from around the world, we have lost any connection with the cuisine from our own region. We do not know what foods naturally grow here, or what locally unique dishes have been popular among our home cooks, creative chefs, and native-food enthusiasts. Our food is devoid of story or connection with peoples or places.

Therefore: We seek to discover the food history of our region and its peoples from the distant past to the present. We seek to uncover the provenance of ingredients and recipes, whether they come from near or far. We bring the stories of people and place to our food, whether invented or preserved.

A local food culture is the heart of community in Europe and much of the world. This is what needs to be developed here as well, and it's beginning to emerge in some places. This can be seen as true local culture based around local food and agriculture, and it's appearing in the form of agritourism, farm dinners, local food festivals, community potlucks, food banks, and faith-based communities. It includes entertainment, music, and storytelling, but it's all about building community around food.

We need to learn to love our foodshed and what's emerging within it, to nurture it, to give to it, to allow it to give to us. This is a relationship of a profound order. *It's really about loving our foodshed into existence.* We are touching the realm of the sacred here, and we do not know the ways to speak about this yet. Words fail. But we do know that this is sacred work we're doing together, and through this work, the sacred moves in us and through us. The relationships that are thereby created are nothing less than sacred. Food is sacred—and mysteriously sacramental.

15. Cultivating Community Seed Saving

> The desire to save seeds comes from an ethical urge to defend life's evolution.
>
> —Vandana Shiva

Problem: Gardeners and farmers alike have gradually ceased the ancient practice of saving and trading their own seeds. In the process of commercialization, many heirloom varieties adapted to regional conditions have disappeared. Commercial seed producers increasingly cater to large-scale food processors and marketers. Biotechnology has almost completely displaced classical plant breeding. This has created a dramatic loss of genetic plant diversity, and it has diminished food producers' ability to adapt to environmental stresses such as disease or global warming.

Therefore: As a community of eaters, we inspire and encourage our farmers and gardeners to save and share the seeds from what they produce, renewing an age-old partnership with plants that preserves biodiversity and regional adaptability.

STAGE THREE: INCREASING PRODUCTION CAPACITY

> Over the next 40 years, land, energy, water, and weather constraints will place unprecedented pressure on mankind's ability to access its most basic goods—food, fuel, and fiber. Humanity must now produce more food in the next four decades than we have in the last 8,000 years of agriculture combined. And we must do so sustainably.
>
> —"The 2050 Criteria," World Wildlife Fund

> Recently, Oxfam commissioned modeling to make estimates about what food prices would look like twenty years from now, and determined that under normal circumstances, food commodity prices are likely to increase about 50 percent between now and 2030. And if estimates of climate change are factored in, food prices could be up to 100 percent higher than they are at present. This would put enormous pressure on the world's population and especially its poor.
>
> — Suren G. Dutia, "AgTech: Challenges and Opportunities for Sustainable Growth"

Introduction

With global food demand expected to increase 70 percent by 2050 and food prices expected to perhaps double during that time, increasing food production, efficiency, and diversity everywhere will be critical, especially in the face of significant environmental constraints and challenges. Food localization offers a powerful alternative to the strategies of industrial agriculture.

Stage Three Patterns

1. Identifying opportunities and barriers
2. Supporting direct marketing

3. Introducing permaculture, restoration and regenerative agriculture, agroecology

4. Rebuilding and cultivating soil

5. Training and supporting new producers

6. Recruiting and training the labor pool

7. Encouraging diversity of food production approaches

8. Incentivizing conversion of commodity-crop or export production to production for local consumption

9. Cultivating value-added producers

10. Channeling local capital

11. Supporting restaurant and retail sales of local food

12. Emphasizing controlled-environment agriculture

1. Identifying Opportunities and Barriers

Problem: There is great ignorance, misunderstanding, and confusion about the current state of our region's food supply and its potential for food localization. We are profoundly disconnected—intellectually, emotionally, spiritually, and physically—from our food supply system, and we are unconscious of how it works.

Therefore: From existing sources and original research, along with observation and interaction, we gather enough data to build realistic and useful perspective. Much of our emerging understanding will take the form of stories.

❧

"Doing the homework" is really the starting place. We often hear it said that all of us involved in local food suffer from inadequate or outdated or nonexistent data. The need is to apprehend current realities in our food systems, the downsides and upsides, the good, the bad, and the ugly. Research is needed, both formal and informal—including conducting focus groups or listening sessions.

Any entrepreneur will agree that you may do your best to understand market forces and trends—try to gain the best picture of reality that you can—but you will never arrive at definitive answers to any of your questions. Nevertheless, the best data available *will* serve to guide intuition and decision making.

Opportunities

Social entrepreneurs are generally skilled in sensing how to transform challenges into opportunities. They are also attuned to changes in marketplace dynamics, and they learn how to build flexibility into their plans to respond to such changes.

For social entrepreneurs, activists, and policy workers in food localization, there are certain fundamentals that we'd like to know about current conditions.

- How much food is being produced within the foodshed, on how many acres? How much of this food is being produced for local consumption (categorized by sector—direct, restaurants, wholesale distribution, and so forth)? How much for export?
- How much of food consumption is being sourced locally?
- What are the nutritional needs of our local population? How much of what types of foods meet these needs? How much will the local population grow over the next twenty-five years, and what will projected nutritional needs be?
- How many acres of local food production would be needed in order to meet the population's nutritional needs?
- In our region, how many acres of agricultural land exist? How is this land being used?
- What is the state of the region's soils?
- What is the state of the region's water supply for agriculture (current and future)?
- What is the state of the region's government policies that could hinder or support expansion of local food production?

The resulting data, even if significantly incomplete, will help to provide greatly needed perspective and will begin to identify challenges and opportunities. Projects will emerge. From a social-entrepreneurial perspective, every challenge reveals opportunities. Quantifying these, wherever possible, is a useful exercise, even though definitive numbers can almost never be achieved.

Barriers

In any region, there exist numerous barriers to the expansion of local food production. Understanding the specifics of each of these barriers will help yield a useful map of the terrain.

- onerous or nonsupportive local government policies and regulations (such as regarding land use)
- high cost of land
- lack of available land suitable for farming
- lack of access to capital
- shortage of experienced farmers
- shortage of experienced farm labor and labor housing
- price competition with the industrial food system
- lack of infrastructure
- lack of water availability, high cost of water
- short growing season
- increasingly unpredictable climate
- vulnerability to extreme weather events
- high risk as business venture (no insurance, no federal aid, lack of state support)
- competition (for resources) from commodity-crop and export agriculture

This resulting data and perspective will serve as a guide to all those who are involved in localizing a foodshed. A key challenge will be to make this data easily accessible and comprehensible to a diversity of stakeholders.

Many local food efforts have been forced to rely on USDA census data published every five years, the most recent from 2012 (which became available in May 2014, after a long and frustrating wait). Market conditions have been changing so rapidly that much of that information is already out of date. Reporting systems are notoriously inaccurate.

We often hear, "Well, it's the best data available, so we have to use it." Of course we need to pay attention to these numbers, but we also need to resist assuming that they provide us an accurate picture of reality. We must balance all this data with our actual experience in regional foodsheds and our deepest intuition.

It's important to realize that no amount of data will substitute for direct observation. More than anything else, we need to learn *to see*— to apprehend what is happening in our emerging foodshed. Students of permaculture are often taught that before they attempt developing any design for a specific site, they should first intensely observe all the dynamics (biological, geological, climatic, and so forth) occurring within that site for at least a year. This is also known as *reading the landscape.*

> Good design depends on a free and harmonious relationship to nature and people, in which careful observation and thoughtful interaction provide the design inspiration, repertoire, and patterns. It is not something that is generated in isolation, but through continuous and reciprocal interaction with the subject.... There is little value in continuous observation and interpretation unless we interact with the subject of our observations. Interaction reveals new and dynamic aspects of our subject and draws attention to our own beliefs and behavior as instrumental to understanding. The interplay between observer and subject can be thought of as the precursor to design. The accumulation of the experiences of observation and interaction build the skill and the wisdom needed both to intervene sensitively in existing systems and to creatively design new ones.[142]

We will return to the topic of this kind of interaction and observation in chapter twenty-eight.

2. Supporting Direct Marketing

Problem: Producers need to be able to produce revenues and profits from what they grow and make.

Therefore: As a first step, we inspire, encourage, and support markets and market structures to facilitate sales directly to eaters.

〜

A few years ago, as we were having a delightful early-summer outdoor lunch at one of our favorite local restaurants—Tangerine, in north Boulder—a pickup pulled up right in front of where we were sitting, and a farmer got out to deliver two bags of freshly picked greens to the chef inside. It was a beautiful thing to see. But as we watched this transaction unfold, we couldn't help but wonder how many other such deliveries he had to make that week, and how many other farmers were doing exactly the same thing—when they all really needed to be in their fields, farming!

One farmer told us that he made as many as fifty such deliveries in a day. We started thinking about the huge inefficiencies in direct marketing, which a couple of years later led to our capitalizing one of the first local food distribution companies in Colorado.

Direct marketing is an essential method of operation for most small farms, and this approach needs to be expanded almost everywhere—including selling via CSAs, at farmers markets, at farm stands, and through direct delivery to homes or scheduled drop-off points. Even commercially oriented midsize farms may maintain a strong direct-marketing component in their overall market mix as a matter of ensuring diversity of income streams.

Profit margins for direct marketing are much higher than wholesale or retail channels, but labor costs are high and inefficiencies can absorb much of the profit. Direct marketing has accounted for much of the growth in local food production and sales in our area over the last several years, but this growth has flattened out recently, perhaps a signal that the inefficiencies of selling directly to eaters are taking a toll and that it may be time to begin focusing on building infrastructure (see stage five).

Direct marketing makes strategic sense for a small farm or ranch attempting to maximize revenues and profits. Elimination of the middleman increases profits. But it can also mean increased costs that are rarely tracked. (We heard from a small local producer in Brighton, CO, who was selling his eggs for $6 a dozen. But as he did an in-depth analysis of everything involved, much to his surprise, he discovered that his direct costs were close to $6 a dozen.)

The main avenues for direct marketing:

- *Farmers markets.* Often seen as the most visible indicator of the growth of the local foods sector, with some 8,500 farmers markets in the United States. The farmer-owned Boulder County Farmers Markets (with locations in the cities of Boulder and Longmont)[143] together generate about $5 million in producer sales in a season (April 1 to October 15). For many local producers, this is a very important outlet. For perspective, however, note that this amount of food could feed the entire population of Boulder County (roughly three hundred thousand people) for only two days. Farmers markets are extremely labor intensive for producers, especially if they are attempting to sell at multiple markets. For instance, a goat dairy in Denver participates in nineteen farmers markets every week. Experienced producers seem to be relying less on farmers markets, looking to sell their output more efficiently.

- *Community supported agriculture (CSA).* For many small producers today, the CSA model of selling shares in advance of the growing season is the core of their operation. While this approach provides much-needed cash early in the season, it requires growing a great variety of items (as many as fifty species of vegetables or more). This is the fastest-growing sector of direct marketing. When we started our food work in 2006, we could find only about 125 CSA shares available throughout Boulder County. Today there are many farms in the area that individually have several times as many shares (such as Monroe Farms, with 650 members, and Red Wagon Organic Farm, with 450). We estimate that there are at least two thousand CSA shares available in the county today, representing exponential growth.

- *Farm stands.* An increasing number of farmers in our area are discovering the value of having customers come to the farm to shop for their food needs. This builds lasting relationships ("Know your farmer, know your food"), and provides customers direct farm experience for their families. Farm stands also provide a solid revenue stream, as they can be open on most days and don't require shipping harvested product to a centralized farmers market.

- *Agriculture supported community.* Some farms have launched programs to provide access to lower-income customers by offering shares on a sliding scale, based on means, or "work shares."

- *Neighborhood supported agriculture (NSA).* These are "super-local" CSA operations based on multi-plot neighborhood gardens or co-ops. In Denver, Sprout City Farms cultivates urban farms on underutilized land, thereby bringing good food to neighborhoods.

- *Buying clubs and co-ops.* Buying clubs allow citizens to pool their financial resources to purchase bulk foods at wholesale prices. They often form around interest in particular types of foods (meat, cheeses, local) or in a clutch of specific producers.

- *Virtual farmers markets and food hubs.* This is largely a rapidly changing technology-driven development, as producers seek to diversify ways to reach new customers. For instance, modeled after Oklahoma and Nebraska Food Cooperatives, the High Plains Food Co-Op is an online platform that connects a network of about forty producers in the Rocky Mountain Front Range and high plains with customers interested in locally produced food and nonfood products. Arkansas Valley Organic Growers is a cooperative of producers in the Pueblo area who, in 2013, launched their own food hub, the first in the state, allowing them to offer centralized pickup of CSA shares and other direct sales.

- *Farm-to-table dinners and agritourism.* Many producers are discovering that hosting on-farm events such as farm dinners, weddings, and tours can not only provide additional revenue but also build community and increase direct customer sales. Some farmers, such as May Farms in Byers, CO—home of the "Zombie Crawl"—have reportedly managed to generate more cash with such events than through crop production.

- *Faith-based CSAs.* Some congregations and interfaith groups are adopting farms to build CSA subscriptions. New York–based

Hazon, a Jewish organization, has the largest network of CSA farms in the country (among them Red Wagon Organic Farm in Boulder County).

While direct marketing builds sales—and needs to be further developed—it does little to expand production capacity. With the increased profits, farmers may lease additional acreage or offer more CSA shares, but this amounts to *incremental increase* in production capacity, nothing on the scale of what is needed to reach a larger commercial market.

3. Introducing Permaculture, Restoration and Regenerative Agriculture, Agroecology

Problem: Much conventional agriculture is profoundly unsustainable; agriculture in any region generally lacks a holistic or systemic perspective, leading to unnecessary negative impacts on the natural systems upon which it depends. Soils are generally depleted and need amendment.

Therefore: We encourage agricultural philosophies, methodologies, ethical and design frameworks that are modeled from natural ecosystems, applying a whole-systems approach to sustainable agriculture and food systems based on traditional knowledge, alternative agriculture, and experience in local food systems.

ॐ

Permaculture

To understand the profound importance of regenerative agriculture, the kind of farming that builds natural capital, we need to see it not as a fringe or retrograde activity—unable to feed the world, as conventional agronomists would claim—but as a heroic and under sung achievement in the face of overwhelming institutional neglect, cultural dissipation, economic monopolies and dire ecological challenges from chemical, nuclear and genetic pollution, climate change and an eroding resource base in the land and in society. Tracing the threads of progressive agriculture and ecology against the backdrop of the rise of a consolidated industrial food system will, I hope, show how the former carry a true populist mandate which we must now champion to reclaim the common wealth of the earth itself and to secure a future for ourselves and our descendants.

—PETER BANE, *THE PERMACULTURE HANDBOOK: GARDEN FARMING FOR TOWN AND COUNTRY*

As many others have noted, Cuba's experience of surviving a harrowing shortage of fossil fuels (caused by the collapse of the Soviet Union in the early 1990s) provides poignant lessons in rapidly shifting from a traditional petrochemical-based food system to one that is organic, relies on human labor rather than mechanization, and is primarily vegetarian. Cuba successfully made this transition through what they call "The Difficult Period" (the average citizen lost twenty pounds) largely because of the significant number of permaculture practitioners who were already working there. Partly due to their influence, the Cuban food system became 80 percent organic in only eighteen months. Today, Cuban *urban* gardens produce 50 percent of the nation's vegetables.

We organized and promoted a permaculture design certification course in Boulder—"Permaculture through the Seasons"—and today there are some five hundred recently certified graduates in the area, along with at least one hundred certified permaculture teachers. This represents a powerful force in the community. Many of our newest farmers have a background in permaculture, which helps ensure that the future of local agriculture will not succumb entirely to the industrial model. And some farms and ranches are being revamped with a long-term permaculture design plan.

Restoration and Regenerative Agriculture

While many permaculture projects are focused on the small scale, Mark Shepard is applying permaculture principles to large-scale operations. Shepard runs New Forest Farm, a 106-acre perennial agricultural forest in southwestern Wisconsin, considered to be one of the most ambitious sustainable agriculture projects in the United States, a conversion of a typical row-crops grain farm into a commercial-scale, perennial agricultural ecosystem. This is regarded as one of the first attempts to develop restoration agriculture in the United States. Shepard described the essence of restoration agriculture in his recent book.

> It is absolutely possible for human beings to produce their staple foods using perennial, agricultural ecosystems that actually improve the quality of the environment. This can be done on a backyard scale, it can be done on the farm and ranch scale, and is needed on a global scale—without a minute to lose.
>
> While producing an abundance of food for humankind, these systems remove carbon dioxide from the atmosphere, purify water, increase the depth and fertility of topsoil, provide wildlife habitat and create incredible beauty which is increasingly necessary in our "modern" world of concrete, steel, plastic, and glass.
>
> In an incredibly short period of time, we can restore and heal our farmland. We can recreate some of the abundance that our ancestors saw when they first moved to this continent. Instead of just stopping the insult ... we can become active participants in the transformative, restoration process. We can do it while still farming and producing food. As we heal our farmland we can heal our planet. And when we heal our farmland we heal ourselves and our families.[144]

Shepard is the founding president of Restoration Agriculture Institute, the CEO of Forest Agriculture Enterprises, and teaches agroforestry and permaculture around the world.

Agroecology

> The transition to an ecologically-based agriculture is obligatory if we hope to feed ourselves during the wrenching economic, social, and climatic troubles ahead.
>
> —DAN ALLEN, *COME ON HOME! ECOLOGICAL AGRICULTURE AND SIXTEEN WONDERFUL FARMS THAT POINT THE WAY*

> If we don't get sustainability right in agriculture first, it won't happen anywhere. It won't happen in the materials sector nor the industrial sector, in general. Agriculture is fundamentally ecological in nature. Agriculture has the science of ecology standing behind it, a science devoted to discovering how ecosystems work. The material and industrial sectors do not.
>
> —WES JACKSON

The industrialized food system has been developed with the complicity and support of land-grant universities, but now even they are being forced to reinvent themselves. Some are experimenting with the discipline of agroecology, which promises to combine science-based knowledge with experience-based information, well-executed social dynamics, and political support. Fred Kirschenmann says, "Proponents of agroecology argue that these alternatives may not only produce as much or more food from the same acreage, but also could do so while enhancing rather than destroying biodiversity and the myriad of environmental and agricultural services biodiversity provides. These new production systems, however, would require a rather significant redesign of our food system."

A good example of an agroecological approach is the Land Institute in Salina, Kansas, where Wes Jackson leads research in the development of perennial crops (especially grains) that could replace many current crops. The application of ecological science to the study, design, and management of sustainable agriculture, agroecology offers a model of agricultural development to meet this challenge. Recent research demonstrates that by scaling up the practice of agroecology, we can sustainably improve the livelihoods of the most vulnerable and thus contribute to feeding a hungry planet.

4. Rebuilding and Cultivating Soil

Problem: In most areas, significant amounts of soil have been lost, and soil fertility has been seriously depleted.

Therefore: We seek to rebuild and cultivate soil wherever possible, developing this as part of our local culture.

℘

Soil regeneration, which is going to be necessary almost everywhere, takes intensive, well-planned practices and knowledge of how soil life works. In animal production, it means looking at the kinds of grazing that maximizes root growth with a biodiverse plant mixture in grasslands or pastures (exemplified by Allan Savory's Holistic Management, which uses rotational grazing to restore pastureland). In farming, it means utilizing cover crops (green manures) and composts to build organic matter at a fast rate without losing productivity, and keeping soil planted (with food crops or cover crops) as much as possible.

While individual producers may be committed to rebuilding and cultivating soil on their own lands, this will be insufficient for an emerging foodshed. The entire community needs to learn about soil and nutrition and their relationship, and there is a great need for community composting efforts. But rarely is soil made the centerpiece of a food-localization strategy.

Some entrepreneurs are discovering that soil regeneration provides an important opportunity. For instance, in Denver, a company called Waste Farmers is developing soil supplements for gardeners. Their flagship products are sold under their Maxfield's brand: soil conditioner, planting mix, and potting soil. They have also launched a product for commercial marijuana growers named "Batch 64."

Just as modern, chemical-based industrialized agriculture was taking hold in the 1940s, Sir Albert Howard's groundbreaking book, *An Agricultural Testament,* took a more systemic view toward soil.

> If we regard erosion as the natural consequence of improper methods of agriculture, and the catchment area of the river as the natural unit for the application of soil conservation methods, the various remedies available fall into their proper place. The upper reaches of each river system must be afforested; cover crops

including grass and leys must be used to protect the arable surface whenever possible; the humus content of the soil must be increased and the crumb structure restored so that each field can drink its own rainfall; over-stocking and over-grazing must be prevented; simple mechanical methods for conserving the soil and regulating run-off, like terracing, contour cultivation and contour drains must be utilized. There is, of course, no single anti-erosion device which can be universally adopted. The problem must, in the nature of things, be a local one. Nevertheless, certain guiding principles exist which apply everywhere. First and foremost is the restoration and maintenance of soil fertility, so that each acre of the catchment area can do its duty by absorbing its share of the rainfall.[145]

Those involved in food localization would do well to follow Howard's guidance.

Holistic Range Management

> Humans are a desert-making species.
>
> —Elisabet Sahtouris

Every civilization that's collapsed in the past, as you know, has collapsed because of an agricultural disaster. And soil and food, in many ways, [are] ground zero of any sustainable economic system. And the prognosis on our food system is not good. The decline in soils, the increase in deserts, the increase in desertification [are] not that well known in the mainstream, but it's very frightening. And it has all kinds of other consequences, like soil goes from being the second largest carbon sink in the world, after the oceans, to [being] a source of carbon. As soils degrade, carbon is released, and on a scale that matters to the global climate change challenge.... I think healing the land is a central principle of this new economic system. And whether that's done in organic farms near cities, or on massive grasslands across Australia, that has to be a part of this new paradigm. We need to think differently about the way we treat and manage the land.

—JOHN FULLERTON, CAPITAL INSTITUTE, "THE GRASSLANDS STORY"

Ultimately, the only wealth that can sustain any community, economy or nation is derived from the photosynthetic process—green plants growing on regenerating soil.

—ALLAN SAVORY

If you could wave a magic wand and stop all fossil fuel emissions worldwide tomorrow, what effect would it have on climate change? None. It's baked in.

—TOM NEWMARK, *THE CARBON UNDERGROUND*

Developed by Allan Savory, holistic range management uses proper management of livestock as the key to reversing desertification, conserving water, and sequestering carbon on grasslands. This is a decision-making and planning process that generates the insights and management tools needed to understand and align with nature, resulting in grounded decisions that balance key social, environmental, and financial considerations. The underlying emphasis is not just regenerative agriculture, but with the way we make decisions.

The Savory Institute is dedicated to facilitating the large-scale restoration of the grasslands of the world—one-third of the earth's surface. Holistic management is a key strategy in a global plan to have "five billion hectares of hope" by 2025—that is, rangelands under holistic management.

This approach may be the most radical, effective, and revolutionary approach to regenerative agriculture available today. As Tre' Cates, COO and CFO of Savory Institute says, "We believe this needs to be a revolution—in the soils, in the souls, in society."

5. Training and Supporting New Producers

The new farming future means that we will need to invest in a new kind of training at all levels of our education system.

We should begin now to involve all elementary school children in school gardens, agriculture in the classroom programs, and other learning experiences that engage them in the experience of growing food and the excitement of learning about the web of relationships and energy exchanges that can provide their food for them. Such education would "leave no child inside." We also need to introduce more college courses in agroecology and provide internship opportunities for experience-based learning in ecosystems management on real farms.

—Fred Kirschenmann, *Cultivating an Ecological Conscience*

Problem: An extreme shortage of farmers.

Therefore: We encourage and inspire training, mentoring, capitalization, and support networks to recruit and cultivate new farmers. We also promote farming as a viable career choice.

∾

In the last several years, Richard Heinberg, senior fellow at the Post Carbon Institute, and Sharon Astyk (author of *A Nation of Farmers: Defeating the Food Crisis on American Soil*) have rather dramatically proclaimed that, because of the looming energy crisis, we need at least fifty to one hundred million new farmers in this country (for comparison, currently about 1 percent of the population is involved in farming). They're talking about something unprecedented, a massive shift to small-plot, bio-intensive, labor-intensive, local farming. They're talking about this nation learning to feed itself again.

But the barriers to entry for new farmers are significant. It's not just that farmland is expensive. Successful farming, even at a small scale, requires an extraordinary combination of skills and knowledge. New farmers need training and experience, mentoring, and capital. A number of programs have been launched to meet this need. For instance, Adrian Card and his team at Colorado State University Extension for Boulder County developed a Building Farmers Program to educate producers on building capacity and opportunities through business development and management training, with a focus on mentoring from successful farmers. The program was successful, and a seven-state collaborative program emerged, now called Building Farmers in the West, available to new and beginning specialty producers from Colorado, Idaho, Oregon, New Mexico, Nevada, Utah, and Washington.[146] Even the venerable Future Farmers of America is beginning to encourage young people to consider local food production.

Finally, as conventional farmers apprehend the financial upside of production for local consumption, they too will need training, mentoring, capital, and support. Making this transition is not easy, but it may turn out that these commodity-crop farmers and their progeny represent the largest potential source of new producers within a local foodshed. They already have land, certainly love the land, and they have many years of farming experience, albeit of a variety that is increasingly becoming outmoded. These traditional producers will need a great deal of community support and encouragement in making the local food shift.

6. Recruiting and Training the Labor Pool

Problem: A shortage of farm workers makes expansion of production difficult.

Therefore: We encourage and support training and employment opportunities on farms and ranches.

❧

Local agriculture is extremely labor intensive. As farmers attempt to expand, they often run into a shortage of skilled farm workers. Immigration laws have significantly disrupted the supply of seasonal laborers from Mexico, and young Americans are often unwilling to work at the low wages that farmers are accustomed to paying.

Efforts to integrate returning military veterans, prison parolees, and recovering drug addicts or alcoholics are promising, but training programs for these kinds of people are still in early stages of development. Training programs for greenhouse production are currently being

launched by the nonprofit Veterans to Farmers (founded by social entrepreneur Buck Adams, himself an ex-marine).

Worldwide Opportunities on Organic Farms (WWOOF) provides
many people with invaluable on-farm experience in fifty states and
internationally. Visitors exchange labor for room and board, plus education. Many CSA farms will offer whole or partial shares in exchange
for labor. Volunteering, work-for-food programs, and internships can
all help.

7. Encouraging Diversity of Food Production Approaches

Problem: Dependence on single approaches to food production (i.e.,
soil-based organic produce farming) has some of the same weaknesses
as monocropping—such as vulnerability to pests, disease, crop failure,
and catastrophic weather events—which can leave a regional food supply at risk.

Therefore: We encourage and inspire diversified food production methodologies and cropping patterns. This begins with educating ourselves.

❧

No single approach to food production will be adequate to the challenge of greatly increasing the local food supply, and rigid insistence
on a particular approach will weaken the resilience of a regional foodshed. It's important to implement a diversity of approaches. Organic
may be the preferred method for local food production, but the costs
and administrative complexities of USDA certification are forcing many
small farmers to forego the process, opting instead to position their
farming as "beyond organic" (adhering to practices more rigorous than
the USDA requires) or to adopt standards agreed upon by local producers. On the other hand, some farmers are devoted to biodynamics,
a spiritual-ethical-ecological approach rooted in the work of Rudolf
Steiner, founder of the Waldorf Schools.

In areas of climate instability or drought, controlled-environment
agriculture will become increasingly important—aquaculture, aquaponics, hydroponics, aeroponics, hi-tech greenhouses, hoop houses, and

high tunnels. The greater the diversity of agricultural production methods, the more resilient a foodshed will be.

8. Incentivizing Conversion of Commodity-Crop or Export Production to Production for Local Consumption

Problem: Far too much agricultural land is tied up in conventional commodity-crop production for export.

Therefore: We seek ways to offer financial and social incentives for conventional producers to begin the conversion process.

❧

Conventional farmers transitioning to organic production face a daunting task. They have to learn to do just about everything differently. The soil on their farm has become sterile and essentially incapable of supporting life, and they will have to spend years rebuilding the soil biologically, increasing the natural biota that support life. There won't be much food production going on during the conversion process—and none of it will be organic. To make this conversion, they will need incentives and support. They will also need to see convincing evidence that conversion makes financial sense and that there will be a market for the food they intend to produce.

This may require the assistance of local, state, and federal government. But more importantly, it will require farmers collaborating with the emerging local food industry to find the ways to support such a transition.

It's important that local food communities actively support such transitional farmers. Many conventional producers have become so focused on export production that they have little connection to their local community.

9. Cultivating Value-Added Producers

Problem: There is a great need and demand for processed or value-added food products to provide diversity and resilience in the local food system.

Therefore: We seek ways to reduce barriers to entry and increase resilience and profitability.

༄

Local food is not just about the crops grown in field or greenhouse. It includes a variety of processed products that add value for the customer and results in a higher return to the producer: processing meat into sausages, turning milk into cheese, milling grain into flour, preserving and canning vegetables and fruits, fermenting raw foods, and using locally grown ingredients in pastas, sauces, and soups for the retail market. These kinds of foods provide numerous opportunities for local food businesses and add to the diversity and value of the local food supply chain.

Value-added producers face particular challenges, however, including finding access to commercial kitchen space,[147] sourcing ingredients locally, securing startup capital, and getting their products in appropriate retail locations.

MM Local in Denver is the first cannery in Colorado since the disappearance of the canning trade some forty years ago. They source local vegetables and can them in attractively labeled clear glass jars. They are pursuing direct sales, as well as wholesale, and offer a CSA-style Harvest Share in the fall. Boulder-based Ozuké is another significant value-added producer, buying local produce to create fermented foods such as kimchi and sauerkraut. Both companies seek to market nationally, but MM Local plans to source locally wherever they have a canning operation (they have recently opened in the Pacific northwest).

10. Channeling Local Capital

Problem: Little affordable capital is accessible to local food producers through traditional channels, making expansion difficult.

Therefore: We encourage and support the development of pathways and structures to facilitate moving local money into the local food system. We move a portion of our personal capital from Wall Street into our local food economy.

∾

Localizing the food supply in a particular foodshed requires many things, but it most especially requires a considerable amount of money. Farmers need to expand operations, infrastructure needs to be built, new businesses need to be financed, and eaters need to be educated. Farmers and small food-related businesses generally have a tough enough time getting credit, and the situation has become especially difficult since the 2008 financial crisis. Even those with excellent track records for borrowing and repaying are having difficulty today obtaining credit from mainstream banks or credit unions. Equity capital for small business today is virtually nonexistent. Access to capital is one of the biggest barriers to achieving 25 percent food localization.

We know it is possible to capitalize 25 percent food localization in Colorado with local money. As discussed earlier, economist Michael Shuman calculated that it would require $1.8 billion, which represents less than one half of 1 percent of the money that local citizens hold in nonlocal stocks, bonds, and various investment and retirement funds—"fast money," in Woody Tasch's terms. And that doesn't even include the additional cash that people have in bank accounts. The challenge is to create the pathways for that capital to flow into the emerging local food economy.

- *Slow Money investment clubs:* Patterned after No Small Potatoes in Maine, these are generally groups of citizens who each place an equal amount of money into a pool, form a limited liability company, and decide how their pooled funds will be invested in local food and farming enterprises, guided by Slow Money principles. There are about a dozen such groups operating in the United States, four of them in Colorado. (The subject of slow money will be addressed more completely below, in chapter thirty-three.)

- *Crowdsourcing platforms:* It's now possible for local food and farming entrepreneurs to raise capital online through crowdsourcing, especially via Kickstarter-type contributions, but it's not easy to apply this to a local scale. Newly released SEC guidelines will make it possible for certified platforms to offer crowdfunded equity investments to both accredited[148] and unaccredited investors.

- *Self-directed IRAs:* Individuals can now convert their IRA funds to be self-managed, so they can invest their money directly as desired.

Local investing is a rapidly evolving industry, and myriad options are emerging. The learning curve is fairly steep, financial risks are relatively high, and we encourage thorough research.

11. Supporting Restaurant and Retail Sales of Local Food

Problem: Locally sourced foods are rarely available at restaurants and retail stores.

Therefore: We encourage retailers and restaurateurs to offer more locally sourced foods to their customers, and we reward those who do with our patronage.

∞

From a food system perspective, this is a *pull-through strategy,* that is, one that encourages retailers and restaurateurs to respond to increasing eater demand for local food. Grocers and restaurants can gain a competitive market differentiation by sourcing locally and emphasizing their connection to their farmers and ranchers and value-added producers.

Furthermore, grocers and restaurants are in a position to influence eaters more than almost anyone else (the 10% Local Food Shift Pledge is one tool that can be useful in this regard). In Boulder, local independent grocers are taking the lead in this arena, while natural foods grocers emphasize local sourcing far less, preferring to offer lower price points on organic food. Whole Foods is a prominent market leader, even though they are often accused of localwashing, while supporting few local producers.[149] Whole Foods says that they have a hard time finding local producers who can deliver sufficient quantities of products they need; on the other hand, producers often complain that Whole Foods demands lower prices than they can afford to accept. Traditional supermarkets are beginning to respond as well.

The growth of online grocery delivery services provides a promising outlet for local producers. Door to Door Organics has pledged to purchase 20 percent local food in Colorado (increasing from their previous pledge of 10 percent).

12. Emphasizing Controlled-Environment Agriculture

Problem: Restraints on access to land and water, plus increasingly unstable climate, limit soil-based production in some areas.

Therefore: We encourage the exploration and utilization of a variety of forms of controlled-environment agriculture, which require far less land and water.

❧

We already know that small farms are quite a bit more efficient in raising food than conventional or commodity-crop agriculture. Standard commodity-crop commercial agriculture yields, on average, somewhere in the range of $1,000 worth of product per acre per year. That's a ballpark number, but it's a pretty good rule of thumb. Meanwhile, small farms—from a few acres to a few hundred acres, using bio-intensive methods, primarily organic (though not necessarily certified)—are producing (conservatively) about $10,000 worth of produce per acre per year. That's a whole order of magnitude above what's usual with commodity-crop agriculture.

So already we know that this kind of local food production is a much more efficient way of growing food than conventional agriculture. But we also know that this kind of production is especially vulnerable to land prices, labor shortages, and various climate and other disasters. Besides, there's just not enough production going on at this scale, such that now demand for local food is far greater than supply. So if our global food supply is suddenly interrupted—which it inevitably will be—we will face food shortages right here in our home territory, because there is simply not enough supply.

Land and water shortages, along with climate instability, are challenges to local food production. Home gardening and community gardening and urban agriculture can help, but how could we greatly increase local food production in just a few years, in the event of a disruption to the global food supply? One solution is *controlled-environment agriculture* (CEA)—hoop houses, low tunnels, high tunnels, greenhouses, hydroponics, aquaponics, and aeroponics. For more on CEA, see chapter thirty-two.

Demand and Consumption Are Not Givens

While it's true that demand for local food is currently outstripping supply, there are many factors that could reduce demand and cause a reversion to conventional food, such as price increases. And other factors can also be involved. After the September 2013 flood, the Boulder County Farmers Markets saw a dramatic reduction in sales—just when farmers greatly needed the income—because of customer fears of crop contamination. In this case, the problem was really people not knowing their farmers and therefore not being able to trust their food, which reveals a weakness in the emergent local food system.

A number of potential future scenarios are worth considering.

- The drought in the Central Valley in California causes food prices to significantly increase and even results in actual shortages of some organic food items. (We often hear that the Central Valley is the source of 50 percent of the fruits, nuts, and vegetables Americans consume, but it is also likely the source of as much as 90 percent of organic ingredients.)

- Local climate disasters, such as the 2013 flood in northern Colorado, dramatically reduce local food production, so that commercial buyers committed to local sourcing are forced to substitute nonlocal or conventional food items.

- The global food crisis escalates, causing food prices to rise sharply. Since Americans allegedly spend something like a mere 6 percent of their discretionary income on food, this causes eaters to reduce the amount they spend on local food.

These scenarios reveal a delicate tension between demand and supply.

STAGE FOUR: A LOCAL FOOD REVOLUTION

We don't really know what patterns might naturally emerge in stage four of the emergence of a foodshed, because we're all experiencing this process for the first time. We are in uncharted territory here, and there is little precedent anywhere to draw from. This is especially true at the Turn, where nearly everything is chaotic and unpredictable.

My sense is that there will be a compelling call for a local food revolution during this stage, but this could come from unexpected sources. Thomas Paine was not regarded as a political leader or even an activist when he published *Common Sense*. Who he was in society was not significant. His message had its own power. In fact, at first there was considerable debate about who the author might be. In the end, authorship probably did not matter much. Paine might as well have remained anonymous.

The primary precondition for the call to revolution was a widespread dissatisfaction and unease among the people, though it did not have a coherent voice. We certainly can see that today in how we relate to our current industrial food system. We're not happy, but our dissatisfaction lies mostly below the surface of our awareness. *Common Sense* stated the obvious, though it was rarely spoken of. Once stated, the reality was undeniable. Once heard, neutrality was not an option. In July 1776, what finally emerged in the colonies was a consensus agreement not only to declare independence from the Crown but also to form a new sovereign nation.

From this I gather that it will be necessary for a critical mass of people within an emerging foodshed to declare their independence from the industrial food system and to unite around the project of building a regional foodshed. We can only guess what this critical mass might be.

It will be a dangerous enterprise, for there will be a high risk of reverting to the familiar modes of trying to *make* it happen. To successfully negotiate the Turn will require the emergence of foodshed catalysts who understand that the foodshed must arise organically and who will guard against the use of influence, manipulation, or violence. Who among us really knows how to serve in this way?

Here we can perhaps utilize the power of story. This means identifying critical emerging centers of aliveness and giving them visibility. The revolution is already underway, but is almost entirely invisible. Once seen, it will gain momentum.

There is also a great need to convene and connect centers of aliveness. This can be done in the form of gatherings and events. The key here is foodshed catalysts correctly understanding the underlying purpose of such events.

And I cannot ignore the need for catalytic publishing in this environment—in whatever forms are most appropriate or available, including consulting and coaching. This is about transmission and ignition.

As it becomes clear that a local food revolution is emerging in our midst, a critical question will arise: how will this revolution be funded? The need for capital will become urgent, and it will become clear that the local food revolution will be funded primarily by individuals who understand that this simply must happen—at any cost.

STAGE FIVE:
BUILDING SUPPLY-CHAIN INFRASTRUCTURE

> An ideal regional food system describes a system in which as much food as possible to meet the population's food needs is produced, processed, distributed, and purchased at multiple levels and scales within the region, resulting in maximum resilience, minimum importation, and significant economic and social return to all stakeholders in the region. This is known as "self-reliance" as opposed to "self-sufficiency" wherein everything consumed is supplied from within the target area.
>
> —Northeast Sustainable Agriculture Working Group

Regional food systems strive to increase local sales and consumption of food that is produced, processed and distributed within the same region or foodshed. Although the promise of modern regional food systems has yet to be fully tested or proved, both history and current research point to the potential for regional food systems to deliver significant value for local communities and for society as a whole.

—JIM COCHRAN AND LARRY YEE, *FOOD COMMONS 2.0*

Introduction

Across the country, communities are beginning to understand the profound economic, environmental, and social benefits of increasing the production and consumption of fresh, locally grown food.

In order to grow in a highly competitive food marketplace, where demand for local food far exceeds supply, the emerging local food industry requires an integrated regional infrastructure of aggregation, processing, distribution, and other services that can efficiently connect small and midsize local producers with the larger commercial buyers—retailers, restaurants, schools, and institutions—who serve major consumer markets. This is the "missing middle" of the foodshed supply chain.

Building such an infrastructure in a highly integrated and collaborative manner can expand and preserve regional agriculture on a larger scale, allow for sustainable farming practices to proliferate, and give a greater number of eaters access to local food. Processing and storage infrastructure will allow farmers to meet the standards required by wholesale buyers for food safety, quality, and consistency. Aggregation and distribution services will give producers access to markets some distance from their farms.

The intention is to modify the best efficiencies and business models of larger, global supply chains to create a shorter, small-scale version. A regionalized system can also address the failures of the larger supply chains, such as poor wages and mistreatment of workers, low prices for farmers, and high barriers to entry for small and midsize farmers. Access to larger retail and institutional markets, where general demand for local food is rapidly growing, is especially important for midsize farms, which can provide a larger volume of food to wholesale outlets and currently have more difficulty selling that volume through direct-to-consumer sales like farmers markets and CSAs.

The resulting regional supply chain will provide a more direct connection between producers and buyers than is currently possible in a large-scale supply chain, allowing producers to retain a higher portion of the sale price of their produce. Properly designed and managed, this system can give farmers a fair price and create more communication through the chain between producers and buyers. This can lead to better relationships and trust between producers and the businesses buying their products, as well as greater understanding of the needs on both ends.

This infrastructure can also provide significant opportunities for economic development and job creation, including the potential to repurpose defunct or abandoned manufacturing and processing sites, which will, in turn, support businesses that produce related equipment and inputs.

❧

What distinguishes the work in stage five is that the advent of the local food revolution in a particular region has galvanized the community around the common goal, and there is an understanding of the crucial need for an integrated, collaborative, values-based system to connect food producers and entrepreneurs with their larger commercial markets. The community rallies together to construct this missing local food infrastructure.

Many of the components of the supply-chain infrastructure may have been initiated much earlier, especially during stage three, but those early efforts generally lacked cohesion, cooperation, and unity. What happens during stage five is markedly different. And this infrastructure network will make possible the growth and expansion of the local food supply chain, bringing more local food to local eaters.

Stage Five Patterns

1. Identifying opportunities and barriers
2. Introducing slow money and restorative economics
3. Supporting the drivers and social entrepreneurs

4. Channeling local capital

5. Constructing local investment vehicles and platforms

6. Organizing technical assistance

7. Recruiting and training management

8. Organizing collaboratively

9. Building a new local food industry and economy

10. Building a foodshed alliance

11. Encouraging innovation

12. Building a local brand

13. Increasing institutional procurement

14. Engaging local government

15. Developing institutional support

16. Guiding and influencing needed policy changes

17. Cultivating a local food culture

1. Identifying Opportunities and Barriers

Problem: There remains considerable ignorance and confusion about the current state of our region's food supply and its potential for food localization.

Therefore: From existing sources and original research, along with observation and interaction, we gather enough data to build realistic and useful perspective. Much of our emerging understanding will take the form of stories.

ॐ

At each stage of the process, we take the time to identify opportunities and barriers to deepen our understanding and perspective. This is a discipline we constantly cultivate.

At stage five, the issues we consider include identification and evaluation of

- potential, existing, and developing assets (growers and producers, aggregators, processors, distributors, and other related ventures);

- potential strategic partnerships; and
- strategies for development of the infrastructure network.

We develop access to critical knowledge, insight, and perspective through feasibility studies and market research, exploration of best practices and new technologies, and economic-development approaches.

2. Introducing Slow Money and Restorative Economics

> Today, ours is an economy of separation: standard commodities that bear no relationship to the individual user, buildings that bear no relation to the land they occupy, retail outlets that bear no connection to local production, and products made in obliviousness to their effects on nature and people. None of these can possibly be beautiful, alive, or whole... Right investment is to array money in sacred vestments: to use it to create, protect, and sustain the things that are becoming sacred to us today.
>
> —CHARLES EISENSTEIN, SACRED ECONOMICS

Problem: Our local economy is held hostage by a global commerce of extraction and consumption that erodes community capacity for resilience and self-reliance and depletes local resources. This system is highly resistive to food-localization efforts. For food and farming enterprises, access to capital is one of the primary barriers to development.

Therefore: We seek to rebuild our local economy by making the transition to a form of commerce that supports preservation, restoration, and regeneration. We seek to understand and apply core slow money principles[150] of carrying capacity, cultural and biological diversity, sense of place, care of the commons, healing the biosphere, building soil, and nonviolence. This means, especially, investing a significant portion of our money in local farming and in the enterprises that are needed to support a healthy local food and farming system.

☙

This transition to a localized economy, inspired most visibly by the work of Woody Tasch, represents the beginnings of restorative economics.

"Advocacy is one thing, investing another," Tasch proclaims. "We are here because we recognize that increasing the flow of capital to small food enterprises, to local food systems, to the production, processing, distribution and marketing of local, fresh, organic food is one of the most fundamental things we can do to begin fixing our economy, our country, our culture, from the ground up."

In my experience, the slow money approach is simply essential in the emergence of a regional foodshed. Localizing our economy and localizing our food supply are interdependent processes. Local food and farming enterprises need capital, certainly, but it must be patient, "nurture capital"—capital that seeks to maximize impact, has a high tolerance of risk and reduced expectations of returns, and has a longer time horizon than "fast money."

Nurture capital is required to strengthen local food systems and to scale up food production. Funding needs to be provided to small and midsize farms for operations, purchases, and expansion. In addition, funding is needed for the infrastructure to connect food producers and consumers.

It could be appropriate to begin introducing slow money at stage three, to help increase production. But the investments at that stage are very high risk, because they are not yet connected to a larger system of support.

3. Supporting the Drivers and Social Entrepreneurs

The most powerful force in the world is a pattern-changing big idea—if it is in the hands of a social entrepreneur of equivalent ambition. Each such major pattern shift triggers cascades of follow-on innovations, adaptations, and local applications. The railroad and today's digital revolutions are prime business examples. The job of the pattern-change social entrepreneur is to recognize whenever a part of society is stuck in an inefficient or harmful pattern, to conceive a better and safe alternative, to make that vision realistic and then a refined reality, and then to persuade his or her entire society to make the leap to this new way.

—WILLIAM DRAYTON, FOUNDER OF ASHOKA

Problem: Emerging centers of aliveness are often virtually invisible and unsupported, limited in their impact.

Therefore: We encourage, inspire, and support social entrepreneurs who feel called to help build the local food system. They can be found at the heart of emerging centers of aliveness.

∾

The local food revolution is being led on two fronts: first, by a sprawling and largely spontaneous grassroots movement that includes informed eaters and passionate activists, who have driven demand to unprecedented levels (remarkably, without the benefit of classic marketing techniques), and second, by an emerging local food industry that is just beginning to find its feet and is hungry for capital to fund both expansion and new ventures. Spearheading both fronts are social entrepreneurs—community leaders, organizers, and business owners who are committed to disruptive systemic change in the way our society feeds itself.

In our area, we have noticed that the real drivers of change are the social entrepreneurs who recognize needs and opportunities—farmers who want to expand their operations, chefs who want to source locally, community grocers who want to vertically integrate, the myriad value-added food processors who have been springing up in recent years, and the experienced business people who are drawn to establishing significant enterprises in food aggregation, processing, and distribution. Some of these entrepreneurs have the vision of taking their operation to a national scale. It doesn't seem to matter if their operation is for-profit or nonprofit, their values are essentially the same.

Social entrepreneurs, especially millennials, have a way of just getting things done, and we have learned a lot from them. They are somehow attuned to what is needed and wanted, what is possible, and what it will take to get it built and made successful. And they don't have much patience with public process or government involvement. They're used to moving quickly and being flexible.

4. Channeling Local Capital

> People are hungry for food that's produced by farmers, ranchers and artisans they know and trust. They want to spend a larger share of their food dollars in their own communities.
>
> —ERIKA BLOCK, FOUNDER OF LOCAL ORBIT

> We can engage in conscious, purposeful money destruction in place of the unconscious destruction of money that happens in a collapsing economy. If you still have money to invest, invest it in enterprises that explicitly seek to build community, protect nature, and preserve the cultural commonwealth. Expect a zero or negative financial return on your investment—that is a good sign that you are not unintentionally converting even more of the world to money.
>
> —CHARLES EISENSTEIN, *SACRED ECONOMICS*

Problem: The emergence of the local food system infrastructure requires considerable capital. Dependency on institutional sources of capital skews how investments and returns are made—consistently away from the local economy. While individuals within the region hold great wealth in nonlocal stocks, bonds, and various investment funds, they often possess neither the motivation nor the mechanisms to move a meaningful portion of their money into the local economy.

Therefore: Develop a diversity of pathways through which local capital can flow directly to local food and farming entrepreneurs. Encourage equity participation and philanthropy over lending.

∽

A key part of the work of this stage will be to help channel or direct local capital where it can make a significant difference in the localization effort. This is a huge challenge, but it's also an opportunity to engage members of our communities in the local food revolution. Look for ways to provide local investors with access to opportunities for engagement and impact in food localization and the local food industry. And here it is important to remember that we're *all* investors. Organizing a Slow Money investment club is a great way to start. There are numerous other pathways beginning to open up, such as equity crowdfunding, while others will need to be pried open, like local credit unions, which will need a lot of effort.

5. Constructing Local Investment Vehicles and Platforms

With investment crowdfunding you can raise capital from your own community, however you may define it—your neighbors, customers, affinity groups, or even your professional network. And their investment decisions may be based on much more than just profit or a quick exit. This opens the door for true impact investment for everyone.

—Brian Beckon, *Cutting Edge Capital*

Problem: There is a dearth of vehicles to enable individuals to directly invest in local food and farming enterprises, and those that do exist are generally accessible only to accredited investors or are not local.

Therefore: We seek to develop a diversity of local investment vehicles and platforms that prioritize funneling capital to food and farming enterprises.

❧

Financial investments at this stage should be prioritized around building the critical infrastructure that will allow producers to expand and will allow commercial buyers to efficiently source increasing amounts of local foods. The focus is to make affordable capital available to businesses all along the supply chain, from growers and value-added producers to commercial buyers and infrastructure enterprises.

Investment Vehicles

It should be understood that investment vehicles are highly regulated by federal and state securities laws, and expert legal counsel should be engaged in considering any of these options.

On the smallest level, Slow Money investment clubs are an easy way to begin. In Boulder, Local Food Investments LLC was modeled after No Small Potatoes in Maine, a simple LLC structure that allows up to twenty people to pool their money—$5,000 each—to begin making investments. The caveat—to avoid SEC scrutiny—is that everyone in the group must be actively involved in each investment decision. This is essentially a low-interest loan fund. Other forms of investment clubs are possible, including a nonprofit approach, as 2Forks Investments in Western Colorado has adopted, providing zero-interest loans.

At a larger level, say $10 to $50 million, some are considering the *business development company* (BDC)—a model that has been utilized in other economic-development work, but not yet for local food economies. This is a legal structure that allows up to five hundred accredited and unaccredited investors to pool their funds to invest in local food enterprises.

At the high end of the scale, the $50 to $100 million level, we've begun exploring what Michael Shuman calls a *Regional Food Authority*,[151] an entity that can issue bonds, providing loans and mobilizing in-kind support for those local enterprises with the greatest strategic potential to help the community realize its food-localization goals. With local government support, the food authority could issue municipal "food bonds" with interest payments to bondholders exempt from federal taxation. Anyone, including unaccredited investors, could buy shares. This could greatly stimulate lending to food and farming businesses. The idea, as Shuman says, is to deploy "the full faith and credit of a community" to stimulate economic activities that serve the entire community. The food authority can prioritize assistance for

- meta-businesses that support a number of local businesses in the region;
- infrastructure businesses, including incubators, food hubs, and shared-use facilities;

- clusters of businesses involving one or more food businesses, such as industrial ecology operations, where the waste of one business serves as the input to another;
- clusters of businesses from multiple counties that span the supply chain; and
- any other local food business that, if it succeeds, can strengthen the value chains and bottom lines of many food businesses in the region.

Finally, an *intrastate direct public offering* is a mechanism for a food-related enterprise (either for profit or nonprofit) to offer securities to both accredited and unaccredited investors within a state—essentially a form of crowdfunding. There is no cap to the amount of capital that can be raised this way, and it does not require federal registration.

Suggested Guidelines for Investment

We should look for a number of factors when deciding whether a business or enterprise ought to receive investment funds.

- *Local/regional:* The enterprise is based in the region or has operations that can significantly impact the regional food supply chain.
- *Local sourcing:* The enterprise produces or sources food ingredients grown in the region.
- *Organic or transitional:* Food products are organic (not necessarily certified) or from a farm transitioning to organic production.
- *Sustainable practices:* The enterprise utilizes and supports practices that contribute to sustainable local food production in the region.
- *Localization:* The enterprise is committed to contributing to localization of the food supply chain.
- *Financial viability:* Financial projections are reasonable and well supported.
- *Fundability:* The enterprise is not eligible for (or would not benefit from) affordable financing from more traditional sources.

- *Diversity and fertility:* The enterprise is committed to promoting diversity and building fertility, both of the soil and the local economy.
- *Preservation and restoration:* The enterprise actively participates in accelerating the transition from an economy based on extraction and consumption to an economy based on preservation and restoration.

Investment activities need to be guided by individuals with significant expertise in agriculture, organic foods, business development, and capital investments, who are all dedicated to the mission of localizing the food supply chain.

6. Organizing Technical Assistance

Problem: Almost no one is experienced in building local food systems or the enterprises that will emerge within them. In the beginning, as the local food economy is being built, its foundation will be weak and will lack resilience—as will many of its early enterprises.

Therefore: We seek to connect seasoned experts with emerging food and farming entrepreneurs, and we try to keep the costs of such expertise from being prohibitive. We encourage volunteerism.

ॐ

Through consulting, workshops, seminars, conferences, and webinars, we provide access to best agricultural and business practices (including conversion to organic production), along with resources and skill development in finance, marketing, management, technologies, certifications, and food safety.

Moving money into the local food economy requires many hands—many levels of experience and expertise—to ensure that it all works reasonably well: due diligence for investors, consulting, financing, business planning, strategic development, business partnership development, management expertise, and mentorship.

Such involvement reduces investment risk, increases business success, and creates an integrated structure for entrepreneurs and investors. This is all part of a coordinated approach to replicate and scale successful business models and best industry practices throughout the emerging foodshed.

7. Recruiting and Training Management

Problem: Many who initiate or inherit food and farming enterprises have limited management experience. As the enterprise grows and the local food system becomes more complex, a lack of management expertise can be a significant limiting factor.

Therefore: We develop programs to train entrepreneurs in management skills, and we incentivize the migration of managers from other industries to local enterprises.

∿

Growing businesses—whether they be farms, processing facilities, or food hubs—requires management skills that are not common in the local food system. But those skills can be acquired or hired. And solid business and financial management practices will be essential in making the much-needed investments in local food and farming enterprises successful. This is a significant learning curve, one that is not at all unusual in a newly emerging industry.

8. Organizing Collaboratively

Problem: Like most entrepreneurs, food and farming venturers greatly value independence and are accustomed to making their own way. This can hamper the emergence of a healthy local food economy.

Therefore: We seek to cultivate a culture in which collaboration and cooperation are among the highest values.

∿

Research demonstrates that networks of social entrepreneurs working together can accelerate and increase impact. We engage communities of entrepreneurs and develop patterns of effective collaborations that accelerate the emerging local food industry. Entrepreneurs working together in "open, competitive-yet-collaborative relationships" (value chains) can evolve a network of incalculable power. We support the development of a national trade association for the local food industry, comprised of regional foodshed chapters.

One of the challenges among farmers and other food entrepreneurs is the misconception that they are competing with each other, which is both inaccurate (since demand outpaces supply) and undermines the whole foodshed. The real competition is the industrial food system, which seeks 100 percent domination. The only way we can begin to effectively compete with this, and the only way we can achieve any significant degree of food localization in our foodshed, is if we work together. Yes, this is often seen as a radical and even dangerous idea in some circles. But none of our local producers or buyers is big enough to make it on his or her own. The only way we'll get there is together.

We support the emergence of a trade association for the local food industry, composed of all the key producers, buyers, and everyone in between.

9. Building a New Local Food Industry and Economy

> The diner and the shopper willing to pay prices considered fair to the farmer justifiably expect to connect dollar value with appropriate farm practices. Such consumers are all the more intrigued when they feel the entire supply chain that got the food to their plate or their grocery basket is well grounded in its ethics and its commitment to the local and regional community.
>
> —Philip Ackerman-Leist, Rebuilding the Foodshed

People are trying to find ways to shorten the distance between producers and consumers, to make the connections between the two more direct, and to make this local economic activity a benefit to the local community. They are trying to learn to use the consumer economies of local towns and cities to preserve the livelihoods of local farm families and farm communities. They want to use the local economy to give consumers an influence over the kind and quality of their food, and to preserve land and enhance the local landscapes. They want to give everybody in the local community a direct, long-term interest in the prosperity, health, and beauty of their homeland... Without prosperous local economies, the people have no power and the land no voice.

—Wendell Berry, "The Idea of a Local Economy"

A sustainable, democratized food system is decentralized and benefits from a network of farms, highly local distribution channels and motivated consumers.

—Douglas Gayeton, *Local: The New Face of Food and Farming in America*

Problem: Local food is portrayed by the Unholy Alliance as a tiny niche market or, at best, an insignificant subset of the total food industry. At the same time, because most agriculture is based on exports, local food is usually considered economically insignificant.

Therefore: We seek to acknowledge and support local food as a new emerging industry, one that is creating a new kind of economy in our society.

☙

Some think of food localization as a form of activism or see it as a mere expansion of the local food movement. That may all be partly true, but increasingly we're coming to understand that we're witnessing (and catalyzing) the birth of a new industry—the local food industry. When we look through this lens, something shifts. It's rather enlivening to think this way, and we're just beginning to adjust to this reality. It is sometimes said that local food is simply a segment of the larger food industry, just as organic food is considered an industry segment. But since in localizing our food supply, we are opting out of the industrial food industry, we actually stand apart, creating something new. So it's useful to think of local food as an emerging industry.

At the same time, we're experiencing something even deeper, which is the development of a local food *economy*. This is unlike our usual conception of economies, because it is a naturally occurring web of highly localized relationships that touches every aspect of how our food moves through the supply chain. At the core of this local food economy is a shared dedication to the well-being of the land, soil, biota, animals, and people.

10. Building a Foodshed Alliance

Problem: The emerging foodshed has no identity, no name, no formal recognition, no acknowledged existence as a living being.

Therefore: We seek to catalyze an alliance comprising all the key producers, buyers, and everyone in between. This is a collaborative organization—essentially a trade association—devoted to the increasing localization of food and farming in our region and the cultivation of our emerging foodshed.

Essentially, the alliance is a values-based supply-chain partnership, a strategic collaboration of business relationships between farms, processors, distributors, and buyers. Shared values create a collective business opportunity and customer allegiance. Such value chains are among the most promising developments in rebuilding local food infrastructures and in increasing local food consumption.

Initially, members of the alliance will include farmers, ranchers, restaurants, retailers, value-added processors, aggregators, food hubs, distributors, food-related community organizations and nonprofits—as well as other local businesses who support the alliance's goals and values. In the future, the alliance may also open membership to individuals. Members are expected to share business and market information with one another so that all can make better decisions to maximize the economic, environmental, and community benefit to all the members of this value chain.

11. Encouraging Innovation

Problem: Meeting the challenges, obstacles, and opportunities of building a local food infrastructure under difficult conditions will require a diversity of approaches in every aspect of the supply chain, from production to distribution. Many established methods will be insufficient to achieve the levels of yield, scale, and efficiency that are needed. This will be especially true as the impacts of global warming take hold and as our economy becomes increasingly unstable.

Therefore: We encourage and reward innovation. We find who the innovators are in our foodshed and support them every way we can. We encourage adoption of innovations from other foodsheds. We avoid reliance on technologies that subvert or compromise emergence and block healing and regeneration.

ॲ

The need for reducing reliance on fossil fuels, reducing or eliminating carbon emissions, and sequestering carbon will all require radical changes in the way we feed our local population. We may have to leave some traditions behind, maybe even some sacred cows.

As noted earlier, typical commodity-crop production yields something like $1,000 an acre per year, while a well-managed organic production can produce around $10,000 of food per acre. But much more is possible—and probably necessary. We've seen business plans for organic greenhouse production, utilizing a combination of controlled-environment technologies, capable of producing about $1 million worth of food per acre each year—year-round. These are said to be very energy efficient and use only about a tenth of the water that soil-based production consumes. Controlled-environment agriculture (CEA)—including aquaponics and hydroponics—will be an important strategy in areas that are constrained by limited water supply and a short growing season. CEA is discussed in greater depth in chapter thirty-two.

12. Building a Local Brand

Problem: Food has become almost a fungible commodity, so that its provenance and life cycle are anonymous and unknowable, thus creating a food culture of disconnection.

Therefore: We seek to build a distinct identity or brand for the food produced by our region, which can include provenance (specific producers), quality, terroir, life cycle, and supply-chain cycle. We find ways to connect the stories of our food from seed to plate.

∽

Branding campaigns like "Colorado Proud" and "Buy Fresh, Buy Local" are notoriously nonspecific and do not really help build a regional foodshed. They do not satisfy eaters' intense hunger to understand their food.

Developing a regional brand is difficult; it may need to support several hyperlocal brands within it to identify specific farms, grower cooperatives, food hubs, or alliances. This branding must go beyond mere labeling, so that the stories of our food are carried through every aspect of the supply chain.

Once we define our regional foodshed, we may choose to develop regional standards or guidelines that must be met to qualify for the foodshed brand. We will have to wrestle with the meaning of terms like *certified organic* and *beyond organic*. We will need to guard against inadvertently supporting monoculture production of local crops. And we will also be careful to support conventional producers who are in the risky and expensive process of converting to local food production, ensuring there are suitable markets for "transitional crops."

13. Increasing Institutional Procurement

Problem: Institutional food buyers (schools, universities, large employers, hospitals, and hotels) increasingly want to supply local food to their customers but face a plethora of hurdles—including inadequate supply, lack of efficient purchasing and delivery mechanisms, regulatory and policy limitations, producer certification requirements, and budgetary restrictions based on industrial supply systems.

Therefore: We seek to reduce barriers and obstacles while supporting customer demand for local food. We convene stakeholders gatherings and facilitate understanding and awareness.

❧

In a given foodshed, institutional food buyers may represent the largest potential for extending the reach of local food. Historically, they have relied on food-service corporations (e.g., Sodexo, Aramark, Bon Appetit) that have built a massive but largely invisible industry; food in this context is truly a faceless commodity. But with a growing commitment to the health and well-being of their customers, institutional food buyers are beginning to understand the possible benefits of sourcing as locally as possible.

At the same time, their customers increasingly express their preference for local food and expect their institutions to respond. For instance, the student-based Real Food Challenge has precipitated major procurement shifts in many schools and universities.

While there are leaders in this shift (such as the Kaiser Permanente health system in Northern California), no regional foodshed has yet successfully learned to meet this challenge. We are all at the early stages of institutional procurement.

14. Engaging Local Government

Problem: Local government has significant power and influence over the local food system. Current food policies were generated decades or generations earlier, usually designed to support industrial-scale agriculture, and are out of sync with an emerging regional foodshed.

Therefore: We seek to engage local government in supporting the project of localizing our food supply, developing needed policies and structures.

❧

When considering the appropriate role of local government in food localization, often the easiest answer is that it needs to get out of the way. The truth is that local government is often slow to join the process.

We do not wait for it and do not rely on it. We simply move ahead, but we also assist government in joining the conversation farther down the road, educating and informing it along the way. We create relationships. Some of us may even choose to become part of local government ourselves. This is a long-term strategy.

Here it's also important to emphasize the vision of food localization as economic development. It's possible that those charged with economic-development policies may be inspired by the opportunities that food localization can provide.

15. Developing Institutional Support

Problem: Major foundations and charitable institutions within a region are often charged with investing a certain amount of their endowment locally, but their involvement in food is usually limited to addressing hunger or the health of children.

Therefore: We promote a food-system perspective among the leaders of local foundations and institutions. We cultivate a willingness to channel institutional funds into the development of the local foodshed.

16. Guiding and Influencing Needed Policy Changes

> The realities we face in rebuilding local food systems are formidable, and there are citizens, policymakers, and corporations dead set against any push for relocalization.
>
> —PHILIP ACKERMAN-LEIST, *REBUILDING THE FOODSHED*

Problem: Existing government food and agricultural policies, often crafted by representatives of the Unholy Alliance, are among the most resilient barriers to the development of a regional foodshed.

Therefore: We take a proactive role in local, state, federal, and industry policy related to food and farming, pursuing appropriate policies in food standards, land use, food safety, health, fair labor, water, and economic development.

17. Cultivating a Local Food Culture

What makes food—something tangible—a vehicle for the sacred? It is grown by someone who cares deeply about its nourishing and aesthetic qualities. It is grown in a way that enriches the ecosystem, soil, water, and life in general. Its production and processing contribute to a healthy society. In other words, sacred food is ensconced in a web of natural and social relationships. It is grown with a love for people and earth that is not an abstract love but a love for this land and these people. We cannot love anonymously, which is perhaps why I've always gotten a somewhat cold feeling from anonymous charity that doesn't create connection. Somebody grew sacred food for me!

—CHARLES EISENSTEIN, *SACRED ECONOMICS*

Everything about eating—including what we consume, how we acquire it, who prepares it and who's at the table—is a form of communication rich with meaning. Our attitudes, practices, and rituals around food are a window onto our most basic beliefs about the world and ourselves.

—PATRICIA HARRIS, DAVID LYON, AND SUE MCLAUGHLIN,
THE MEANING OF FOOD

Foods that are chosen from local ingredients also have a distinctive story. Whether invented or preserved, local foods help define, and give flavor, to our places.

—GRACY OLMSTEAD, *THE AMERICAN CONSERVATIVE*

Food is intrinsic in our culture and our daily lives. It is a part of our heritage—where we have been and where we are going.

—WILL MORIN, *UPSTATE BUSINESS JOURNAL*

Problem: Most of us have lost our connection with the foodways of our region's past. In addition, we have often lost the foodways of our ancestors, wherever they came from. We are a people without a food culture.

Therefore: We seek to recover appropriate food traditions from our past and include them in the emergence of a new local food culture that is enlivened by the foods and food practices unique to our region.

⁕

A local food culture arises from the intersection of food with culture—current and historical. This includes a diverse array of local food traditions and customs—food production and gathering, preparation and presentation, preservation, and buying and selling, as well as food folklore, whether transmitted through written or oral history. The local food culture is the heart of community in many parts of the world. It needs to be developed here as well.

Certain foods and food practices connect us to a culture or history that has been passed down for generations, while others were invented in our lifetimes. A local food culture connects us to our geographic region, our climate, our period of time, our history, our ethnic or religious diversity, our families, and our community.

STAGE SIX:
SCALING THE REGIONAL FOOD SYSTEM

Introduction

> We can no longer import our lives in the form of food, fuel, and fundamentalism. Life is homegrown, always has been. So is culture. And so too are the solutions to global problems.
>
> —PAUL HAWKEN

To farm and live sustainably, is to farm and live spiritually. Sustainability certainly is not a religion, but it is fundamentally spiritual. Sustainable farming and sustainable living are attempts to work and live "in harmony with an unseen order of things"—to work and live spiritually. To farm and live sustainably, we must be willing to openly proclaim the spirituality of sustainability. We must reclaim the sacred in food and farming.

—John Ikerd

The next phase of localizing a foodshed is expansion, which will ensure its long-term resilience. If a local food system is to feed a significant portion of its population, reaching levels of 10 to 25 percent food localization, or more, it will be necessary to achieve a level of scale and efficiency far beyond what we're seeing almost anywhere in the United States today. This means that stage six is unknown territory; nobody in the local food revolution has gone there before.

Stage Six Patterns

1. Identifying opportunities and barriers
2. Securing and restoring land and water
3. Scaling production
4. Building a comprehensive data infrastructure
5. Channeling institutional and government capital
6. Trading with other regional foodsheds
7. Developing a regional seed bank

1. Identifying Opportunities and Barriers

Problem: Scaling the local food system to the point where it is the dominant food supply chain in our region (stage seven) could easily be a project lasting decades or even generations.

Therefore: During stage six we will need to evolve permanent structures that will hold the mission and vision of the regional foodshed, will perpetually identify the emerging opportunities and barriers to its development, and will provide long-term catalytic guidance for the regional effort.

2. Securing and Restoring Land and Water

Problem: With the impacts of global warming—which are just becoming visible but will continue to unfold dramatically for hundreds or even thousands of years—the threat to arable land and fresh water in our region will be great.

Therefore: We will learn to protect and restore the lands and waters in our region to support our local food economy and our ability to feed our people.

ॐ

In Colorado, at least in the Front Range, we live in a short-grass prairie bioregion with a shrinking water supply. Aquifers are being depleted. Municipalities, anticipating future population growth, are buying farmland in order to secure water rights. They're buying water from far outside their region. Even China is buying agricultural land in the United States. And now the rise of fracking as a key component of oil and gas production is an additional threat, driving up competition for water and rendering much water unusable due to permanent contamination. Meanwhile, land prices are skyrocketing, making it nearly impossible for new farmers to get started. Developers are snatching up land in anticipation of a near doubling of the state's population by 2050.

Land trusts and cooperatives are already forming to begin to respond to these challenges.

3. Scaling Production

Problem: Local food production is far below demand and long-term need. We lack land, farmers, methodologies, and financial resources. Meanwhile, with the coming collapse of the industrial food system, with the increasing impacts of global warming, and with the projected increase of the local population, we can see a massive food crisis on the horizon.

Therefore: For a significant amount of food localization to be achieved in our foodshed, we will find the ways to greatly expand and intensify food production, to levels where efficiencies of scale become available. We will be reluctant to adopt technological solutions.

4. Building a Comprehensive Data Infrastructure

Problem: We have no way of even reasonably estimating the realities of our current local food system and its various components—including per capita consumption, acreage deployment, soil conditions, crop and animal production, local versus nonlocal consumption and sales, projected demand, and so on—let alone its development in the future. This seriously hampers our ability to adequately plan and measure progress.

Therefore: As a community, we will build a comprehensive data resource—open to all stakeholders, including producers, buyers, food entrepreneurs, policy makers, funders, investors, and government officials—which will provide the perspective and metrics that will justify the policies, decisions, commitments, and investments that will be needed to meet the needs and unleash the enormous opportunities that are associated with a significant level of food localization.

All of us working on food localization suffer from lack of good data. Nearly every foodshed will likely need to build a data system that supports the entire supply chain—from projected production capacity to projected eater demand.

5. Channeling Institutional and Government Capital

Problem: Hundreds of billions of dollars of capital are controlled by government and institutional investors who fail to support local food economies.

Therefore: We will persistently encourage government and institutional investors to increasingly provide capital for our emerging foodshed.

Ultimately, because of the huge amounts of capital that will be required to build the foodshed ($1.8 billion in Colorado alone), government and institutional capital must be brought into the mix. There are few models for this.

6. Trading with Other Regional Foodsheds

Problem: It is probably not possible for us to meet all our essential food needs from within our own foodshed, especially while we're scaling our food system and in the early stages of developing its resilience and self-reliance.

Therefore: We will seek to trade our production surplus (if we have any) with other regional foodsheds.

ॐ

A key principle of localization is to meet the local population's essential food needs first and then to export any surplus, trading with other nearby regional foodsheds who have achieved some measure of resilience and self-reliance. This is a radical departure from current export-based agriculture, which has made resilience and self-reliance in food an oxymoron.

7. Developing a Regional Seed Bank

Community systems of seed supply are increasingly coming under pressure. In the first instance, factors such as droughts, crop failure, conflict, difficult storage conditions, and poverty are eroding both the quantity of seed and number of plant varieties available to farmers. Second, as a result of agricultural modernisation, farmers are increasingly purchasing more of their seed requirements. Not only does this mean that local seed storage could become less important, but as this bought-in seed replaces older, local varieties, these varieties become increasingly unavailable in many communities. In consequence, interventions to strengthen informal seed supply systems, such as establishing seed banks, and seed breeding and multiplication are gaining popularity among NGOs and public sector institutions engaged in the area of seed supply.

—V. Lewis and P. M. Mulvany,
"A Typology of Community Seed Banks"

Locally produced seeds yield hardier, more delicious crops. When seeds are grown, saved, and replanted in a particular location year after year, remarkable adaptations develop. Growers can select and save seeds from standout specimens with traits like resistances to pests and diseases, brighter colors, and tastier flavors. In essence, they are carrying the best from one growing season into the next. This is how our ancestors farmed sustainably for over 10,000 years—and it's the only way to recreate such a system today.

—Rocky Mountain Seed Alliance

Most of us now have no connection to the earth or the food we eat, some of which may never have been touched by a human hand. But native Americans used to sing to their corn to get it to grow. An American seed saver once came across a patch of corn which was growing much better than anything else nearby and he asked the Indian who had planted it why that was. "It's because I remember the song" the Indian said. But the seed saver took seeds from the corn and when he grew them, he found that the strain had a tap root which went several feet into the ground so it was able to get to moisture that was unavailable to the other farmers' plants. That seed was taken to Africa so that the taproot could be bred into native varieties and the result was so successful that the breeder won a UN prize. That Indian hadn't just remembered the song. He'd saved the seed as well.

—Anita Hayes, founder of Irish Seedsavers

Problem: At least 75 percent of the world's seed supply is controlled by a handful of transnational agrochemical corporations,[152] who are diminishing crop diversity and the possibilities of seed self-reliance for farmers and gardeners. Without taking back our seed supply, we cannot take back our food supply.

Therefore: We will develop a regional network of seed growers, distributors, educators, resources, and storage facilities. We will inventory the existing seed diversity in our foodshed and learn what other varieties are needed for climate resilience and food security. We will identify growers and stewards to conserve and expand this diversity. Our vision is a foodshed with local farmers and gardeners producing an abundant diversity of crops—food, herbs, wildflowers, and native grasses—from locally adapted seeds.

BEYOND STAGE SIX

> There is no place for government in agriculture. It's the work of the people.
>
> —ALLAN SAVORY

Localization of the region's food supply must eventually become the responsibility of the people as a whole. We do not know how to do this now, for we long ago ceded control of our food supply to corporate interests. In truth, we live in a nation where we have surrendered control of almost everything. Our democracy has been deeply eroded. But in food localization, we are recovering our agency and our sovereignty. In this, perhaps, we have an opportunity to begin building the kind of democracy that we all long for.

Perhaps we are in the process of reorganizing our society around a local food economy—our food commons—making the health and well-being of our people and lands our primary project, the foundation of our society. This is how radical and fundamental the local food revolution really is! We are rebuilding our society from the ground up.

We must realize that this will be a long and sustained process and that the effort will be opposed by the forces of the Unholy Alliance, who built the global food system as their primary way to control and exploit humanity for their own ends.

Remember that the warnings about global warming began appearing in the 1970s and have steadily increased in evidence and urgency. But for decades, the powers that be have resisted the drive to reduce greenhouse-gas emissions and the exploitation of fossil fuels. This should be a lesson to us. We cannot wait for governments and corporate interests to be persuaded to take the actions that are needed to ensure the future of humanity regarding food. Our future is in our hands, not theirs.

Perhaps what will eventuate is the emergence of regional nation-states—local, independent democracies that are interdependent, organized around food. They would exist in parallel with prevailing government structures, not in opposition. But they would, over time, build their own sovereignty, their own resilience.

PART 7

REVOLUTION IN PRACTICE

We are in a dangerous time of transition from separation to communion. We are between two major stages and moving rapidly into a time of planetary initiation. We are entering a world systems crisis and we must choose whether we will pull together in creative cooperation or pull apart in profound conflict. The coming decades will reveal the soul of our species and provide the opportunity for a rite of passage from one great trajectory of learning and development to another.

—DUANE ELGIN, *THE LIVING UNIVERSE*

CHAPTER 26

From Theory of Change to Theory of Revolution

The battle for independence from global industrialized food systems is being fought with words. Marketing spin cannot compete with authentically arising memes. People are opting out of being consumers—economic targets—and are now learning to be responsible food citizens. *Feeding the world* is an anachronism; feeding local populations first is the new mission. Sustainability is passé. Say hello to regenerative agriculture and restorative economics. It's a spontaneous revolution, shifting from the global to the local, profoundly changing how humanity will feed itself in increasingly uncertain times.

For the last couple of decades, in movements and organizations bringing about social change, one of the defining questions has been "What's your theory of change?" People proudly consider themselves to be *changemakers,* and whole disciplines have been developed about being agents of change. These are all expressions of stage three of evolution (including stages one and two, which overlap), when we're intent on *making things happen.* Well, when we make things happen, we might be somewhat successful in the short term, but there are often unintended consequences.

The revolution I'm speaking of is completely different. *We can't make revolution happen. We can't plan it.* It's spontaneous, emergent.

MICAH WHITE AND THE NEW REVOLUTION

As alluded to earlier, prominent changemaker Micah White, one of the cocreators of the Occupy movement, is now introducing a new theory of revolution.

> Protest is broken. We are living through a period with the largest protests in human history. But they are not working. And when you reach that point, instead of repeating the traditional protest behaviors, screaming and holding posters, you have to *innovate*....
>
> We live in a time when activists are so focused on what seems possible that we do not achieve anything. We need to disturb the power and not act only in safe ways.
>
> REVOLUTIONS HAPPEN WHEN PEOPLE LOSE THEIR FEAR.
>
> The trigger for the next revolutionary movement will be a contagious mood that spreads throughout the world and the human community.
>
> The next generation of activists will abandon a materialistic explanation of revolution—the idea that we need to put more and more people in the streets—in favor of learning how to spread that kind of mood, how to make people see the world in a fundamentally different way.[153]

These are prophetic words. Powerful. Catalytic. Revolutionary.

In a recent interview, White discussed some of what he's been working on. This is radical stuff, and there's a part of us that already knows and understands it, even though we might not express it the same way. White sees four types of revolution.

- Voluntarism: The actions of humans create social change.
- Structuralism: Economic forces, such as food prices, cause revolution.
- Subjectivism: Revolutions are an inner process inside the individual.
- Theurgism: Revolution is a supernatural process, a *divine intervention.*

We've all seen examples of the first three types of revolution. But now we're beginning to see revolutionary encounters of the fourth kind— which, to me, represents a special kind of emergence.

I would submit that the local food revolution—as a revolution— exhibits characteristics of all four.

Micah White's perspective could only appear at stage four, at the Turn. It is a powerful example of *emergence*. And it is an example of the fourth kind of revolution. This is very encouraging.

NEW LANGUAGE FOR
THE LOCAL FOOD REVOLUTION

I'll share one more example of revolutionary communication, a demonstration of how new language is being created to fuel the local food revolution. Douglas Gayeton is an award-winning American multimedia artist, filmmaker, writer, and photographer who divides his time between a farm near Petaluma, California, and the medieval town of Pistoia in Tuscany, Italy. He's the author of a most amazing book, called *Local: The New Face of Food and Farming in America*.[154]

Along with his wife, Laura Howard, Douglas directs the Lexicon of Sustainability, a massive project that's been going on for several years. The Lexicon of Sustainability is really a response to climate change, beginning with food. Next is water, he says, and then energy.

Here's how Douglas and Laura work: through careful research and constantly plying a vast network of contacts, they look for food innovators and disruptors—people we might think of as evolutionary catalysts or even revolutionaries—people who are discovering and applying new approaches that have great potential for addressing Peak Everything, often in unexpected ways.

I had an opportunity to interview Douglas in the fall of 2015. He explained that once he finds such a person, he spends days or weeks with him or her, conducting interviews, gaining a complete understanding of what the person is doing, and sometimes taking thousands of photographs—if he senses that the person's work is really significant.

Then he goes back to his studio, has the interviews transcribed and the images processed, and looks for the fundamental emerging pattern. When and if he finds it, he then writes to that person and asks a series of questions about this pattern. He asks the person to name the pattern—with a simple word or phrase—and to write just a few sentences about his or her work.

From there, he adds lettering to a final, multilayered image, sometimes writes a longer story to accompany it, and makes the work available online and in print. He's planting seeds of catalytic communication, accelerating their emergence in the world. The results are astonishing.

Below, for example, is Anne Cure of Cure Organic Farm, a local food hero here in Boulder, representing the innovation of community supported agriculture. The image itself is powerful and intriguing, and then we begin to notice the words. Revolutionary words. Catalytic words. Transformative communication.

> Community Supported Agriculture = CSA. Buying a CSA membership means entering into partnership with a local farmer. The member buys a subscription at the beginning of the season. This cash infusion allows farmers to pay for seed, water, equipment, and labor in the early season when farm expenses are high, and farm income is low. In return, the farm provides its members with a box of fresh picked seasonal produce each week. CSAs build community by reconnecting their members to the seasons and fostering relationships between members and the people who grow their food.

There are also quotes from Anne Cure: "We want to connect with these families and provide a place where they can experience the farm," "Our goal is not to grow food for the whole world. It's to grow really good food for 175 families," and "When people learn about their food, how vegetables and animals are raised, they form a deeper relationship with the land."

Around the edge of the image, Gayeton says,

Figure 7: Anne Cure

I ask Anne Cure what led her to create this CSA for 175 local families and she says, "There's nothing better than knowing who you're growing your food for: Alicia and Quentin who love the fava beans. Mark and Anne who can't wait for the San Marzanos. Or Oliver and Eu, who will eat these carrots before they leave the farm. We want to share the farm's stories and create a place people feel a part of. We commit to feeding as many families as our land can healthily provide for. This includes over a hundred varieties of vegetables and flowers grown during the year."

In less than 250 words, with carefully selected images, a wonderful story is told that can change people's lives. Imagine this image enlarged to the size of a billboard, which actually happened a few years ago—when it was displayed on the side of a grocery store in Boulder.

And below is Benzi Ronen, the founder of Farmigo, representing the innovation of Economies of Community (EOC). Farmigo is an online farmers market that connects eaters directly to local producers. In this image we find the blueprint for, as the text says, "what a 'networked' food hub looks like."

An industrialized food system is highly centralized and benefits from economies of scale. Local food systems benefit from a sustainable, democratized food system that is decentralized and benefits from a network of farms, highly local distribution channels and motivated consumers.

At Farmigo, Benzi develops web software to power local food systems.

Three Principles of Economies of Community

- Transparent: equal access to information
- Democratized: equal voice and ability to take action
- Frictionless: simple transactions and feedback.

The system connects Producers and Consumers through disruptive Distribution.

For Producers:

- More Profit: receive higher price per pound compared to wholesale
- Greater Security: not dependent on 1 or 2 wholesalers
- Build Community: cultivate direct relationships with consumers

On the Consumer side:

- Value locally grown food
- Create and maintain local distribution sites
- Perform quality controls, validating all producers in food chain
- Recruit others to join the movement

They are linked by Distribution: Many to many (multiple producers to an entire food community)

And all this is supported by Internet software, websites and social media

And around the edge of the image, is a final message.

Figure 8: Benzi Ronen

How can software enable the scaling of a decentralized food system so it feeds more households with locally sourced food? The Internet helps local food producers and consumers find each other easier; software-enhanced systems further leverage this power of the internet by allowing consumers to join scalable, location-specific networks of farms and food producers. Targeted knowledge-sharing has transformed the purchasing of food into an intimate conversation between consumers and food producers. It strengthens local economies and results in more secure local food systems.

There's an entire MBA in food hubs packed into this image—again in about 250 words. It is worth studying and contemplating. I can tell you that a lot of producers and food entrepreneurs have been making themselves familiar with what is expressed here.

These two images represent Gayeton's way of capturing what's emerging in the local food revolution and sharing it widely—the essence of the lifework and learning of evolutionary catalysts who are dedicated to localizing our food supply.

LOCAL FOOD SHIFT

Finally, I would be remiss if I didn't include *Local Food Shift* magazine. We're taking everything we have learned since we began localization work—from organizing reskillings to introducing the Transition movement in the United States to declaring a goal of 25 percent food localization in Colorado—and all the relationships we have developed, and wrapping them into one single enterprise, a seasonal magazine.[155] It appears in print and online and is intended to serve as a catalyst—to be a voice for the local food revolution, to celebrate our awakening foodshed, and to help build real food security and food sovereignty in Colorado.

In September 2015, we printed our first edition, twenty thousand copies of a beautifully designed 160-page magazine (on matte stock recycled paper), which we've been distributing throughout the state and beyond. As I write this, we're in classic startup mode—standing shoulder to shoulder with all those who are working to rebuild soil and foodsheds and regenerate local economies.

The role of *Local Food Shift* is to hold the vision of a local food-shed coming into consciousness, to tell the stories of our awakening foodshed, and to ignite other catalysts for food localization within our own foodshed and beyond. With the launch of *Local Food Shift,* we are now taking our work to a whole new level. More directly than any other strategy, we feel this magazine will help catalyze the local food revolution, along with its emerging industry, and also support the birth of a true local food culture. We hope to cultivate Colorado's regional foodshed *as a living being* and nurture the centers of aliveness emerging within it. Our promises to our readers, advertisers, and investors spell it out.

- We give voice to the local food revolution. We understand that this kind of communication may be as important and fundamental to our community as farming.

- We are storytellers. We write and publish the stories that we ourselves want to read.

- We never claim to know the whole story. We do not claim to be completely objective, but do our best to be completely honest and candid. This doesn't necessarily mean that others will always consider our work balanced or fair. We receive feedback and input gracefully, and learn from it.

- We are part of the living foodshed, not apart from it. We are engaged, just as we want our readers to be engaged. We are not on the sidelines of the local food revolution, but on the front lines. We are part of the *local food experience* in our foodshed, present and active. We garden, cook, and eat as locally as we can wherever we go. We are intimately involved in the activities and events of the local food movement. We are very conscious that our lives are changing in tandem with the emergence of our foodshed.

- We nourish, nurture, inspire, inform, instigate, investigate, explore, cultivate, connect, harvest, and share. We save seeds and grow sprouts. In spirit, we tend to and care for the soil, the biota, the animal laborers (including humans)—all those who the foodshed serves and all those who serve it. In this manner, we too are farmers.

- We hold the essential sacredness of food and farming at the very center of our work, endeavoring to infuse the Sacred into everything we do.

CHAPTER 27

Christopher Alexander and the Evolutionary Catalyst

Perhaps more than anyone else, Christopher Alexander has opened the door on how to be an evolutionary catalyst (or foodshed catalyst or deep revolutionary). For this I am grateful, though I am sad that so few people know his work. We need to know it; I'm certain he created it for you and me.

Alexander's particular medium as an evolutionary catalyst is *architecture*—creating structures and buildings that actually give life. But what he has discovered applies to what I have been pointing to throughout this book, *becoming agents of evolution*. What he is showing us is timeless, universal. And essential for us.

He teaches that "the task of making, the task of building itself," is to be understood as "a *spiritual exercise*, a direct attempt to come face to face with the ground of the universe."

What Alexander has learned is that the process of catalyzing what he calls "living structure"—and this can apply to a permaculture site, a community, or a foodshed as much as to a building—is a process of infusing what we are creating with *wholeness* and *relatedness* that are *contagious*. This brings about *healing* that ripples throughout the structure and far beyond. This requires great intentionality and devotion. And discipline.

In other words, as an evolutionary catalyst, I am not the one who is creating. I am but a vehicle through which wholeness and relatedness and healing are emerging as a manifestation of God. I serve not my own vision, but the unfolding vision of living structure that is being mysteriously revealed.

> Careful construction of the world ... will result in a world which is practical, harmonious, functional. If this is true, astonishingly then it appears that the safest road to the creation of living structure is one in which people do what is most nearly in their hearts: that they make each part in such a way that it reflects their true feelings, that it makes them feel wholesome in themselves, and is, in this sense, related in the deepest way to their own true I....
>
> This is enigmatic, if not ridiculous. It means that a world constructed in the most personal and individual fashion, made by people who are searching deeply to follow the nature of their own true selves, will be—in the most public, objective, and universal sense—a world which is functional, adequate, and harmonious.
>
> The enigma which arises, then, is that the process by which human beings create the world, in their own image, gradually creates a living world, and this is—I have come to believe—the best and most efficient way a living world *can* be created.
>
> Of course, the phrase "in their own image" requires that it be the *true* self, and the personal search for the true self cannot be separated from this process which each person strives for. This means, then, that the making of a living world cannot be separated from each person's search for the true self.[156]

This is as clear a description of what it means to be an evolutionary catalyst as I have ever found.

Near the end of *The Luminous Ground,* the fourth volume of *The Nature of Order,* there is a chapter titled "Making Wholeness Heals the Maker." That's worth taking in for a moment. *Making wholeness heals the maker.*

In chapter four, I mentioned Alexander's *A Pattern Language,* published in the mid-1970s, and described how he realized that this earlier work was largely misunderstood. What he was attempting to point to was how certain elements in living structures awaken something deep within us—deep and true feelings that we did not even know we had—and he was saying that we can fashion these elements intentionally. In *The Luminous Ground,* he finally becomes more transparent. "Taken to its ultimate," he says, "a living structure brings us face-to-face with God." Yes, God.

Perhaps it's relevant to explain that I have provisionally come to the place where I can say that the force that has guided the process of the evolution of our universe over the last fourteen billion years—whatever that force is—I consider to be an expression of God (not God per se, but a profound expression of what God is). Another way of saying this might be that through the process of evolution, God is entering the universe and ending separation. This relates closely to what Christopher Alexander has been saying in recent years. This is not God as a supernatural creator, but God as a process, God as the unfolding natural creativity in the universe. Perhaps this is as much as we can comprehend of God at our rather primitive stage of evolution.

> This quality, when it appears in things, people, in a moment, in an event *is* god. It is not an indication of God living behind all things, but it is actually *God itself.* This is spirit made manifest.... We have contact with actual spirit in that thing.
>
> And this is the ultimate aim of all making: to make a thing which *does* manifest spirit, which shows us feeling, which makes God visible and shows us the ultimate meaning of existence, in the actual sticks and stones of the made thing.[157]

What if this became the fundamental—if perhaps secret—*intention or design parameter* for an emerging foodshed? Or a relocalization plan? A potluck dinner? A restaurant? A business or organization or investment? A revolution? A community? A regional democracy? Or a world?

What Alexander shows us is *how spirit becomes clothed in matter,* how God manifests in our universe—and how we can become engaged in the process. *This changes everything.* Alexander is teaching us to see ourselves as evolutionary catalysts.

Once I accept that what is happening is actual spirit, it helps me to make a whole thing. Once I understand it, I can seek to do just that. I take everything I know about centers [of aliveness], feeling, and so on, and focus on my inner knowledge of what it means for spirit to appear.

This is a direct humility. Then I am close to making a gift to God.

But my acceptance is more than just humility. Somehow it helps me. If I know that I have to make spirit—I cannot fool around with that. It is a great weight, and a great joy. I keep at it. It is hard work, emotionally. I can do it at any time. But it is so much easier to ignore it, not to do it. Not doing it is easy. Doing it is hard. Concentration, attention, effort—it is all very hard.

But when I actually do it, I pay attention to what I am doing and allow myself to go only in that direction where I can say it is an emerging spirit. That cuts many things out. The inner knowledge that I carry in me, which already knows what is spirit and what is not, will let this instruction, or this knowledge, guide me quite surely toward certain kinds of things.

This brings me, then, to a last aspect of the process which produces life in things, a necessary state of mind. The core of this necessary state of mind is that you make each building in a way which is a gift to God. It belongs to God. It does not belong to you. It is made to serve God, to glorify God. It is not made to glorify you. Perhaps, if anything, it humbles you.[158]

Now we're getting down to it. This is the core of our work as evolutionary catalysts in cultivating emergence.

It is very hard to allow the wholeness to unfold.[159] To do it, we must pay attention, all the time, only to the wholeness which exists in what we are doing. That is hard, very hard. If we allow ourselves the luxury of paying attention to our own ideas, we shall certainly fail. The things which can and do most easily get in the way, are my own *ideas,* my thoughts about what to do, my desires about what the building "ought" to be, or "might" be, my striving to make it great, my concern with my own thoughts about it, or my exaggerated attention to other people's thoughts. All this can only damage the building, because it replaces the wholeness which actually exists at any given stage with some "idea" of what it ought to be.

The reason why I must try and make the building as a gift to God is that this state of mind is the only one which reliably *keeps me concentrated on what is,* and keeps me away from my own vainglorious and foolish thoughts.[160]

Well, this is real work, difficult work. But it is the work of an evolutionary catalyst. And we may go on a long time before we realize that this is what we're actually doing.

Sometimes, when I make something, my mind is so concentrated on it that it becomes different. It becomes a pure thing. I am not concerned with showing off, but only with making the thing itself. How can I set my mind in this egoless direction? At every step in the 10,000 steps during the making of a building, I am always, at each step, asking which of the things that I can do next is the one which will be the best gift to God....

The trouble is, it is immensely hard work asking this question. It is a bore. It is troublesome. It is pedantic. It is too pious. I can't be bothered with it. It is absurd to keep on asking myself this question. Besides, this question finds me out, and keeps on showing me—what I don't want to know—that my natural inclinations are no good, that my work is too puffed up with pride, that my judgment is imperfect.

So, even just *asking* the question, 10,000 times, is almost impossible.[161]

Yes, as Christopher Alexander says, it's almost impossible. But given the stakes we're dealing with, it's worth striving in this direction. And we can learn to support each other in doing this work. And perhaps we can learn to draw on the support of the angels of evolution themselves, the "Unseen Ones" who attend to emergence on this planet and beyond. And perhaps we can consider that the process Alexander describes—which we are learning as evolutionary catalysts—is one of the great gifts of humanity and that it can be carried far beyond this troubled time and even far beyond this beleaguered planet.

May we dedicate our lives to the possibility of being catalysts for what is emerging in our world.

CHAPTER 28

The Secrets of
Cocreative Collaboration

All localization work requires collaborative group process. This chapter explores an approach to group process rooted in an understanding of the seven-stage process by which the universe has evolved. This is a brief, practical introduction to how emergence can move through intentionally formed groups and how leadership is transformed into catalysis.

In any given process, there is often an unfolding pattern that is not immediately apparent. If we don't know what the pattern is—or if we don't even know that there *is* a pattern—we are flying blind. We stumble around in uncertainty; success is slow at best, and at worst, seemingly random—or even impossible. Once we see an evolutionary pattern, however, we have a whole new way of looking at our challenges. Suddenly, things begin to make sense. With practice, we can learn to allow the pattern to emerge in us and through us. Knowing the underlying pattern and aligning with it makes our task much easier, more fun, and more productive. Perhaps more than anything else, the pattern gives us a way of organizing what we learn and how we learn.

Collaborative group process often follows an evolutionary pattern that mirrors the evolution of the universe. This was the key insight of David Sibbet, founder of the Grove and the entire discipline of graphic facilitation. He once said to a group of his students (including me), "You can tell what stage a company or organization or group is at by the kinds of meetings they are having." His understanding was guided by the breakthrough work of Arthur M. Young, who identified seven major stages in the evolution of the universe (and their substages) and

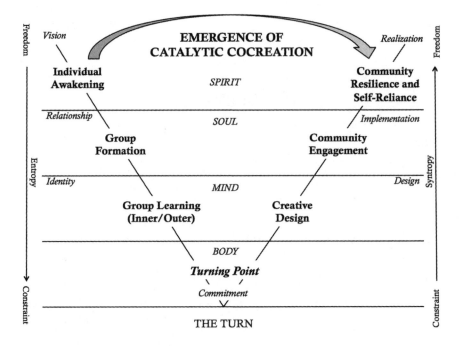

Figure 8: The Emergence of Catalytic Cocreation

demonstrated that the pattern of these stages is mirrored in any evolutionary process—or could be. Young's insight was that a deep understanding of how humans can create together can be rooted in this same process.

It is possible to synthesize the framework that Sibbet employs so that it is accessible for small groups, where collaborative cocreation can become a conscious process.

Cocreative group process comprises seven stages, each a multifaceted process.

Stage one: individual awakening. It begins with an individual catalyst who experiences a pressing need and at once is possessed by a vision of what is possible. Passion is kindled to the point that inaction is no longer an option.

Stage two: group formation. For the vision to begin moving into the world, the catalyst must share it to attract a resonant group of individuals who will become cocreators. This is often difficult.

Stage three: group learning (inner/outer). Before the group can accomplish anything, it must become aligned around the vision and attuned to current reality. Through this process, which can take a long time and is often stormy (and often fails), the group forms a common identity that is the seed for a new organism.

Stage four: turning point. Eventually, the group begins to focus on the need for action, precipitating a crucial moment when decisions and commitments must be made. This launches the group into a whole new phase of existence, unleashing power that is capable of bringing a new creation into the world.

Stage five: creative design. The group decides on and designs a specific project that has the potential for bringing their vision into reality. The major design breakthrough is discovered, not figured out; it is not primarily an intellectual process.

Stage six: community engagement. The group attempts to implement the project design within the target community. Here the group is focused on learning from feedback, developing necessary course corrections. It's an iterative, emergent process.

Stage seven: community resilience and self-reliance. If the group has been aligned with the vision, with each other, and with current reality—and if it has been faithful in being a vehicle for what is wanting to emerge—the vision will ultimately become a reality. This is cause for celebration—a process that gives birth to new visions and provides fuel for the next levels of conscious collaborative cocreation.

A group that has learned to follow this process is nothing like what we have come to understand as a *committee*. Through this process, a new organism comes to life, a vehicle through which the forces of evolution can move. The group itself becomes an evolutionary catalyst.

EMERGENCE IN ACTION: THE PATTERNS OF COCREATION

Stage One: Individual Awakening

Every project must first be experienced, and then expressed, as a vision which can be seen in the inner eye (literally). It

must have this quality so strongly that it can also be com-
municated to others, and felt by others, as a vision.

—CHRISTOPHER ALEXANDER, *A New Theory of Urban Design*

All human enterprise begins with inspiration. Someone—usually an individual—has a vision, a spark of an idea that is powerful and compelling,
unexpected, illuminating. This is equivalent to the explosion of light we
see at the beginning of the universe. The person who has this vision is
an evolutionary catalyst.

A vision may not always occur as a flash of light. It may emerge
gradually, first appearing dim and hazy and incomplete, slowly becoming clear and bright and intricately detailed. Nevertheless, in the end, it
brings light to the darkness, lights up the world with a new possibility.

Like light in the creation of the universe, the vision represents potential. The occurrence of a vision is a profound and mysterious event, no
less strange and inexplicable than the cosmic genesis itself. As human
beings, we cannot explain the meaning of vision. We cannot make it
happen. It happens in us, to us. It occurs unexpectedly, suddenly, often
when we are not looking for it. Vision is essentially involuntary, the
irreducible quantum of human creation. Oddly, it seems to choose us,
to seek us out.

Vision is fundamentally a way of seeing—seeing what is possible,
seeing what the future can be. It also opens up a new way of looking at
what exists, in terms of its capacity to give birth to what does not yet
exist. And when it presents itself to our consciousness, we are caught
up, fired up, *en-lightened*. We see the world anew. We can *en-vision* a
future that has not been seen before.

The occurrence of a vision means that something wants to come into
being. Visions are given to us as gifts that we, in turn, are called to give
to the world. Being gifted with a vision is a *calling*, giving one a mission
and purpose, a focus. The power of vision is impersonal. It is not our
property. We belong to it, if we choose. If we do not accept the vision,
or if we fail to bring it into existence, it will choose someone else.

Once we apprehend a vision, our task is to bring that vision into reality. With this in mind, we can begin to see that the process of creation

is one of moving through the seven stages from potential (stage one) to reality (seven).

Stage Two: Group Formation

The vision begins to have power—it begins to move—only when it is shared with other people. A vision kept inside, secret, can never manifest. Thus, those who experience a vision are compelled to enroll others in midwifing it into reality. This usually involves painting a picture of the future, planting it in the minds of those whose support and involvement will be necessary in bringing the vision into reality.

A vision has the power to motivate people. It gives them a focus. Most importantly, a vision brings people into relationship with each other. People are very much like the particles of the early universe, racing about without purpose, generally encountering each other briefly, each either positively or negatively charged. Each person possesses tremendous energy, but that energy, without a focus, cannot be channeled. But when people are drawn to a vision, inspired and motivated by a compelling picture of the future, all this chaotic movement changes dramatically. Galvanized by the light of potential, they are attracted to relationships with each other centered on the vision. United by a single spirit, they discover a new way of seeing, a purpose and direction for their lives, a way of relating with others who share the same vision.

This calls forth enormous power and energy. Vision binds people together. In a very real sense, vision calls forth people and transforms them into a group. In responding to the call of the vision, they begin a journey together. Thus, *relationship* is the fundamental principle of stage two of human creation.

Stage Three: Group Learning (Inner/Outer)

Once individuals become a group, they begin a process of exploration and discovery. No matter what the endeavor, there is much to be learned. They begin asking questions—of themselves, of each other, of the world around them. There is much information that must be sought, analyzed, and shared. Usually, this process is unstructured at first, chaotic and riddled with false starts. This happens because people do not understand the nature of the task they face—discovering it is the essence of stage three work. Gradually, structure does appear. What creates the structure is information itself. Information produces form—it *in-forms*. This is a key insight into the nature of the creation process for human beings.

The Power of Questions

There are essential questions that must be explored during this phase of the creation process.

- What is the vision? What are its implications?
- Is it possible to make this vision a reality? What will be required?
- Does the vision need to be modified? Is it realistic?
- Who are we in relation to this vision? That is, what are our roles and responsibilities? What is our level of commitment to actually having this happen?
- What do we know about the world in relation to the vision? Is the world ready for it? Is this something that is truly needed or wanted?
- What do we need to find out?
- What do we need to do for the vision to become a reality?

Many more questions will also arise. And for some participants, the sheer number of unanswered questions may, for a time, make the vision seem unattainable.

The How Question

There is one question that almost inevitably arises at this stage: "How shall we do this?" But this is not the question that will move the process forward. In fact, the *how* question can be deadly; it can kill the vision.

We seem to believe that unless we know how to do something, we cannot do it. And if we cannot readily see how to bring a dream or vision into reality, we deem it impossible. This limits the potential for discovery and learning that is needed, from which the vision can be built. Many great visions are abandoned as hopeless causes simply because the visionaries listen to the voice that tells them that they do not know how to create the reality that they foresee. Or, perhaps even worse, they seek to *figure out* how to bring their vision into being—they try to force an answer into being. This is actually an abuse of human mental power, a distortion of our creative nature, which arises from a profound (and usually unconscious) belief in the fundamental scarcity and hostility of the universe.

One of the most important secrets of the creation process is that the *how* is never figured out; it is *revealed*. We discover the answers to the *how* question in a learning process that cannot be forced or hurried, manipulated, or controlled. If people realize that their fundamental purpose at this stage is to welcome all the questions that come up and to learn everything they need to learn, they will be able to move forward with focused intensity.

The Discovery of Reality

One of the tasks in stage three is to discover and discern *current reality* in relationship to the vision of the future that is emerging—because without being fluent in the current reality, it is very difficult to create a new reality.

Becoming aware of current reality—what is so—means also becoming aware of what is *not* so. This is awareness of what management consultant Robert Fritz calls "structural tension,"[162] the relationship between the vision and current reality. This tension seeks resolution—and it generates energy for the creative process.

The Transforming Role of Information

What occurs during the process of discovery in stage three is the uncovering of information. Information is the fuel that will power the project. The quality of information acquired, expressed, and exchanged will determine the quality of the relationships that are formed between the project's participants, the participants and the vision, the participants and current reality, and the participants and the future. A number of activities are used to uncover and exchange this information.

- *Research*—a persistent effort of testing assumptions, verifying discoveries, and excavating new information

- *Report*—exchanging the information derived from research with other participants

- *Recheck*—looking to see if the current strategy and activity—and indeed the vision itself—are consistent with what is being learned

- *Reformulate*—clarifying and adjusting the vision, plans, and strategies to harmonize with the view of reality that is developing

- *Restate*—communicating the reformulated vision, plans, and strategies to other participants

- *Regroup*—adjusting the roles and relationships of the participants to the reformulated vision, plans, and strategies

Living with the Unknown

In our effort to discover current reality, many new questions arise. We become increasingly aware not only of what we know but also of what remains unknown. It is more important for us to live in the questions than to arrive at the answers. All too often, in not being able to arrive at verifiable answers, we settle for what we (or others) believe. This is destructive to the process of creation. The capacity for living with the unknown, for being in a perpetual state of questioning and discovery, is essential for those who choose to create together.

The Formation of Identity

The subtlety and efficacy of the insights discovered during stage three may be difficult to grasp at first. On a basic level, people are in process of discovering current reality as regards the vision. But on a deeper level, as the participants gain a clearer picture of reality, they are also gaining a new sense of identity. They are defining themselves in terms of the vision they are helping to bring to birth in the world of time and space. And the process of making explicit their shared assumptions, distinctions, values, and worldview gives both the individuals and the group as a whole a distinct identity, with unique qualities and characteristics. This is precisely parallel to the formation of atoms with all the properties they possess.

Of course, most groups of people engaged in a project do not create their identity consciously. But it is useful to be aware that at this stage of any creation process, part of what is going on is the formation of this identity. If this aspect of the process can be conscious, the effect is truly transformational. The group is becoming a living being.

Stage Four: Turning Point

The stage three process of information discovery cannot go on forever. The energy produced by the accumulation of information will reach a critical mass, when what has been learned precipitates a turning point in the creation process. There comes a moment of decision, for the crucial question is finally unavoidable: Will we do this? Knowing what we now know about the vision, about what is so in the world, about what is not so, and what we have discovered about ourselves, shall we now choose to actually bring this vision into reality?

If this question is not confronted and responded to consciously, the vision will be stillborn. For the envisioned future to be given life, we must decide to make it a reality.

From one standpoint, this moment is much like the moment just before liftoff, as a plane races down the runway. The pilot must choose, as the plane increases in speed and the air begins to lift its wings, whether to commit to flight or abort the takeoff. So it is with stage four. The momentum of energy created by the first three stages eventually demands that those involved either commit to the vision or abandon it.

We have all seen how such decisions and commitments can be put off repeatedly—justified by a desire to refine the vision or to seek more information. But inevitably, the moment of truth comes. And putting off a decision too often will, at some point, become a decision to abort.

Decision and Commitment: The Distinction

The Turn is actually a two-phase process. First, we decide to take responsibility for bringing the vision to life. *We will do this!* But the decision alone will not be sufficient to reverse the entropy of the left side of the process arc. The project is now mired in the muddle of limitations and constraints. Enormous energy—energy of a radically different sort than what we have expended to date—will be required to begin the long return to freedom.

If the decision is to have any impact, make any difference, it must be accompanied by a *commitment*. This means bringing physical resources to bear—committing the time, materials, money, and human power that will be necessary to make the vision a reality. And this commitment must often be made without knowing precisely what will be required to do the job. All we can do at this stage is rely on our experience and the vast amount of information we have already accumulated. We have no choice but to *estimate* what will be required. This is a simple reality that we must come to terms with, that no matter how well we may be informed or prepared, no matter what amount of brilliant analysis or strategy we may have produced, the future is largely unpredictable and unknowable.

So it is that commitment is a supreme act of faith, stepping out boldly and determinedly into the unknown. There is a memorable and instructive scene in the movie *Indiana Jones and the Last Crusade:* Jones faces a bottomless chasm he must cross in order to find the Holy Grail (and thereby save his mortally wounded father). There is no way around it, and it is too wide to jump across. Suddenly he remembers that it is a test and that what is required is an act of faith. He must step out into the abyss. We can see in his eyes the moment he makes the *decision* to step out. But he has not yet moved. He makes his *commitment* at the moment he actually steps out into what appears to be open space. His foot comes to rest on a solid bridge that was invisible before. It was not his decision that enabled him to cross, but the commitment he made—in the physical, in the here and now.

Creation simply cannot occur without conscious decision and commitment. In fact, it is reasonable to say that decision and commitment is the fundamental *quantum of action,* the basis of all potential creations made manifest. At this stage, creation becomes purely an act of will or intentionality. Here, the vision becomes our own, not something that has come to us. We make it ours, giving ourselves over to it. Otherwise, it will remain but a dream.

Stage Five: Creative Design

Indiana Jones did not know *how* he would cross the chasm. Only when he actually committed himself irreversibly—when he stepped out into apparently empty space—did he discover the solution. He did not figure it out. The *how* was revealed—and after he made his commitment.

Asked too early, the *how* question can kill a vision, bring an enterprise to a screeching halt. At stage five, however, the question finally becomes appropriate and, in fact, essential. But we cannot analyze or rationalize our way to the answer. Rather, the task here is to open ourselves up, so the answer can appear.

Those who regularly engage in creative endeavors know what we are speaking of here. Jazz improvisation comes to mind—a process of discovering and unleashing the flow of music within certain agreed-upon limitations (key, tempo, rhythm, chord progression). At one time, this was considered an activity exclusive to artists, but now it has become virtually institutionalized as part of the planning and development process for all kinds of endeavors. Formal brainstorming is an example—a group convenes to develop a creative solution or design for a specific project (usually with fairly well-defined parameters—constraints).

In a brainstorming session, it often happens that, after a period of unstructured meandering, chaos, and sometimes even conflict, a creative idea emerges that is so compelling that it elicits instantaneous and often unanimous consent. This is the *aha* moment common to true discovery. The solution is *revealed*. It just shows up. True, we create the conditions in which it can appear, but we don't create the revelation. We merely facilitate its appearance.

The object of this elusive pursuit is a kind of creative blueprint or design for the envisioned future. This design is the basic plan that will be followed in the rest of the creative process. It takes into account what was learned during the discovery (stage three) about current reality, and it is fully informed by the limitations and constraints of the environment or milieu in which the vision is intended to manifest. The design is no less than the compilation of all stages of the creation project coalesced into a form that has life, generative power—the DNA that will infuse everything in the next stages of the creation. This generative center of the design is embedded in the detailed plan that is developed—which will include the more external aspects of the plan in terms of allocation of resources, scheduled milestones, projected expenses, review points, and so forth.

Stage Six: Engaging the Community

Design in hand, those engaged in the project can now proceed to bring the vision into visible form. They move forward as a body to implement the plan. While stage five was intensely creative, stage six is essentially a straightforward task of implementation. Everyone involved in the project knows what must be done, by whom, when, within what constraints of resources, and with what qualities. If the work of the previous five stages has been thorough, stage six is relatively easy, almost routine. The work moves out to the physical level.

Alignment

For the project to flow smoothly at this stage, careful attention must be given to the relationships that began forming in stage two. Effective implementation requires effective relationships. And effective relationships depend on alignment—alignment with the vision, with the distinctions and values discovered during stage three, with the decision and commitment to move the vision into reality, with the plan as it has been developed, with those engaged in the project together, and with the intended result.

Course Correction

No matter how well planned a project may be, no matter how brilliantly conceived and designed, things will go awry. Estimates and projections will prove to have been inaccurate. Assumptions will be challenged and changed. Accidents will occur. People will make mistakes. And the plan will have to be adjusted.

Creating a new future is, after all, an uncertain and unpredictable process—an emergent process. Thus, the critical task at stage six is to pay attention to feedback and learn from it. Measuring progress is important.

An analogy is perhaps helpful here. Sailing across the ocean is a difficult task, requiring adjustments and course corrections. One must frequently get a fix on one's position, compare this to where one intended to be at a certain time, and calculate strategies to get back on course. I find the methods used in traditional navigation instructive. A sailor uses a sextant to measure the position of the sun in the sky relative to the horizon and the compass. The precise moment of this measurement is carefully recorded. With this information, the sailor can determine his or her position anywhere in the world in terms of longitude and latitude.

The essential discipline of stage six is much the same. We reference the vision of the future (the objective) and see where we are in terms of the plan (the timeline). This is a matter of tracking current reality. With this information in hand, we can see how far off course we might be and begin to discover what we need to do to get the project back on track. We could call this process of experimentation and learning from feedback the *circle of discovery.*

Stage Seven: Community Resilience and Self-Reliance

If the work of the previous six stages has been faithfully performed, success will inevitably be achieved. The project will arrive at its goal, the actualization of the vision. The intended future has at last arrived.

What was envisioned finally makes possible a certain kind of *condition* in the world that was needed. (Some planning processes even take care to define as part of goal development "conditions of satisfaction.")

Of course, achieving stage seven is not a single event, but itself a process. There are no doubt seven identifiable substages, but we have not yet clearly defined them (more work for future creators).

Celebration

Celebration is an aspect of creation that is often overlooked. The importance of celebration is not simply acknowledgment of the achievement. Nor does it merely give us an excuse to have a grand party. Rather, the primary creative function of celebration is to allow for reflection.

We reflect on what we have accomplished and what we have learned.

In our celebration, it is important to reflect on the past, to review where and how we began and to recall the milestones along the way. This often involves sharing anecdotes and stories. This allows us to see the entire process for perhaps the first time and to appreciate the significance of what has been accomplished. And we recognize the knowledge we have gained through the project.

We then reflect on the present and behold our creation, the real-world manifestation of what began as a vision, a spark of light. The realization of the vision has brought about many changes, and bringing those changes to consciousness provides us crucial information. Perhaps the most important change to recognize is that we ourselves have changed. We are not the people we were when we began. We have learned together. We have grown together. We have experienced ourselves as powerfully creative beings, capable of achieving what we envision. Creation is no longer a mere concept. We have experienced our cocreatorship and have taken a major step toward conscious oneness with the Creator. What is most important about going through the process is not what we accomplish, but what we become. As results transform situations, people's consciousness evolves. This creates a context for the perception of new opportunity, new vision.

Based on what we have learned together, we finally reflect on what is now possible in the future. To the extent to which we have created consciously, we will have opened up possibilities that were hitherto unimagined. In the course of reflecting on the future, new visions and dreams are spawned. We stand on a substantial foundation. We know that we will create whatever we choose—that is, whatever is given to us to bring into the world. Our potential for creating is without limit.

Sustaining the Group

Nurturing the cocreative group is essential. You're going to be working closely together for quite a while. It is challenging work. It will take everything you have to give. But if this is what you're called to, nothing else will satisfy you like this work. There are many things that will support the group.

- *Keep the learning going.* Put on events that you want to go to. Support each other in taking classes, courses, and workshops. Share skills, books, articles, and information.
- *Find activities that deepen you and the group.* Consider Joanna Macy's work,[163] Heart and Soul work (from the Transition movement), outdoor group activities, and shared meals (especially potlucks) with no agenda.
- *Review your balance of giving and taking.* Take steps to keep yourselves sustainable, resilient, and self-reliant.
- *Deepen your own preparation (inner and outer).*

Remember, the work you're doing is on all levels—body, mind, soul, and spirit.

QUESTIONS FOR EMERGENCE

- *Stage one:* What am I seeing or hearing? What wants to be born through me?
- *Stage two:* What am I feeling about this? Who is this for? Who is with me in this?
- *Stage three:* Why would I do this? What will be required of me? What is the current reality for me, for my community, for this vision, for this unborn creation? What do I need to know? What skills do I need to develop? What relationships must I cultivate?
- *Stage four:* Will I do this? Will we do this?
- *Stage five:* What is being revealed to me? What is being revealed to us?
- *Stage six:* Is this working? Am I (are we) being true to this creation, to this partnership? Do I (we) need to make any course corrections? Do I (we) need to adjust my (our) understanding of current reality? Is the vision evolving?
- *Stage seven:* Who have we become in the process? What's possible now? What's next?

PART 8

THE FUTURE OF FOOD

This courage of seeing, of being unafraid to see the suffering of our world, is needed in our work. We're rediscovering this capacity. We live and we can't avoid living with tremendous uncertainty. The Great Turning is underway, but no one can tell what will unfold or if it will unravel first. We need to look squarely at the uncertainty. If we can't be with that, we [will be swept away with the tide]. The warrior stands and does not demand the assurance of a happy ending.

—Joanna Macy

CHAPTER 29

Preparing for Climate Collapse

The climate of the future is already here, but it's here in pieces, very unevenly distributed. We don't yet know which of those pieces will become more common until they become normal, which will become less common until they disappear from our lives. That's how the weather changes, not by a gradual wave of average change, but in the unevenly distributed events that generate those averages, heat waves becoming more common, snows disappearing. The future is arriving, one broken piece at a time, each piece made out of the broken bits of the past, each piece breaking things as it comes.

—Frank Landis, *Hot Earth Dreams*

This final part of the book is not to provide answers or solutions, but to offer potentially useful lenses to look through, ways to hold the issues. As discussed in part three, there is perhaps no greater or more unpredictable challenge to our food supply (whether industrial or local) than the potentially devastating impacts of climate change. We need to quickly prepare our food production for eventual climate collapse, as well as for short-term changes and even sudden weather events.

Northern Colorado's thousand-year rain and five-hundred-year flood in the late summer of 2013 brought this realization to the forefront in our state, causing many to begin considering a haunting question: how can we significantly increase local food production in the face of increasingly erratic weather and a shrinking water supply? In some areas, such as Phoenix and Tucson, Arizona, food localization advocates are wondering if it's even remotely possible to meet this challenge.

It's a harrowing situation we face with global warming, certainly, but there are actions we can take. Food localization can play a crucial role, offering a powerful way to reduce greenhouse-gas emissions and reverse the profound damage already done to our environment.

In Colorado, producers are exploring ways to increase local food production while sequestering carbon, reducing the use of fossil fuels, and utilizing growing methods that require less water. For instance, we are witnessing a dramatic rise in controlled-environment agriculture (greenhouses, hydroponics, aquaponics, and aeroponics), which makes possible efficient, large-scale food production on small acreage.

Local entrepreneur Buck Adams has pioneered greenhouse technologies in the two companies he founded: Circle Fresh Farms, which was a major supplier of tomatoes to Whole Foods in Colorado; and Veterans to Farmers, a nonprofit organization that trains veterans in greenhouse production and management and offers them opportunities in cooperative ownership. Hoop houses and high tunnels are popping up on local farms at a record pace, despite regulatory resistance to non-permanent structures. Veterans to Farmers, for example, is involved in plans to build forty acres of greenhouses on city of Denver land.

The Savory Institute—through its holistic range-management process—is demonstrating that properly managed herds of cattle and sheep can actually restore grasslands otherwise headed toward desertification. Hundreds of thousands of acres in Colorado are already under some form of holistic management.

In his latest book, *Growing Food in a Hotter, Drier Land: Lessons from Desert Farmers in Adapting to Climate Uncertainty,* Gary Paul Nabhan advocates the use of locally produced compost to increase the moisture-holding capacity of fields, orchards, and vineyards; reducing bureaucratic hurdles to rainwater harvesting and gray water on private lands; and transitioning to perennial agriculture, especially tree crops and grass pastures. Nabhan notes that investing in such measures would be far more effective than doling out billions in crop-insurance payments—in 2012, the United States gave $11.6 billion to farmers hit with diminished yields or all-out crop failures.

Finally, permaculture practitioners are demonstrating scalable food production and water conservation methods in areas previously considered unsuitable for farming.

Beyond mitigation and remediation, local food systems must become resilient enough to withstand an increasing number of extreme weather events, as well as rapid climate change more generally. Some scientists warn that global temperature increases of 4 to 6 degrees Celsius are possible within the next decade or so. Agriculture as we have known it would cease to be possible at those temperatures, so it is imperative that resilient production methods be quickly developed. And at the same time, it is important to realize that it is highly unlikely that industrialized agriculture will be able to continue under such conditions, which could lead to widespread famine and conflict if local food systems do not increase production in time to meet these challenges.

CHAPTER 30

The Moral Challenge
of Biotechnology

If we are going to live so intimately with these chemicals—
eating and drinking them, taking them into the very marrow
of our bones—we had better know something about their
nature and their power.

—RACHEL CARSON, *SILENT SPRING*

There are deeply disturbing parallels between the (often well-intentioned) effort to control runaway global warming through technology (e.g., geo-engineering) and the effort to feed the world through biotechnology (bio-engineering). Both resort to methods that attempt to address symptoms but ignore underlying causes. Both are incredibly dangerous, often born of desperation and unchecked greed.

The difficulty is that humans are inserting themselves into evolutionary processes of nature that they neither comprehend nor appreciate. To do so is a violation of the *precautionary principle* and is potentially reckless, immoral, and unethical—a fundamental violation of the sacredness of life. To do so merely for the sake of *profit* is particularly reprehensible, outrageous. To do so to "feed the world" is just a lie.

How do we know these things? Because the obvious result of such practices is to further disconnect us from life itself and to make human technology the solution to all the problems we ourselves have created.[164] It is precisely this kind of self-serving striving that has led humanity— and the entire biosphere—to the brink of quite possibly irreversible disaster, including global climate collapse, which will keep unfolding for centuries and perhaps millennia, and has caused the largest mass extinction of species in sixty-six million years, wiping out as many as two hundred species a day.

The debate over the use of GMOs has been explicitly confined to two aspects, the scientific and the economic. But as Wendell Berry says, these are "only two sides of an eight-sided coin." The economic issues are usually stated in simple terms: protecting the profitability of commodity-crop export farmers and preserving their way of making a living. The scientific issues are usually framed by the idea that any decision about GMOs must be based in science. Besides the reality that much for what passes as scientific research is nothing but corporate-sponsored propaganda, it needs to be said that science is not capable of giving us answers to the questions of how we should live on the planet. It can give us perspective, understanding, and insight, and it can produce tools, but it cannot tell us how to live. We must draw upon deeper resources for that. These are not issues that can be decided based on materialistic science or short-sighted economics alone, for the consequences of our actions here are far reaching.

GMO OMG, a documentary by Jeremy Seifert, tells the symbolic story of Haitian peasant farmers who rejected and burned Monsanto's offer of GMO seeds after the devastating 2010 earthquake, taking to the streets ten thousand strong. It was this story that drove Seifert to explore why the reaction to GMOs was so powerful. What he discovered is compelling: "It's such a personal and intimate threat, not only financially, but to the land, to the air, to the water and to the food—the most intimate interaction we have with the world around us. When that gets taken over and the culture associated with food is removed because their seeds are replaced with these foreign seeds, they become essentially enslaved to these companies. It touches so many areas of life and culture that it's a very important issue to the entire movement."[165]

The battle over GMOs has become emotionally charged to the point that rational debate is nearly impossible. Attempts to establish GMO labeling have been met with powerful and well-funded industry campaigns.

One of the chief (and highly cynical) arguments of proponents of biotechnology is that consumers should be given a choice and that GMO labeling has the undesirable effect of limiting consumer options—as if anyone would deliberately choose to eat foods that might be damaging to one's health and the environment! A special food issue of *Scientific American* illustrates the problem. In the lead editorial, "Fight the GM Food Scare," the editors abruptly depart from the realm of science: "Instead of providing people with useful information, mandatory GMO labels would only intensify the misconception that so-called Frankenfoods endanger people's health."[166]

They continue: "Many people argue for GMO labels in the name of increased consumer choice. On the contrary, such labels have limited people's options. In 1997, a time of growing opposition to GMOs in Europe, the E.U. began to require them. By 1999, to avoid labels that might drive customers away, most major European retailers had removed genetically modified ingredients from products bearing their brand. Major food producers such as Nestlé followed suit. Today it is virtually impossible to find GMOs in European supermarkets."

Polls show that almost no one will intentionally seek out foods containing GMOs. It's clear enough that most eaters, given the choice, will avoid GMOs. General Mills recently announced that their legacy Cheerios brand will no longer contain GMOs. Whether this is merely a cynical marketing scheme or a serious move toward corporate responsibility remains to be seen.

For those of us involved in localizing the food supply, we can confidently hold to moral and ethical principles to guide our choices about biotechnology. Here is what I've concluded over the last several years.

We must say no to GMOs, to those who seek to use them, and to those who have become dependent on them.

We must say no to public officials, appointed or elected, who will not stand firmly against GMOs and the corporations who seek to control our food supply.

We must say no to corporations who use GMOs in their products.

We must say no to corporations who seek to own GMO patents on seeds—as if life itself could be patented and owned!

We must say no to governments who allow this to happen!

CHAPTER 31

The Role of Animals in
Local Food and Agriculture

One of the great dilemmas to be addressed in the development of local food systems is the role of animals in local food and agriculture. Here we find a heated debate—ranging from vegans, who insist that humans should not exploit animals in any way, to practitioners who contend that animals must be an integral part of any food production system.

In this debate, we should all beware of statistics that do not distinguish from industrially produced meat and meat that comes from small, conscientious, and compassionate producers who hold themselves to high standards.

Some scientists claim that the current industrial animal-agriculture system is the single greatest human cause of climate change on the planet. That's worth considering, and it raises deep and difficult questions. In *Meatonomics,* David Simon frames the challenge well. "Compared to plant protein, raising animal protein takes up to one hundred times more water, eleven times more fossil fuels, and five times more land. Animal food production now surpasses both the transportation industry and electricity generation as the greatest source of greenhouse gases. Even worse, the system fosters financial incentives that encourage the relentless destruction of land and the routine contamination of air and water. Without dramatic reform, the end game in the conflict between fixed resources and ever-increasing demand is likely to have a group of clear losers—the planet's inhabitants."[167]

Given that meat consumption is rapidly increasing throughout the world, particularly in China and India, this constitutes a nightmarish dilemma. To meet this demand, producers are raising animals in concentrated animal feeding operations (CAFOs), which rely on copious amounts of antibiotics, chemicals, and GMO corn and soybeans to keep costs low and profits high. Such systems externalize costs, making it difficult for smaller producers who care about quality to compete.

Industry consolidation has exacerbated the situation. Reportedly, four corporations now own 83 percent of the beef market; the top four firms own 66 percent of the hog industry; and the top four firms control 58 percent of the poultry industry. These corporations are far more interested in profits than they are in human health or environmental integrity, and government regulations are skewed in their favor.

Recently a major Chinese processor, Shuanghui International, bought Smithfield Foods, the largest pork producer and processor in the world. At the same time, the USDA has approved U.S.-grown chicken to be shipped to China for processing (without benefit of USDA inspection), then shipped back to U.S. markets for sale.

Local food planners will need to determine the extent to which animal production should be a part of their agricultural mix. Integrating grass-fed bison, cattle, sheep, and goats; pastured poultry; and forest-raised pigs provides numerous economic incentives for producers, but it also raises issues that must be carefully dealt with to manage carbon and waste outputs, as well as health impacts for the local population.

❧

Allan Savory tells vegans that he doesn't care whether they eat meat, but that they should feel compelled to actively support the holistically managed grazing of livestock to restore grasslands, end desertification, save water, and sequester carbon.

❧

I've heard ranchers say, "Our animals only have one bad day in their lives." Is it compassionate to allow our livestock to die of illness or old age? Or is it more caring to ensure that they have a full and natural life and, without stress or pain, gently end their lives when we decide it's time.

What is the appropriate role of animals in our local agriculture and in our diets? Every one of us—and all of us together—will need to evolve our own answer to this question.

CHAPTER 32

The Promise of
Controlled-Environment Agriculture

> To feed nine billion people in 2050, the ratio of food pro-
> duced per unit arable land must be increased substantially.
> Greenhouses will be part of the solution. Greenhouse hor-
> ticulture is a resource-efficient and environmentally friendly
> production system with enormous yield per unit area.
> Greenhouse-grown food products have consistently high
> nutritional value, and greenhouse operation is economically
> profitable.
>
> —LEO F. M. MARCELIS AND SILKE HEMMING

In the effort to localize the food supply in the Colorado Front Range,
with a goal of 25 percent food localization within the next decade, one
of the most significant challenges is limited production capacity. Demand
for local food far outstrips supply, forcing commercial buyers to rely on
out-of-state producers (California), out-of-country sources (Mexico),
or even U.S. conventional growers for access to "fresh" healthy food.
Export-oriented commodity agriculture dominates the economic landscape, which is true in most regions throughout the nation.

Despite the growth of the organic food industry, which reached a
reported $39 billion in 2014, there is concern that farmland is not being
converted to organic production at a pace that will continue to support
demand. The local food industry—now at an estimated $12 billion—has
been growing more rapidly than the organic food segment, but unless

local food production capacity is significantly increased, that growth rate could stall.

CHALLENGES TO PRODUCTION CAPACITY

Several factors in the Front Range combine to significantly inhibit the growth of local food production.

- *Lack of affordable land.* Of the nine million acres of farm and ranch land in the region, most are committed to commodity-crop production, animal pasturing, and hay production. Conventional producers, who are supported by federal subsidies and other forms of support, see few incentives to produce food for local consumption—especially since the distribution and marketing infrastructure is limited. Meanwhile, land prices are prohibitive for many prospective farmers, as well as for established farmers who wish to expand operations.

- *Short growing season.* The growing season (April to September) limits food production to half of the year. Buyers do their best to adapt to seasonal availability by relying on distant producers. Meanwhile, local producers struggle to find supplemental sources of revenue during the off-season, complicating their ability to attract and retain labor.

- *Increasing drought and decreasing water supply.* State officials say that about half of Colorado is currently in some level of drought. Most areas of the state normally receive less than twenty inches of natural precipitation each year, so most agricultural production requires irrigation, with the majority of water supplies coming from unpredictable snow-melt runoff. Meanwhile, water demands by rapidly growing municipalities and proliferating fracking operations create severe pressure on agricultural producers.

- *Increasing climate chaos.* With global warming, seasonal weather patterns are becoming unreliable, forcing producers to rapidly attempt to adapt their cropping plans. Extreme weather events are also increasing, such as the rains and flood of September 2013, which inundated more than 28,000 acres of cropland (mostly conventional) and 39,000 acres of pastureland and destroyed much of the 150-year-old ditch irrigation system. Climate projections indicate that these trends will worsen in the coming decades.

- *Lack of trained labor.* Every year, food producers must face the increasing challenge of hiring skilled workers on a seasonal basis. Immigration restrictions have greatly constricted the traditional supply of labor coming from Mexico.

- *Competition with marijuana industry.* Legalization of both medical and recreational cannabis in Colorado makes this cash crop an attractive priority for growers, governments, and investors. Most available warehouse space in the region has already been snatched up, compelling marijuana entrepreneurs to erect large-scale greenhouses on agricultural land. Because of its revenue potential, marijuana production is often prioritized over food production.

- *Bioregion not ideal for land-based food production.* Most of the Colorado Front Range is in a semiarid short-grass prairie bioregion, where shale-based soils are sandy and more conducive to animal grazing than vegetable production. Native populations followed the buffalo through this area but scarcely relied on any kind of agriculture for food. Even though these factors arguably make the Front Range a less-than-ideal location for a population of 4.5 million people, the region is expected to increase to more than seven million by 2050[168]. Feeding such an increasingly urban population as locally as possible will become an enormous challenge, but one that will also create tremendous opportunity for economic development.

- *Lack of financial incentives.* Low farm profits and limited infrastructure for distribution and marketing discourage many producers from attempting local food production at any appreciable scale.

These challenges are, of course, not limited to Colorado.

ADVANTAGES AND DISADVANTAGES OF CONTROLLED-ENVIRONMENT AGRICULTURE

> CEA offers ecologically sensitive food production through a combination of ancient and recent technologies that focus on the preservation of waste streams into productive resources.
>
> —EMMANUEL PRATT, SWEET WATER FOUNDATION

In this context, controlled-environment agriculture (CEA)—whether via hoop houses, low and high tunnels, hydroponics, aquaponics, or aquaculture—offers advantages and benefits (ecological, economic, and social) that are only beginning to be recognized in this country, though other nations have adopted CEA extensively. For instance, in the Netherlands, only 0.5 percent of arable land is used for greenhouses, but the production value is 22 percent of total Dutch agricultural production value.[169] Around the world, the top ten greenhouse producers are China (with an estimated 2.8 million hectares), followed by Korea (57,000 ha), Spain (52,000 ha), Japan (49,000 ha), Turkey (33,500 ha), Italy (26,500 ha), Mexico (11,800 ha), the Netherlands (10,300 ha), France (9,600 ha), and the United States (trailing with 8,400 ha—only about 21,000 acres).

Nevertheless, adoption of CEA is beginning to accelerate in the United States. According to a 2013 Rabobank study, while "greenhouse produce is estimated to only represent 1 to 2 percent of overall U.S. fresh fruit and vegetable production," certain crops, like greenhouse tomatoes, today account for as much as 70 percent of sales.

While still in its early stages, "the U.S. greenhouse industry has been steadily growing over the past decade," says the Rabobank study. "This growth, driven in part by the need for more intensive production due to limited land, water and labor, has pushed sales over $3 billion and is estimated to reach over $4 billion by 2020."

The local food industry has generally been slower to adopt CEA than commercial agriculture. Some of the earlier commercial-scale greenhouses were developed in conjunction with supermarkets, mostly growing commodity tomatoes (not organic).

Greenhouse Food Production Advantages

- *Small footprint.* In terms of output, greenhouse production can utilize as little as 1 percent of the land needed for equivalent land-based production. With farmland increasingly scarce and expensive, this is a tremendous advantage.

- *Energy efficiency.* While greenhouses are often considered energy intensive, the reality is that they use far less in fossil fuels than soil-based market farming methods. In the future, agricultural engineers anticipate that greenhouse production without fossil fuels can be achieved in the future by using heat pumps, geothermal heat, waste heat from other industries, and green electricity. Current natural gas consumption, used for heating greenhouses in cooler weather, can be offset by lower fuel needs in other areas—growing for local customers reduces or eliminates the need for refrigeration and shipping

- *Water conservation.* While the industry literature regularly claims that greenhouse production uses less than one-tenth the water used by soil-based production, that figure is actually conservative. Much of the water in a CEA unit is recycled within the system. Evaporation is extremely limited. Rainwater capture and near closed-loop irrigation recirculation can further improve water conservation.

- *Reliable year-round supply of produce.* CEA breaks the cycle of seasonality, which often forces buyers to rely on imported products.

- *Environment control.* CEA systems are designed to maintain near-optimum climatic and nutritional conditions for the plants being cultivated, thus eliminating most of the uncertainties of commercial-scale food production.

- *Input control.* Plant nutrients, carbon dioxide, light, and water can all be tightly controlled (via computers) for maximum efficiency and quality and to maximize the photosynthesis process.

- *High production capacity.* High-tech hydroponic greenhouses are capable of annually producing in the range of $1 million in revenues per acre—roughly two orders of magnitude greater than soil-based market farming.

- *Stable nutrient composition.* Consistent product quality, particularly in terms of nutritional value, is difficult to achieve in soil-based production. CEA provides an unmatched level of stable nutrient composition.

- *Pest and disease control.* Using biological agents, it is possible to keep production free from synthetic pesticides, herbicides, and fungicides.

- *Waste reduction.* Other than organic plant residues, this production method does not produce waste materials.

- *Reduced labor costs.* Greenhouse production is far less labor intensive than soil-based production.

- *Scalable.* Production can easily be scaled to meet growing demand for local, sustainably produced food—especially in urban settings.

- *Ultra-short supply chain.* Greenhouses can conveniently provide local populations with their daily supply of vegetables and nutrients. Delivery to customers can take place within hours of harvest, eliminating the 1,500-mile transport chain that imported produce travels through.

- *No agricultural runoff.* This type of food production is basically done in closed-loop systems, thus greatly reducing pollution.

- *Dramatically reduced delivery time.* Greenhouses can be placed near population centers, so food can be purchased and consumed within a few hours of being picked.

Greenhouse Food Production Disadvantages

- *Capital intensive.* Capitalization of greenhouses averages approximately $1 million per acre.

- *Training required.* Successful greenhouse production demands skill and experience, as these are sophisticated facilities. To keep up with market demand, adequately training new growers will be a high priority.

- *Limited crop variety.* The most common greenhouse crops are tomatoes, leafy greens, microgreens (especially for restaurants), cucumbers, peppers, herbs, green beans, and squash. Strawberries and raspberries are likely to be popular in the near future. Root crops and melons are usually impractical.

- *Carbon dioxide must be added as a system input.* Plants can quickly reduce carbon dioxide concentration in the closed greenhouse environment, which can slow plant growth. It must be introduced and monitored.

IS IT ORGANIC?

Both producers and eaters are increasingly concerned about the quality of their food, and in recent years, they have demonstrated a preference for local and organic food, traditionally produced in soil. Hydroponic food production is mildly controversial and often misunderstood. Greenhouse producers are often asked if their produce is organic. Lufa Farms in Montreal provides valuable insights into these concerns.

> Short answer: no. We practice sustainable hydroponic agriculture by using no synthetic pesticides, herbicides, or fungicides; capturing rainwater and recirculating 100% of irrigation water; using half the energy to heat as a ground-level greenhouse; composting green waste; choosing cultivars for their taste and nutritional value instead of durability; and delivering our produce on the same day it's harvested to eliminate waste.
>
> From the outset, our mission has been to grow food where people live and grow it more sustainably. One of the major challenges when we started was to decide whether we wanted to use soil-based methods (which are eligible for organic certification in Canada) or greenhouse hydroponics (which currently are not).
>
> In the end we decided to focus on hydroponic growing, even though these methods are not eligible for organic certification, to minimize our environmental impact. Doing so has allowed us to implement systems that recirculate 100% of irrigation water in our greenhouse. Some of the nutrients we use are mined (e.g.,

iron, potassium, etc.). One reason that hydroponics has yet to be certified organic in Canada is because the mined nutrient salts are nonrenewable, but our ability to recirculate cuts down on an estimated 90% of nutrient usage versus standard hydroponic agriculture. By using drip irrigation and other hydroponic methods, we've created a completely closed irrigation loop that grows highly nutritious and incredibly tasty vegetables year-round while keeping water and nutrient use to a minimum.

Early on, we made the decision that we would not use any synthetic pesticides, herbicides, or fungicides in our cultivation. Instead we adhere to strictly sustainable cultivation methods, using only biocontrols (like ladybugs) and biological products (like algae) for pest and disease management.

CHAPTER 33

Shifting Local Capital into the Foodshed

> Innovation and progress are nearly impossible in an under-capitalized industry.
>
> —*Food Commons 2.0*

The restorative economy, says Charles Eisenstein, is nothing less than a facet of an all-encompassing spiritual transformation in our fundamental relationship with the world.[170] The core principles of restorative economics, says Woody Tasch, include carrying capacity, cultural and biological diversity, sense of place, care of the commons, and nonviolence. Localization and democratization of capital begins to reverse the dominant economic paradigm of extraction and consumption, empowering local citizens to direct the flow of capital into a regional food system.

The slow money approach, pioneered by Tasch, initiates new forms of local investment based on the assumption that the best way to begin building a restorative economy is to invest locally in sustainable, small-scale food and farming enterprises. Now a robust national movement supporting an emerging industry, slow money investments are helping to enhance food security, food safety, and food access; improve nutrition and health; promote cultural, ecological, and economic diversity; and accelerate the transition to an economy based on preservation and restoration.

Slow money is an essential strategy, but it is just a beginning. We don't know if it can scale sufficiently to have much impact. Since mid-2010, through Slow Money national gatherings, regional events, and local activities, more than $45 million has been invested in some 450 small food enterprises around the United States. Twenty-four local Slow Money chapters and thirteen investment clubs have formed. Slow Money events have attracted thousands of people from forty-six states and seven countries. Slow Money investing has also begun in Nova Scotia, Switzerland, France, and Belgium.

I've already discussed the reality that localizing the food supply requires moving significant amounts of capital into the local food economy. While slow money and community capital efforts promoted by BALLE and Michael Shuman are important, the reality is that these strategies do not yet come close to the scale of investment necessary to achieve food localization beyond a few percentage points.

What needs to happen? I have become convinced that until we successfully position food localization as the most important and most urgent social cause of our time, it will not attract sufficient capital to get the job done. Why? All too often, local food is seen as a lifestyle choice, an optional way for people to improve their lives. Whole Foods appeals to this set of values, offering a luxury grocery store for upscale consumers where a mere smattering of local food is displayed at premium prices.

Despite the best efforts of slow-money evangelists, social-impact investors do not yet perceive food localization as social entrepreneurship. Much education is needed here. Social-impact investing usually focuses on nonprofits and social enterprises serving disadvantaged or low-income communities in the United States and developing countries. While these efforts must be supported and expanded, they will not result in the kind of economic scale needed to create resilient and self-reliant regional food systems. Given the fragility of the global food chain, all of us are food insecure—not just the economically disenfranchised.

In the high-risk and low-return environment of local food production, where businesses are forced to compete with an industrial food system that externalizes many costs, attracting traditional investors is difficult. Slow money is beginning to open the door here, but it is unlikely to persuade accredited investors to abandon financial return for social return on investment. Tasch wants to awaken investors' biophilia—their innate love for life—a worthy cause. But it might be more effective to target individuals who *don't* think of themselves as investors and awaken in them the realization that they can support a great social cause by shifting small amounts of capital into local food and farming enterprises. This could be revolutionary.

I am convinced that this kind of grassroots approach to capital is where we need to start. It is difficult, and we have almost nothing in the way of precedent to follow. We are essentially starting from scratch.

Among other things, we're up against two intimately related problems. First, we're living in a consumer economy. Seventy percent of the GDP is based on consumer spending. This is no accident, of course. In 1955, economist Victor Lebow wrote in the *Journal of Retailing*: "Our enormously productive economy demands that we make consumption our way of life, that we convert the buying and use of goods into rituals, that we seek our spiritual satisfaction and our ego satisfaction in consumption. We need things consumed, burned up, worn out, replaced and discarded at an ever-increasing rate."

We have come to define ourselves as consumers. Whole industries have been created to provide products for us to consume. Consumerism creates enormous business opportunity, and this is just as true in food as it is anywhere else. In fact, it's useful to remember here that food is the largest industry in the world. It's killing us, literally, but lots of people are making a lot of money from it. It's one more industry dedicated to making and selling us things that we don't really need, things that are ultimately bad for us and bad for our environment—and our economy, apparently.

There is a class of people who have arisen in our consumer economy called *investors*. They don't actually produce anything. They invest their money to make more money so they can invest more money and make even more money. In other words, they have become *consumers of money*—consumers on steroids. Consumerism produces *investorism*. Investorism is *investing money in money itself*.

I think of a cartoon making the rounds on the internet in recent years of some post-apocalypse survivors huddled around a fire in a cave. One of them, dressed in a tattered suit, says, "Yes, the planet got destroyed. But for a beautiful moment in time, we created a lot of value for our shareholders."

It's a strange idea of value, but it's pervasive in our culture.

Investors usually want exit strategies. Exit from what? Exit from engagement? What if there's no exit? What if we do not *want* an exit?

SHIFTING PARADIGMS

One of the great tragedies of our modern culture is that somehow we have all become consumers. We even call ourselves consumers, as if that was our very identity. How did this happen?

The fundamental problem is that "our society is nutrient deficient in the vitamins of purpose, meaning, and value."[171] What is the growing distance between consumers and the source of their food? I'm not talking about food miles, but psychological and spiritual and cultural miles. What is the distance between investors and where their money is being invested? Again, it's a psychological and spiritual and cultural distance.

Why is there a growing tendency to hide how food is produced? Our food supply has been engineered for the profitability and power of the corporations. They create artificial needs. To achieve their goal, they need us to be consumers.

ॐ

If we come to realize that our food supply has essentially been colonized by big agribusiness, and if we discover that our thinking about food has been colonized, and if we learn that the proliferation of GMOs is an extension of this colonization, then we have work to do.

> If we come to realize that our economy has essentially been colonized by the financial industry (by a commerce of extraction and consumption), and if we discover that our thinking about money has been colonized, and if we learn that the destruction of our environment is an extension of this colonization, then we have work to do.

We have ceded control of our food supply to forces we do not know and who do not care about our well-being. We have ceded how we think about food to media and advertising (and the USDA). So we must begin by decolonizing the way we think about food; we must become conscious about our food. This is essentially a spiritual act, and it's going to take some work to root out colonization in our minds and attitudes.

> We have ceded control of our economy to forces we do not know and who do not care about our well-being or the well-being of the planet. We have ceded how we think about money to media and advertising (and the government). So we must begin by decolonizing the way we think about money; we must become conscious about our money. This is essentially a spiritual act, and it's going to take some work to root out colonization in our minds and attitudes.

Next, we must begin radically altering the ways we feed ourselves, with the goal of food sovereignty and food security. We must become independent from foreign powers and distant corporations. The only way this can be accomplished (or at least begun) is by localizing our food supply to the greatest degree possible.

> Next, we must begin radically altering the ways we make and use our money, with the goal of sovereignty and freedom. We must become independent from foreign powers and distant corporations. The only way this can be accomplished (or at least begun) is by localizing our money to the greatest degree possible.

This is perhaps a radical theme, but it seems important, in that it names a fundamental dynamic that is almost completely unconscious in our society. Even Woody Tasch referred to it in his keynote speech at the Slow Money National Gathering in Colorado in 2013: "The grip of buy low–sell high has never been stronger. Television ads show infants in their cribs trading stock on their iPads. This is cute and funny, up to a point, but up to another point, it is a horrible testimony to the colonization of every aspect of culture by the *trading mentality*."

 birds

The consumer culture has given rise to the investor culture. They are intimately related. Consumerism produces *investorism;* consuming goods leads to consuming money itself. And the whole thing is based on an economy of extraction and consumption of earth's most precious resources.

The idea that money itself should earn money is nothing less than *usury.* It is, as James Howard Kunstler says, a kind of Las Vegas mentality, the idea that we should get something for nothing, that we could get lucky, strike it rich.

All this economic activity is devoid of any sense of meaning, purpose, or value. It is empty, totally disconnected from life. It is life destroying, even undermining that which gives rise to life. It recognizes no reality other than the physical and temporal, and it is amoral at best, immoral at worst.

Investorism: n. The movement of money away from purchasing goods and services ("consumerism") toward investing in mutual funds, stocks, and other financial assets.

We need to remember that the economic and financial system that has dominated our culture is dependent on exponential growth, and it is therefore profoundly unsustainable. As Eisenstein says, the end of the Age of Usury is near, the end of the Age of Separation.

Slow money and *locavesting* are signs of an emerging new economy that includes our understanding of the purpose of life, humanity's role on the planet, and the relationship of the individual to the human and natural community.

birds

When we ask people to invest in food and farming enterprises—even with slow money—they usually want to know what the return will be on their investment. Insidiously, for all the goodness represented by many of our slow-money entrepreneurs, the conversation always seems to turn around money and how much can be made (by the entrepreneurs and their investors).

Local food businesses are forced to compete with a globalized, industrialized system that externalizes much of the cost of production and heavily subsidizes producers. Meanwhile, our local food producers operate without subsidies and without access to crop insurance, and most of them are having a tough time making a living.

This makes local food and farming enterprises high-risk operations. From the perspective of investors, they are not good investments. These are long-term, low- to no-return investments with no liquidity and no exit. But that's the kind of money that is most needed. Is it philanthropy? If it is, should it be tax deductible? Ironically, because local food is about business, it's not attractive to traditional philanthropists either.

There is a special class of investor to whom the idea of low-return to no-return investments is not completely foreign, and that is the social-impact investor. They like to put money in the hands of entrepreneurs who are bringing about social change.

But social-impact investors have not quite caught on to the idea of investing in local food and farming enterprises. They don't see local food as an important social cause. This is instructive. Given what we know about the awesome destructiveness of the global food chain (and its extreme fragility), food localization is certainly one of the most important and most urgent social causes on the planet. There is no better way to improve human health (and reduce health costs), reduce greenhouse-gas emissions, sequester carbon in the soil, and rebuild local economies.

But this is virtually invisible to social-impact investors. Perhaps they assume that local farmers and food entrepreneurs are just businesses looking to make money or that food localization doesn't qualify as a social-impact investment. There's a huge gulf in understanding here.

So restorative economics is hard. I'm increasingly convinced that the marriage between consumerism and investorism is one of our greatest obstacles. It's pernicious.

ᖆ

Woody Tasch has said that he wants to awaken the biophilia of investors. Is that really possible? These days, I'm more interested in awakening the sleeping giant that lives within ordinary citizens—people who don't think of themselves as investors and who don't want to be consumers. They want to be involved. They want to be engaged. They want to help. (As you may know, securities regulations are skewed to regulate these folks out of the flow of capital. There are many hurdles that keep them out of the slow-money game.)

Some of these ordinary citizens are attracted to Slow Money investment clubs, and that's important. It's real engagement. But it's going to take a lot more than Slow Money investment clubs. (I sometimes fear we derailed them the moment we called them *investment clubs*.)

It's going to take more than any level of crowdfunding we've seen for any kind of company. It's going to take a revolutionary movement and hundreds of billions of dollars. And it's probably going to take a series of good disasters to kick our butts into gear.

I don't think it's going to be enough to try to slow down fast money (if that was even possible). We're going to need to liberate and redirect money that's currently going nowhere, and we have to do it *soon* (it's ironic how often we hear the phrase "we need slow money, fast!").

We're going to need to find the ways to inspire hundreds of thousands of people across the country to do the unthinkable and invest themselves—along with a bit of their money—in localizing our food supply and rebuilding our local economies. Can you think of something more important to do with your money, whether you invest it or gift it? What's at stake here is nothing less than the future of life on this planet. In the future, we may all be asked, "Where was your money when it all came to a peak and crashed?"

I think we're going to have to learn how to mobilize huge amounts of money. We need to unleash the greatest transfer of wealth that human history has ever seen. How do we do this?

∾

How are revolutions funded? How are wars funded?

How do we capitalize the localization of our food supply?

How do we quickly mobilize hundreds of millions in capital in Colorado? How do we manage how that money is put to work? Can we do all that in time to make enough of a difference? Is it possible for all this to happen in a truly organic, emergent manner?

These are the kinds of questions that keep me awake at night.

∾

In the summer of 2012, a new liquor store opened up in Boulder, Hazel's Beverage World. It started with $7.1 million in capital, raised from forty investors, thirty-nine of whom lived in Boulder. Those forty investors are going to do very well with their investment. And a lot of citizens are going to consume a lot of alcoholic beverages bought at a nice discount. Redirecting that amount of local money into the local food economy could be a game changer.

∾

Revolutions are not funded by institutions, because revolutions run counter to institutional norms. Revolutions are certainly not funded by governments or banks. Instead, they are funded by individuals, people who know that the revolution must happen at any cost and are willing to risk whatever resources or talents they can to it—for the potential *social* return on investment.

For many of us, the slow-money perspective came as a revelation, and it moved us deeply. Suddenly we began to see how the local food revolution could be funded, supported at the most local level, by shifting local money into what is increasingly the most urgent and most important priority for our communities.

For instance, producing the kind of revolutionary publication we're building—*Local Food Shift* magazine—calls for revolutionary investors, people who feel that it must happen. For us, it is community-supported publishing. That's why we launched a Barnraiser crowdfunding campaign to help get our first edition off the ground, and why we're emphasizing membership. It's why the Slow Money investment club in Denver, Local Matters Investments, was one of our earliest investors.

This is why the Slow Money investment clubs are so important, because they represent individuals together directly risking small amounts of capital to fund the local food revolution. This, by the way, is also why investment forms like CSAs are so powerful. They go *outside* the dominant system to directly support those who are growing this revolution from the ground up.

This is not to say that there aren't significant business and financial opportunities in the local food industry. But if these are not connected with the emerging centers of aliveness in our foodshed and developed with the intention of supporting the local food revolution, then they too will ultimately undermine it.

So we need not just impact investors or social philanthropists, but revolutionary investors—and we need tens of thousands of them. We need co-conspirators in this, fellow revolutionaries.

Slow Money investment clubs and crowdfunding campaigns represent just some of the ways revolutions get funded—by people with passion and vision, willing to muster great courage and take extraordinary risks, willing to invest in deep relationships in service to a greater purpose.

CHAPTER 34

What We All Can Do

> Humans are only fully human when we are involved with
> each other, and the majority of us find happiness most eas-
> ily through collective achievement. If we join our neighbors
> in the adventures of building a local economy that supplies
> and supports us all, true happiness, deep joy, is waiting to
> be found.
>
> —RICHARD DOUTHWAITE, *SHORT CIRCUIT*

The intriguing thing about localizing our food supply is that it leads to
confronting many complex global issues that are closely related and that
impact everyone locally. Food is the gateway issue.

Getting involved in food localization can seem overwhelming at first,
leaving us floundering to find a place to start. But here are the things
that all of us must do and that we all *can* do.

- Learn everything we can about our food—where it comes from,
  who grew it, how it was grown, its nutrient properties, how it
  got to our table.
- Learn to grow at least some of our own food.
- Learn how to eat seasonally.
- Learn how to preserve and store food.
- Learn how to waste less food.
- Be prepared to share what we have to eat.
- Reduce our consumption of meat.
- Eat seafood only if it is sustainably raised and caught.

- Demand the labeling of genetically modified food.
- Develop new skills and knowledge—composting, vermiculture, permaculture, soil building, seed saving, cultivating, canning and preserving, cooking, nutrition planning, herbal medicine, and so on.

And we must do all this rather quickly! Fortunately, there are some other practical beginning steps that almost everyone can take.

- Take the 10% Local Food Shift Pledge.
- Buy direct from farmers whenever possible. Join a CSA and shop at farmers markets and farm stands.
- Buy from grocers who source locally.
- Patronize restaurants that serve locally produced food.
- Demand that supermarkets carry more local and organic food.
- Explore the hundred-mile diet.
- Consider keeping chickens, bees, and goats.
- Learn how to save and exchange seeds.
- Share local food with friends and neighbors; have potlucks.
- Volunteer at local farms and gardens.
- Contribute to community food banks.
- Invest in local food and farming enterprises.

From personal experience, we can vouch that taking even a few of these practical steps is life changing. For an evolutionary catalyst called to the mission of food localization, they are doorways to something much more significant.

A CALL TO ACTION

We live in a world in transition, in which we are beset with awesome challenges and unexpected opportunities. We are between stories, between worlds, and nothing seems clear. Just as times of war generate enormous economic opportunities, so does this crisis—an opportunity to correct the very fundamentals of economics. Likewise, we humans have opportunities for contribution, meaning, and purpose that would be unlikely to arise in less turbulent times, opportunities to engage in one of the greatest projects in modern human history, the local food revolution—the healing of much of what afflicts our world today.

- We're calling upon farmers and ranchers and food entrepreneurs new and old, large and small, to participate in catalyzing the local food revolution, one of the greatest transfers of health and wealth we've seen in many decades. We're asking them to see themselves as social entrepreneurs, to become drivers of systemic change, to seize the opportunities that the local food gold rush presents, to innovate the new systems and processes that will be needed, and to forge high common standards for local food production, as well as high systemic standards of fairness, equity, sustainability and stewardship, ethics and accountability, cooperation and collaboration, and food sovereignty.

- We're calling upon chefs, restaurateurs, caterers, and food retailers—who are in a position to influence more eaters than almost anyone—to source a substantial percentage of their foodstuffs from local growers and value-added producers.

- We're calling upon conventional food producers, manufacturers, and service providers to diversify their operations by beginning to meet some of the growing demand for local food.

- We're calling upon eaters everywhere to participate in this historic revolution, which will help turn our troubled world right side up. We're asking them to shift their eating, cooking, and food purchasing patterns; to become homegrown food producers, and to shift some of their money into local food economies. In short, we're encouraging them to abandon the story that they are *consumers* and to begin taking up their role as *engaged food citizens*. As Charles Eisenstein says, "The most direct way to disrupt the Story of Separation at its foundation is to give someone an experience of nonseparation."

- We're calling upon local citizens to activate their economic power and to move a small portion of their money into the local food system.[172]

- We're calling upon institutional food buyers—schools, corporate cafeterias, airports, convention centers, and so on—to make a commitment to devote a significant portion of their purchasing budget to local food.

- We're calling upon local government leaders, policy makers, community activists, and nonprofit agencies to raise awareness, to mobilize public support, to focus priorities, and to help remove barriers.

- We're calling upon holders of significant financial wealth—individuals investors, successful entrepreneurs, philanthropic foundations, capital-investment firms, hedge funds, banks, credit unions, and large corporations—to devote a portion of their capital to help build local and regional food systems.

- We're calling upon experienced legal counsel, entrepreneurs, business and agriculture consultants, and experts of all disciplines to step into the fray to help—without demanding traditional pay rates.

- We're calling for journalists, creative writers, media producers, bloggers, artists, and musicians to investigate, capture, and celebrate the local food revolution, bringing it to center stage, where it belongs.

- We're calling upon faith communities to join together in supporting the local food revolution.

- We're calling for a rebirth of food-based culture and community.

Inhabiting Our Foodshed

We need to think carefully about what's really at stake with the local food revolution. It's important to realize that corporate control of our food supply means loss of food freedom, food security, and food sovereignty. This is an assault on our very humanity.

Corporate agriculture says we need to feed the world. But we're not going to feed the world. *The people of the world are going to learn to feed themselves.*

It seems that there is a lot of controversy about local food these days, especially among so-called experts. This is likely to increase.

We should be seeking guidance not from experts, but from the wisest elders of our human tribe (some of them referenced in this book), those who have deeper connections to what is sacred, deeper connections to life itself—those who can see beyond the urgencies of the moment to behold the broad sweep of evolution itself. From the perspective of the elders—though many seem to remain silent—from a moral and ethical and evolutionary and spiritual perspective, it is obvious that we must end the destructiveness and unfairness of our food supply. It is as obvious as the fact that we must now quickly end our carbon emissions into the atmosphere.

It does not matter how costly it is to do this in the short term, how much lost economic opportunity this causes multinational corporations or conventional agriculture, or how much pain results from making such drastic changes. The choice is clear: we have no choice but to make these kinds of course corrections—or we will ruin life on this planet. It's that simple—and that complex, that difficult. This is our moral and ethical and spiritual dilemma.

It's going to be a long struggle, and we need to be clear inside ourselves about what really needs to happen over the long term. There's a decision and a commitment that each of us will have to make about our food.

What's ultimately at stake here is nothing less than human dignity and freedom. Once we understand this, we have no choice but to do everything we can to reclaim our food sovereignty. The contamination of the biosphere and of our food supply must stop, no matter how long it takes, no matter the cost. And it will take a long time, for we are just beginning to mobilize.

Here in Colorado, we are shaping the future of our foodshed—and it is shaping us. We invite you to join us in this effort by catalyzing the local food shift in your community! Rebuilding and localizing our regional foodsheds is a massive process. The community itself is in control of the process. We're acting primarily as a catalyst for collaboration and as a provider of information, insight, and inspiration—and capital.

In truth, this is a revolutionary experiment. And as Transition movement founder Rob Hopkins says in his cheerful disclaimer, we really don't know if it is going to work. But we do know that if we wait for the government or big industry, it'll be too little, too late. And if we just act as individuals, it will surely be too little. But if we act together, as communities, it might be just enough, just in time.

∾

One of the great pillars in the local food revolution, Joel Salatin, was once asked in an interview, "If you had a microphone that could reach the heart and soul of everyone living on this planet, what would you say?" His answer is illuminating.

> You and I have the distinct blessing and responsibility of being able to participate in earth's redemption. I know the story of civilization following a path of human pillaging, destruction, and

rape. Let's declare that chapter done. I repent for all my ancestors have destroyed. Let's resolve to regenerate, to give restitution. This new path is not up to someone else; not up to those guys over there. Quit pointing fingers and look in the mirror. What can I do, what can you do, today, to rectify the evil we've wrought? … Our privilege to participate is a choice we exercise. And that's the most important exercise of all.[173]

Finally, back in March of 1965, in Montgomery, Alabama, Martin Luther King Jr. said that "the arc of the moral universe is long, but it bends toward justice." In that same spirit, I would offer this as my prayer and plea.

May we align ourselves with that long evolutionary arc of the moral, sacred universe and end the reign of those who would control our food supply, those who would control the very forces of nature, those who would control what is most precious and sacred in our seeds, soils, and souls.

May we restore soils and souls and hearts and minds, and may we reverse this dreadful course that threatens to dominate our humanity and undermine our freedom.

May we truly be people of the earth, connected with land and water and sky and the natural cycles of life, connected with the seasons, connected with each other and connected with the greater community of life, connected with the sun and the moon and the planets and the stars and the galaxies, and may we be connected with that sacred evolutionary spark that dwells within each of us.

Together, we are the local food revolution.

ACKNOWLEDGMENTS

Lynette Marie Hanthorn, whose countless contributions have been instrumental in making this book possible. In many ways, this is *our* book.

Our visionary colleagues and patient investors with *Local Food Shift* magazine, who allowed me to divert so much of my time and attention to this book, in the faith that it might play a catalytic role in localizing regional foodsheds.

John David Garcia's daughter, for placing a rare copy of his book in a Mill Valley bookstore, where it fell into my hands.

Alan Lewis, whose revolutionary writing, speaking, and listening continue to be personally inspirational.

Sister Miriam Therese MacGillis, for opening the door to the seminal work of Christopher Alexander and for believing in us.

David Sibbet, for setting me on fire with his pioneering work in process theory and for introducing the work of Arthur M. Young.

Marshall Vian Summers, whose demonstration continues to guide my life.

Woody Tasch, for breaking new ground in restorative economics, starting with food, and for exemplifying what a book can accomplish.

All those I have quoted or referenced, who have shaped my understanding and perspective.

The farmers, ranchers, visionary entrepreneurs, activists, policy makers, investors, organizers, and foodshed catalysts who are contributing to food localization in Colorado and around the country.

Doug Reil at North Atlantic Books, for placing so much trust in my work, and Marie Goodwin, for making the initial connection.

Recommended Books and Films

Collapse

Carolyn Baker, *Collapsing Consciously: Transformative Truths for Turbulent Times*

William Catton, *Overshoot: The Ecological Basis of Revolutionary Change and Bottleneck: Humanity's Pending Impasse*

Collapse, a documentary film about Michael Ruppert

Jared Diamond, *Collapse: How Societies Choose to Fail or Succeed*

John Michael Greer, *The Long Descent: A User's Guide to the End of the Industrial Age*

Naomi Oreskes and Erik Conway, *The Collapse of Western Civilization: A View from the Future*

Dmitry Orlov, *The Five Stages of Collapse: Survivor's Toolkit*

Joseph Tainter, *The Collapse of Complex Societies*

What a Way to Go: Life at the End of Empire, a film by Timothy Bennett and Sally Erickson

Financial Issues

Hal Brill, Michael Kramer, and Christopher Peck, *The Resilient Investor: A Plan for Your Life, Not Just Your Money*

Amy Cortese, *Locavesting: The Revolution in Local Investing and How to Profit From It*

Carol Peppe Hewitt, *Financing Our Foodshed: Growing Local Food with Slow Money*

Michael H. Shuman, *Local Dollars, Local Sense: How to Shift Your Money from Wall Street to Main Street and Achieve Real Prosperity; The Local Economy Solution: How Innovative, Self-Financing "Pollinator" Enterprises Can Grow Jobs and Prosperity*

Woody Tasch, *Inquiries into the Nature of Slow Money: Investing As If Food, Farms, and Fertility Mattered*

Elizabeth Ü, *Raising Dough: The Complete Guide to Financing a Socially Responsible Food Business*

The Global Food Situation

Wendell Berry, *The Unsettling of America: Culture and Agriculture*

Lester Brown, *Full Planet, Empty Plates: The New Geopolitics of Food Scarcity*

Raymond De Young and Thomas Princen, *The Localization Reader: Adapting to the Coming Downshift*

Richard Heinberg, "Fifty Million Farmers," Resilience.org

Wes Jackson, *Consulting the Genius of the Place: An Ecological Approach to a New Agriculture*

Fred Kirschenmann, *Cultivating an Ecological Conscience: Essays from a Farmer Philosopher*

Anna Lappe, *Diet for a Hot Planet: The Climate Crisis at the End of Your Fork and What You Can Do About It*

Bill McKibben, *Deep Economy: The Wealth of Communities and the Durable Future*

Gary Nabhan, *Coming Home to Eat: The Pleasures and Politics of Local Food*

Michael Pollan, *Omnivore's Dilemma* and *In Defense of Food* and *Cooked: A Natural History of Transformation*

Mark Winne, *Food Rebels, Guerrilla Gardeners, and Smart-Cookin' Mamas: Fighting Back in an Age of Industrial Agriculture*

Permaculture

Philip Ackerman-Leist, *Rebuilding the Foodshed: How to Create Local, Sustainable, and Secure Food Systems*

Peter Bane, *The Permaculture Handbook: Garden Farming for Town and Country*

Darren J. Doherty and Andrew Jeeves, *Regrarians eHandbook*

Ben Falk, *The Resilient Farm and Homestead: An Innovative Permaculture and Whole Systems Design Approach*

David Holmgren, *Permaculture: Principles and Pathways Beyond Sustainability*

Frederick L. Kirschenmann, *Cultivating an Ecological Conscience: Essays from a Farmer Philosopher*

Gary Paul Nabhan, *Growing Food in a Hotter, Drier Land: Lessons from Desert Farmers on Adapting to Climate Uncertainty*

Mark Shepard, *Restoration Agriculture: Real-World Permaculture for Farmers*

Restoring Soil

Allan Savory and Jody Butterfield, *Holistic Management: A New Framework for Decision Making*

David R. Montgomery, *Dirt: The Erosion of Civilizations*

Kristin Ohlson, *The Soil Will Save Us: How Scientists, Farmers, and Foodies Are Healing the Soil to Save the Planet*

Judith D. Schwartz, *Cows Save the Planet: And Other Improbable Ways of Restoring Soil to Heal the Earth*

REFERENCES

Abrams, Nancy Ellen, and J. R. Primack. *The New Universe and the Human Future: How a Shared Cosmology Could Transform the World.* New Haven: Yale University Press, 2011.

Ackerman-Leist, Philip. *Rebuilding the Foodshed: How to Create Local, Sustainable, and Secure Food Systems.* Santa Rosa, CA: Post Carbon Institute, 2013.

Alexander, Christopher. *The Nature of Order: An Essay on the Art of Building and the Nature of the Universe.* Vol. 1, *The Phenomenon of Life,* vol. 2, *The Process of Creating Life,* vol. 3, *A Vision of a Living World,* vol. 4, *The Luminous Ground.* Berkeley, CA: Center for Environmental Structure, 2004.

———. *The Timeless Way of Building.* New York: Oxford University Press, 1979.

Alexander, Christopher, Sara Ishikawa, and Murray Silverstein. *A Pattern Language: Towns, Buildings, Construction.* New York: Oxford University Press, 1977.

Alexander, Christopher, Hajo Neis, Artemis Anninou, and Ingrid F. King. *A New Theory of Urban Design.* New York: Oxford University Press, 1987.

Alexander, Christopher, Hansjoachim Neis, and Maggie Moore. *The Battle for the Life and Beauty of the Earth: A Struggle between Two World-Systems.* New York: Oxford University Press, 2012.

Armstrong, Dan. *Prairie Fire.* New York: IUniverse, 2007.

Astyk, Sharon, and Aaron Newton. *A Nation of Farmers: Defeating the Food Crisis on American Soil.* Gabriola Island, BC: New Society, 2009.

Atlee, Tom. *Reflections on Evolutionary Activism: Essays, Poems and Prayers from an Emerging Field of Sacred Social Change.* N. p.: CreateSpace Independent Publishing Platform, 2009.

Bacigalupi, Paolo. *The Water Knife.* Orbit, 2015.

Bahnson, Fred. *Soil and Sacrament: A Spiritual Memoir of Food and Faith.* New York: Simon and Schuster, 2013.

Bahnson, Fred, and Norman Wirzba. *Making Peace with the Land: God's Call to Reconcile with Creation.* Downers Grove, IL: IVP, 2012.

Baker, Carolyn. *Collapsing Consciously: Transformative Truths for Turbulent Times.* Berkeley, CA: North Atlantic Books, 2013.

————. *Love in the Age of Ecological Apocalypse: Cultivating the Relationships We Need to Thrive.* Berkeley, CA: North Atlantic Books, 2015.

————. *Navigating the Coming Chaos: A Handbook for Inner Transition.* N. p.: iUniverse, 2011.

Baker, Carolyn, and Guy R. McPherson. *Extinction Dialogs: How to Live with Death in Mind.* Oakland, CA: Next Revelation Press, 2014.

Bane, Peter, and David Holmgren. *The Permaculture Handbook: Garden Farming for Town and Country.* Gabriola Island, BC: New Society, 2012.

Bennett, Timothy. *What a Way to Go! Life at the End of Empire.* DVD. Directed by Timothy Bennett. VisionQuest Pictures, 2007. www.whatawaytogomovie.com.

Bergson, Henri. *Creative Evolution.* Translated by Arthur Mitchell, with a foreword by Irwin Edman. New York: Modern Library, 1944.

Berry, Thomas. *The Great Work: Our Way into the Future.* New York: Bell Tower, 1999.

————. *The Sacred Universe: Earth, Spirituality, and Religion in the Twenty-first Century.* New York: Columbia University Press, 2009.

Berry, Wendell. *The Unsettling of America: Culture and Agriculture.* San Francisco: Sierra Club, 1977.

————. *Our Only World: Ten Essays.* Berkeley, CA: Counterpoint, 2015.

Brill, Hal, Michael Kramer, and Christopher Peck. *The Resilient Investor: A Plan for Your Life, Not Just Your Money.* San Francisco: Berrett-Koehler, 2015.

Brooks, Max. *World War Z: An Oral History of the Zombie War.* New York: Crown, 2006.

Brown, Lester R. *Full Planet, Empty Plates: The New Geopolitics of Food Scarcity.* New York: W. W. Norton, 2012.

_____. *Plan B: Rescuing a Planet under Stress and a Civilization in Trouble*. New York: Norton, 2003.

Brownlee, Michael, Barbara Stahura, and Robert Yehling. *Just in Case: Dispatches from the Front Lines of the Y2K Crisis*. Novato, CA: Origin, 1999.

Buzzell, Linda, and Craig Chalquist. *Ecotherapy: Healing with Nature in Mind*. San Francisco: Sierra Club, 2009.

Carson, Rachel. *Silent Spring*. New York: Houghton Mifflin, 1962.

Catton, William R. *Bottleneck: Humanity's Impending Impasse*. N. p.: Xlibris, 2009.

_____. *Overshoot, the Ecological Basis of Revolutionary Change*. Urbana: University of Illinois Press, 1980.

Cohen, Andrew. *Evolutionary Enlightenment: A New Path to Spiritual Awakening*. New York: Select, 2011.

Cortese, Amy. *Locavesting: The Revolution in Local Investing and How to Profit from It*. Hoboken, NJ: John Wiley, 2011.

Desrochers, Pierre, and Hiroko Shimizu. *The Locavore's Dilemma: In Praise of the 10,000-mile Diet*. New York: PublicAffairs, 2012.

Diamond, Jared M. *Collapse: How Societies Choose to Fail or Succeed*. New York: Viking, 2005.

Doherty, Darren, and Andrew Jeeves. *Regrarians eHandbook. Regrarians, 2015*. www.regrarians.org/regrarian-handbook.

Dowd, Michael. *Thank God for Evolution: How the Marriage of Science and Religion Will Transform Your Life and Our World*. New York: Viking, 2008.

Eisenstein, Charles. *Sacred Economics: Money, Gift, and Society in the Age of Transition*. Berkeley, CA: Evolver Editions, 2011.

Elgin, Duane. *Awakening Earth: Exploring the Dimensions of Human Evolution*. New York: Morrow, 1993.

_____. *The Living Universe: Where Are We? Who Are We? Where Are We Going?* San Francisco, CA: Berrett-Koehler, 2009.

Emerson, Jed, and Antony Bugg-Levine. *Impact Investing: Transforming How We Make Money While Making a Difference*. San Francisco: Jossey-Bass, 2011.

Falk, Ben. *The Resilient Farm and Homestead: An Innovative Permaculture and Whole Systems Design Approach*. White River Junction, VT: Chelsea Green, 2013.

Flannery, Tim F. *The Weather Makers: How Man Is Changing the Climate and What It Means for Life on Earth*. New York: Grove Press, 2005.

Fox, Matthew. *Creation Spirituality: Liberating Gifts for the Peoples of the Earth*. San Francisco: HarperSanFrancisco, 1991.

Freudenberg, Nicholas. *Lethal but Legal: Corporations, Consumption, and Protecting Public Health*. Oxford: Oxford University Press, 2014.

Fritz, Robert. *The Path of Least Resistance: Learning to Become the Creative Force in Your Own Life*. New York: Ballantine, 1989.

Garcia, John David. *Creative Transformation: A Practical Guide for Maximizing Creativity*. Eugene, OR: Noetic, 1991.

Gayeton, Douglas. *Local: The New Face of Food and Farming in America*. New York: Harper Design, 2014.

Gebser, Jean. *The Ever-Present Origin*. Translated by Noel Barstad, with Algis Mickunas. Athens, OH: Ohio University Press, 1985.

Gershon, David. *Social Change 2.0: A Blueprint for Reinventing Our World*. West Hurley, NY: High Point, 2009.

Ghose, Aurobindo. *The Future Evolution of Man: The Divine Life upon Earth*. London: Allen and Unwin, 1963.

Gilding, Paul. *The Great Disruption: Why the Climate Crisis Will Bring on the End of Shopping and the Birth of a New World*. New York: Bloomsbury, 2011.

Glendinning, Chellis. *My Name Is Chellis and I'm in Recovery from Western Civilization*. Boston: Shambhala, 1994.

Grace, Stephen. *Grow: Stories from the Urban Food Movement*. Bozeman, MT: Bangtail, 2015.

Greco, Thomas H. *The End of Money and the Future of Civilization*. White River Junction, VT: Chelsea Green, 2009.

Greer, John Michael. *The Long Descent: A User's Guide to the End of the Industrial Age*. Gabriola Island, BC: New Society, 2008.

Gumpert, David E. *Life, Liberty, and the Pursuit of Food Rights: The Escalating Battle over Who Decides What We Eat.* White River Junction, VT: Chelsea Green, 2013.

Hamilton, Clive. *Earthmasters: The Dawn of the Age of Climate Engineering.* New Haven, CT: Yale University Press, 2014.

———. *Requiem for a Species: Why We Resist the Truth about Climate Change.* London: Earthscan, 2010.

Hands, John. *Cosmosapiens: Human Evolution from the Origin of the Universe.* The Overlook Press, 2016.

Harris, Patricia, David Lyon, and Sue McLaughlin. *The Meaning of Food: The Companion to the PBS Television Series.* Guilford, CT: Globe Pequot, 2005.

Harvey, Andrew. *The Hope: A Guide to Sacred Activism.* Carlsbad, CA: Hay House, 2009.

Hauter, Wenonah. *Foodopoly: The Battle over the Future of Food and Farming in America.* New York: New, 2012.

Hawken, Paul. *Blessed Unrest: How the Largest Movement in the World Came into Being, and Why No One Saw It Coming.* New York: Viking, 2007.

———. *The Ecology of Commerce: A Declaration of Sustainability.* New York: Harper Business, 1993.

Hedges, Chris. *Wages of Rebellion.* New York: Nation Books, 2015.

Heinberg, Richard. *Cloning the Buddha: The Moral Impact of Biotechnology.* Wheaton, IL: Quest, 1999.

———. *The End of Growth: Adapting to Our New Economic Reality.* Gabriola Island, BC: New Society, 2011.

———. "Fifty Million Farmers." Resilience. November 17, 2006. www.resilience.org/stories/2006-11-17/fifty-million-farmers. The abbreviated text of a lecture to the E. F. Schumacher Society in Stockbridge, Massachusetts, October 28, 2006.

———. *The Party's Over: Oil, War and the Fate of Industrial Societies.* Gabriola Island, BC: New Society, 2003.

———. *Peak Everything: Waking up to the Century of Declines.* Gabriola Island, BC: New Society, 2007.

———. *Power Down: Options and Actions for a Post-carbon World.* Gabriola Island, BC: New Society, 2004.

Heinberg, Richard, and Daniel Lerch. *The Post Carbon Reader: Managing the 21st Century's Sustainability Crises.* Healdsburg, CA: Watershed Media, 2010.

Hertsgaard, Mark. *Hot: Living through the Next Fifty Years on Earth.* Boston: Houghton Mifflin Harcourt, 2011.

Hesterman, Oran B. *Fair Food: Growing a Healthy, Sustainable Food System for All.* New York: PublicAffairs, 2011.

Hewitt, Ben. *The Town That Food Saved: How One Community Found Vitality in Local Food.* Emmaus, PA: Rodale, 2009.

Hewitt, Carol Peppe. *Financing Our Foodshed: Growing Local Food with Slow Money.* Gabriola Island, BC: New Society, 2013.

Holmgren, David. *Future Scenarios: How Communities Can Adapt to Peak Oil and Climate Change.* White River Junction, VT: Chelsea Green, 2009.

———. *Permaculture: Principles and Pathways beyond Sustainability.* Hepburn, Australia: Holmgren Design Services, 2002.

Hopkins, Rob. *The Transition Companion: Making Your Community More Resilient in Uncertain Times.* White River Junction, VT: Chelsea Green, 2011.

———. *The Transition Handbook: From Oil Dependency to Local Resilience.* Totnes, England: Green, 2008.

Howard, Albert. *An Agricultural Testament.* London: New York, 1940.

Hubbard, Barbara Marx. *Conscious Evolution: Awakening the Power of Our Social Potential.* Novato, CA: New World Library, 1998.

Ikerd, John E. *Crisis and Opportunity: Sustainability in American Agriculture.* Lincoln: University of Nebraska Press, 2008.

———. *Revolution of the Middle and the Pursuit of Happiness.* N. p.: John E. Ikerd, 2014.

Jackson, Wes. *Consulting the Genius of the Place: An Ecological Approach to a New Agriculture.* Berkeley, CA: Counterpoint, 2010.

Jensen, Derrick. *Listening to the Land: Conversations about Nature, Culture, and Eros.* San Francisco: Sierra Club, 1995.

————. *Resistance against Empire*. Crescent City, CA: Flashpoint, 2010.

Johnston, Charles M. *The Creative Imperative: A Four-dimensional Theory of Human Growth and Planetary Evolution*. Berkeley, CA: Celestial Arts, 1986.

Kauffman, Stuart A. *Reinventing the Sacred: A New View of Science, Reason and Religion*. New York: Basic Books, 2008.

Kingsolver, Barbara, Steven L. Hopp, Camille Kingsolver, and Richard A. Houser. *Animal, Vegetable, Miracle: A Year of Food Life*. New York: Harper Perennial, 2008.

Kirschenmann, Frederick L., and Constance Louise Falk. *Cultivating an Ecological Conscience: Essays from a Farmer Philosopher*. Lexington: University of Kentucky Press, 2010.

Klein, Naomi. *This Changes Everything: Capitalism vs. the Climate*. New York: Simon and Schuster, 2015.

Kloppenburg, Jack, John Hendrickson, and G. W. Stevenson. "Coming in to the Foodshed." *Agriculture and Human Values* 13, no. 3 (1996): 33–42.

Kolbert, Elizabeth. *The Sixth Extinction: An Unnatural History*. New York: Henry Holt, 2014.

Korten, David C. *Agenda for a New Economy: From Phantom Wealth to Real Wealth*. San Francisco: Berrett-Koehler, 2009.

————. *Change the Story, Change the Future: A Living Economy for a Living Earth*. San Francisco: Berrett-Koehler Publishers, 2015.

————. *The Great Turning: From Empire to Earth Community*. San Francisco, CA: Berrett-Koehler, 2006.

————. *When Corporations Rule the World*. West Hartford, CT: Kumarian, 1995.

Kunstler, James Howard. *A History of the Future*. New York: Grove Press, 2015.

————. *The Long Emergency: Surviving the Converging Catastrophes of the Twenty-first Century*. New York: Atlantic Monthly, 2005.

————. *The Witch of Hebron*. New York: Grove Press, 2011.

————. *World Made by Hand: A Novel*. New York: Grove Press, 2009.

LaConte, Ellen. *Life Rules: Nature's Blueprint for Surviving Economic and Environmental Collapse*. Gabriola Island, BC: New Society, 2012.

Landis, Frank. *Hot Earth Dreams: What if Severe Climate Change Happens, and Humans Survive?* N.p: CreateSpace Independent Publishing Platform, 2015.

Lappé, Anna. *Diet for a Hot Planet: The Climate Crisis at the End of Your Fork and What You Can Do about It*. New York: Bloomsbury USA, 2010.

Liell, Scott. *46 Pages: Thomas Paine, Common Sense, and the Turning Point to American Independence*. Philadelphia: Running Press, 2004.

Lietaer, Bernard A. *The Future of Money: A New Way to Create Wealth, Work and a Wiser World*. London: Century, 2001.

Lovelock, James. *The Revenge of Gaia: Why the Earth Is Fighting Back and How We Can Still Save Humanity*. London: Allen Lane, 2006.

———. *The Vanishing Face of Gaia: A Final Warning*. London: Allen Lane, 2009.

Macy, Joanna, and Molly Young Brown. *Coming Back to Life: The Updated Guide to the Work That Reconnects*. Vancouver: New Society, 2014.

Macy, Joanna, and Chris Johnstone. *Active Hope: How to Face the Mess We're in without Going Crazy*. Novato, CA: New World Library, 2012.

McGoran, Jonathan. *Drift*. New York: Forge Books, 2013.

McIntosh, Alastair. *Hell and High Water: Climate Change, Hope and the Human Condition*. Edinburgh: Birlinn, 2008.

McKibben, Bill. *Deep Economy: The Wealth of Communities and the Durable Future*. New York: Times, 2007.

———. *Eaarth: Making a Life on a Tough New Planet*. New York: Times, 2010.

McPherson, Guy R. *Walking Away from Empire: A Personal Journey*. Baltimore: PublishAmerica, 2011.

Merry, Peter. *Evolutionary Leadership: Integral Leadership for an Increasingly Complex World*. Pacific Grove, CA: Integral Publishers, 2009.

Merton, Thomas. *Love and Living.* Edited by Naomi Burton Stone and Patrick Hart. New York: Farrar, Straus, and Giroux, 1979.

Mindell, Arnold. *ProcessMind: A User's Guide to Connecting with the Mind of God.* Quest Books, 2010.

Mollison, Bill. *Permaculture: A Designer's Manual.* Tyalgum, Australia: Tagari Publications, 1988.

Montgomery, David R. *Dirt: The Erosion of Civilizations.* Berkeley: University of California Press, 2007.

Morowitz, Harold J. *The Emergence of Everything: How the World Became Complex.* New York: Oxford University Press, 2002.

Nabhan, Gary Paul. *Coming Home to Eat: The Pleasures and Politics of Local Foods.* New York: Norton, 2002.

———. *Growing Food in a Hotter, Drier Land: Lessons from Desert Farmers on Adapting to Climate Uncertainty.* White River Junction, VT: Chelsea Green, 2013.

Newitz, Annalee. *Scatter, Adapt, and Remember: How Humans Will Survive a Mass Extinction.* New York: Anchor, 2014.

Ohlson, Kristin. *The Soil Will Save Us: How Scientists, Farmers, and Foodies Are Healing the Soil to Save the Planet.* Emmaus, PA: Rodale, 2014.

Oreskes, Naomi, and Erik M. Conway. *The Collapse of Western Civilization: A View from the Future.* New York: Columbia University Press, 2014.

Orlov, Dmitry. *The Five Stages of Collapse: A Survivor's Toolkit.* Gabriola Island, BC: New Society, 2013.

Orr, David W. *Down to the Wire: Confronting Climate Collapse.* Oxford: Oxford University Press, 2009.

Osentowski, Jerome. *Forest Garden Greenhouse: How to Design and Manage an Indoor Permaculture Oasis.* White River Junction, VT: Chelsea Green, 2015.

Owens, Matthew B. *Traps: A New Theory on the Origins of Civilization and Modern Economic Climate Traps.* N. p.: CreateSpace Independent Publishing Platform, 2014.

Paine, Thomas. *Thomas Paine: Collected Writings.* New York: Library of America, 1995.

Pfeiffer, Dale Allen. *Eating Fossil Fuels: Oil, Food and the Coming Crisis in Agriculture.* Gabriola Island, BC: New Society, 2006.

Phipps, Carter. *Evolutionaries: Unlocking the Spiritual and Cultural Potential of Science's Greatest Idea.* New York: Harper Perennial, 2012.

Pollan, Michael. *Cooked: A Natural History of Transformation.* New York: Penguin, 2014.

———. *In Defense of Food: An Eater's Manifesto.* New York: Penguin, 2008.

———. *The Omnivore's Dilemma: A Natural History of Four Meals.* New York: Penguin, 2006.

Pritchard, Forrest. *Gaining Ground: A Story of Farmers' Markets, Local Food, and Saving the Family Farm.* Guilford, CT: Lyons Press, 2013.

Quinn, Daniel. *Ishmael.* New York: Bantam/Turner, 1995.

Randall, Lisa. *Dark Matter and the Dinosaurs: The Astounding Interconnectedness of the Universe.* New York: Ecco, 2015.

Robbins, Tom. *Jitterbug Perfume.* Toronto: Bantam, 1984.

Roberts, Paul. *The End of Food.* Boston: Houghton Mifflin, 2008.

Robin, Vicki, Frances Moore Lappé, and Anna Lappé. *Blessing the Hands That Feed Us: What Eating Closer to Home Can Teach Us about Food, Community, and Our Place on Earth.* New York: Viking, 2014.

Roy, Arundhati. *Power Politics.* Cambridge, MA: South End, 2002.

Ruppert, Michael C. *Crossing the Rubicon: The Decline of the American Empire at the End of the Age of Oil.* Gabriola Island, BC: New Society, 2004.

Salatin, Joel. *Everything I Want to Do Is Illegal.* Swoope, VA: Polyface, 2007.

———. *Folks, This Ain't Normal: A Farmer's Advice for Happier Hens, Healthier People, and a Better World.* New York: Center Street, 2011.

———. *You Can Farm: The Entrepreneur's Guide to Start and Succeed in a Farm Enterprise.* Swoope, VA: Polyface, 1998.

Savory, Allan, and Jody Butterfield. *Holistic Management: A New Framework for Decision Making.* Washington, DC: Island, 1999.

Scharmer, Claus Otto, and Peter M. Senge. *Theory U: Leading from the Future as It Emerges: The Social Technology of Presencing.* San Francisco, CA: Berrett-Koehler, 2009.

Schwartz, Judith D. *Cows Save the Planet and Other Improbable Ways of Restoring Soil to Heal the Earth.* White River Junction, VT: Chelsea Green, 2013.

Scranton, Roy. *Learning to Die in the Anthropocene Reflections on the End of a Civilization.* San Francisco: City Lights Books, 2015.

Senge, Peter M. *The Necessary Revolution: How Individuals and Organizations Are Working Together to Create a Sustainable World.* New York: Doubleday, 2008.

Senge, Peter M., C. Otto Scharmer, Joseph Jaworski, and Betty Sue Flowers. *Presence: Human Purpose and the Field of the Future.* Cambridge, MA: SoL, 2004.

Shellenberger, Michael, and Ted Nordhaus. "The Death of Environmentalism: Global Warming Politics in a Post-Environmental World." The Breakthrough Institute. 2004. www.thebreakthrough.org/images /Death_of_Environmentalism.pdf.

Shepard, Mark. *Restoration Agriculture: Real-World Permaculture for Farmers.* Austin, TX: Acres U.S.A., 2013.

Shuman, Michael. *Going Local: Creating Self-reliant Communities in a Global Age.* New York: Free, 1998.

———. *Local Dollars, Local Sense: How to Shift Your Money from Wall Street to Main Street and Achieve Real Prosperity.* White River Junction, VT: Chelsea Green, 2012.

———. *The Local Economy Solution: How Innovative, Self-Financing "Pollinator" Enterprises Can Grow Jobs and Prosperity.* White River Junction, VT: Chelsea Green, 2015.

Sibbet, David. *Visual Meetings: How Graphics, Sticky Notes, and Idea Mapping Can Transform Group Productivity.* Hoboken, NJ: John Wiley, 2010.

Simmons, Matthew R. *Twilight in the Desert: The Coming Saudi Oil Shock and the World Economy.* Hoboken, NJ: John Wiley and Sons, 2005.

Simon, David Robinson. *Meatonomics: How the Rigged Economics of Meat and Dairy Make You Consume Too Much—and How to Eat*

Better, Live Longer, and Spend Smarter. Newburyport, MA: Conari Press, 2013.

Skidmore, Cyril James. *The Truth: The Universe Is a Growing God.* N. p.: Advanced Concept Research, 1995.

Speth, James Gustave. *The Bridge at the Edge of the World: Capitalism, the Environment, and Crossing from Crisis to Sustainability.* New Haven: Yale University Press, 2008.

Stewart, John. *Evolution's Arrow: The Direction of Evolution and the Future of Humanity.* Rivett, Australia: Chapman, 2000.

Stephenson, Wen. *What We're Fighting for Now Is Each Other: Dispatches from the Front Lines of Climate Justice.* Boston: Beacon Press, 2015.

Summers, Marshall Vian. *The Great Waves of Change: Navigating the Difficult times Ahead.* Boulder, CO: Society for the Greater Community Way of Knowledge, 2009.

_____. *Greater Community Spirituality: A New Revelation.* Boulder, CO: Society for the Greater Community Way of Knowledge, 1998.

_____. *The Reality and Spirituality of Life in the Universe.* New Knowledge Library, 2012.

_____. *Steps to Knowledge: The Book of Inner Knowing: Spiritual Preparation for an Emerging World.* Boulder, CO: Society for the Greater Community Way of Knowledge, 1999.

Swimme, Brian. *The Powers of the Universe.* 3-DVD set, 2005. https://storyoftheuniverse.org/store-2/dvd/the-powers-of-the-universe.

Swimme, Brian, and Thomas Berry. *The Universe Story: From the Primordial Flaring Forth to the Ecozoic Era—A Celebration of the Unfolding of the Cosmos.* San Francisco, CA: HarperSan Francisco, 1992.

Taleb, Nassim Nicholas. *Antifragile: Things That Gain from Disorder.* New York: Random House, 2012.

Tainter, Joseph A. *The Collapse of Complex Societies.* Cambridge, Cambridgeshire: Cambridge University Press, 1988.

Tasch, Woody. *Inquiries into the Nature of Slow Money: Investing As If Food, Farms, and Fertility Mattered.* White River Junction, VT: Chelsea Green, 2008.

Teilhard de Chardin, Pierre. *The Future of Man.* New York: Harper and Row, 1964.

Ü, Elizabeth. *Raising Dough: The Complete Guide to Financing a Socially Responsible Food Business.* White River Junction, VT: Chelsea Green, 2013.

White, Micah: *The End of Protest: A New Playbook for Revolution.* Toronto: Knopf Canada, 2016.

Wilber, Ken. *A Brief History of Everything.* Boston: Shambhala, 1996.

Wilson, Edward O. *The Social Conquest of Earth.* New York: Liveright, 2012.

Winne, Mark. *Food Rebels, Guerrilla Gardeners, and Smart-Cookin' Mamas: Fighting Back in an Age of Industrial Agriculture.* Boston: Beacon, 2010.

Young, Arthur M. *The Reflexive Universe: Evolution of Consciousness.* New York: Delacorte, 1976.

Young, Raymond De, and Thomas Princen. *The Localization Reader: Adapting to the Coming Downshift.* Cambridge, MA: MIT Press, 2012.

NOTES

CHAPTER 1

1 Rob Jordan, "Stanford Researcher Declares that the Sixth Mass Extinction Is Here," *Stanford Report,* June 19, 2015, http://news .stanford.edu/news/2015/june/mass-extinction-ehrlich-061915 .html.

2 Fred Bahnson, *Soil and Sacrament: A Spiritual Memoir of Food and Faith.*

3 The goal of that ambitious project, launched in the aftermath of 9/11, is "to help our region feed itself."

4 *Food Commons 2.0*

5 A technology-driven initiative to increase agricultural production in developing countries, which took place from the mid-1930s to late 1960s.

CHAPTER 3

6 Spoken on the steps of Sproul Hall, UC Berkeley, December 2, 1964.

7 Robert F. Kennedy, "The Alliance for Progress: Symbol and Sub-stance," *Bulletin of the Atomic Scientists,* November 1966.

8 Woody Tasch, "Commons Nth: Common Sense for a Post Wall Street World: A Simple, Pragmatic and Neighborly Call to Action for the Age after Rogue Computer Algorithms, CDOs, GMOs, High Fructose Corn Syrup, Food Deserts, Desert Storms, and All Those Endowments, Pension Funds, Mutual Funds and Other Ungodly Humungous Institutional Pools of Capital that Are about to Discover Conscientious Investing, Saying No! to Oil and Yes! to Soil." Available at www.austinfoodshedinvestors.org /uploads/1/7/5/4/17545577/commons_nth_pamphlet.pdf.

9 Daniel Quinn, *Ishmael* (New York: Bantam, 1995).

10 Thomas Berry, *The Great Work: Our Way into the Future* (New York: Bell Tower, 1999).

11 Interview by Terry Tempest Williams, "What Love Looks Like," *Orion* (December 2011).

12 Carolyn Baker, *Love in the Age of Apocalypse: Cultivating the Relationships We Need to Thrive* (Berkeley, CA: North Atlantic Books, 2015).

CHAPTER 4

13 Peter Senge, C. Otto Scharmer, Joseph Jaworski, and Betty Sue Flowers, *Presence: Human Purpose and the Field of the Future* (Cambridge, MA: SoL, 2004).

CHAPTER 5

14 Most of the time, when I use the words *we, our,* and *us,* I am referring to this extraordinary collaboration. Lynette Marie could easily be considered the coauthor of much of the material in this book.

15 Founder of the Co-Intelligence Institute.

16 Cofounder of the Berkana Institute.

17 Dale Allen Pfeiffer, "Eating Fossil Fuels," originally published on *From the Wilderness,* October 2003, www.fromthewilderness .com/free/ww3/100303_eating_oil.html. The website *From the Wilderness* was started by Michael C. Ruppert, author of *Crossing the Rubicon: The Decline of the American Empire at the End of the Age of Oil.*

18 Dale Allen Pfeiffer, *Eating Fossil Fuels: Oil, Food and the Coming Crisis in Agriculture* (Gabriola Island, BC: New Society, 2006).

19 Darley's book was scheduled to be published by New Society Publishers in the fall of 2005, but it was never released.

20 Quoted by Michael Ruppert in "The Paradigm is the Enemy," a presentation at the Local Solutions to the Energy Dilemma Conference, New York, 2006.

21 James Howard Kunstler, "After the Oil Is Gone," interview by Katharine Mieszkowski, *Salon,* May 15, 2015, www.salon.com/2005/05/14/kunstler.

22 "We Can Also Draw on Historical Experience Regarding Denial," *The Oil Drum,* July 2005, www.theoildrum.com /classic/2005/07/we-can-also-draw-on-historical.html.

23 Personal journal notes.

24 Kunstler, *The Long Emergency.*

CHAPTER 6

25 Produced by the Community Solution, April 2006.

26 Veteran oil industry analyst and author of the seminal book *Twilight in the Desert: The Coming Saudi Oil Shock and the World Economy* (Hoboken, NJ: John Wiley and Sons, 2005).

27 Author of *The Weather Makers: How Man Is Changing the Climate and What It Means for Life on Earth* (New York: Grove Press, 2005).

CHAPTER 7

28 Julian Darley, interview by Michael Brownlee, *HopeDance* (July 2006).

29 Campbell published two influential papers with Jean Laherrère: "The Coming Oil Crisis" and "The End of Cheap Oil" *Scientific American,* March 1998.

30 Rob Hopkins, *The Transition Handbook: From Oil Dependence to Local Resilience* (White River Junction, VT: Chelsea Green, 2008).

31 Hopkins, *The Transition Handbook.*

32 The board of Post Carbon Institute had persuaded Darley to leave, had returned to its roots as a think tank, and was now headed by Asher Miller.

33 Tom Atlee, the Co-Intelligence Institute, www.co-intelligence.org /crisis_fatigue.html. Chapter 3

CHAPTER 8

34 There were 159 official U.S. initiatives as of December 2015.

35 Derrick Jensen, *Listening to the Land: Conversations about Nature, Culture, and Eros* (San Francisco: Sierra Club Books, 1995).

36 Thomas Berry, *The Sacred Universe: Earth, Spirituality, and Religion in the Twenty-First Century* (New York: Columbia University Press, 2009), 157.

37 Thomas Berry, "The World of Wonder," *Spiritual Ecology, The Cry of the Earth,* ed. Llewellyn Vaughan-Lee, (Point Reyes, CA: The Golden Sufi Center, 2013), 21.

38 Chellis Glendinning, *My Name Is Chellis and I'm in Recovery from Western Civilization* (Boston: Shambhala, 1994), ix.

39 The book was eventually published as *The Transition Companion,* but is much different from its original conception. Hopkins's website is *Transition Network* (www.transitionnetwork.org /blogs/rob-hopkins). He also has an older website, which is no longer active but is archived, which has a lot of useful information (www.TransitionCulture.org).

40 "Principle 11: Use edges and value the marginal," http://permac -ultureprinciples.com/principles/_11.

41 "Earth Literacy," *Three Eyes of Universe,* www.threeeyesofuni- verse.org/index.php?option=com_content&view=article&id=110 &Itemid=212.

42 Regarded as "an ethical framework for building a just, sustain- able, and peaceful global society," *Earth Charter,* http://earthchar -ter.org/discover.

43 Matthew Fox, interview by Derrick Jensen, in Derrick Jensen, *Listening to the Land* (White River Junction, VT: Chelsea Green, 2002), 70–71.

44 See her website, *The Work That Reconnects,* http://workthatre -connects.org.

45 Both of these statements were made in Transition workshops.

46 Alastair McIntosh, *Hell and High Water: Climate Change, Hope and the Human Condition* (Edinburgh: Birlinn, 2012).

47 David Orr, interview by Derrick Jensen, in Derrick Jensen, *Listening to the Land,* 31.

48 "(Part 1) Indigenous Native American Prophecy (Elders Speak part 1)," YouTube video, 6:36, posted by "MadRazorRay," Sep- tember 4, 2007, www.youtube.com/watch?v=g7cylfQtkDg&list =PL05F4C7427A3AEFA7&index=1.

CHAPTER 9

49 Group self-facilitation techniques developed by Harrison Owen.

50 Michael H. Shuman, "The 25 Percent Shift: The Benefits of Food Localization for Boulder County and How to Realize Them," *Transition Colorado,* 2012, http://community-wealth.org/sites /clone.community-wealth.org/files/downloads/report-shuman12.pdf.

51 Woody Tasch, *Inquiries into the Nature of Slow Money: Investing As If Food, Farms, and Fertility Mattered* (White River Junction, VT: Chelsea Green, 2008).

52 John Ikerd, "The Sustainable Agriculture Revolution: Right and By Nature," paper presented at the 37th Ohio Ecological Food and Farming Conference, Granville, Ohio, February 13–14, 2016 (and available at www.localfoodshift.pub /the-sustainable-agriculture-revolution-right-and-by-nature).

53 Wenonah Hauter, *Foodopoly: The Battle over the Future of Food and Farming in America* (New York: New Press, 2012). Also see www.foodopoly.org.

54 Sharon Astyk, *A Nation of Farmers: Defeating the Food Crisis on American Soil,* 11.

CHAPTER 10

55 David W. Orr, *Down to the Wire: Confronting Climate Collapse* (Oxford: Oxford University Press, 2009).

56 Tony Dokoupil, "Why Suicide Has Become an Epidemic—and What We Can Do to Help," *Newsweek,* May 23, 2013.

57 Michael T. Klare, "The Hunger Wars in Our Future," *Tom Dispatch,* August 2012, www.tomdispatch.com/blog/175579.

58 James Lovelock, *The Vanishing Face of Gaia: A Final Warning* (London: Allen Lane, 2009).

59 Margaret Wheatley, "The Big Learning Event," www.margaret -wheatley.com/articles/Wheatley-The-Big-Learning-Event.pdf.

60 James Gustave Speth, *The Bridge at the Edge of the World: Capitalism, the Environment, and Crossing from Crisis to Sustainability* (New Haven, CT: Yale University Press, 2008).

61 Clive Hamilton, *Requiem for a Species: Why We Resist the Truth about Climate Change* (London: Earthscan, 2010).

CHAPTER 11

62 With Carolyn Baker, McPherson subsequently coauthored *Extinction Dialogs: How to Live with Death in Mind* (Oakland, CA: Next Revelation Press, 2014). McPherson's chapter, "Abrupt Climate Change: Giving New Meaning to 'Hard' Science," may be the best survey of climate change literature currently in print.

The ebook version may be the most valuable, as it is replete with hyperlinks.

63 Nature Bats Last: http://guymcpherson.com.

64 I highly recommend the video of his presentation, which contains much valuable information. All the updates to McPherson's work, including a video of his Boulder presentation, can be found on his website, *Nature Bats Last* (http://guymcpherson.com).

65 By the time *Extinction Dialogs* was published, McPherson had identified an additional twelve feedback loops.

66 The report that this quote is from is no longer on the website of the Arctic Methane Emergency Group.

67   I'm forced to rely on McPherson's research accuracy in this chapter, as I do not have access to most of the documents he references.

68 Timothy J. Garrett, "Are There Basic Physical Constraints on Future Anthropogenic Emissions of Carbon Dioxide?" *Climatic Change,* 104, no. 3 (February 2011): 437–55.

69 Malcolm Light, "Global Extinction within One Human Lifetime as a Result of a Spreading Atmospheric Artic Methane Heat Wave and Surface Firestorm," *Arctic News,* February 9, 2012, http://arctic-news.blogspot.com/p/global-extinction-within-one-human.html.

70 John Howard Kunstler, "Making Other Arrangements," *Orion,* https://orionmagazine.org/article/making-other-arrangements.

71 Arundhati Roy, *Power Politics* (Cambridge, MA: South End, 2002), 7.

72 Bill McKibben, *Eaarth: Making a Life on a Tough New Planet* (New York: Times, 2010), 27.

73 And the people reading this, of course.

CHAPTER 12

74 Steve Grace, *Grow! Stories from the Urban Food Movement* (Bozeman, MT: Bangtail, 2015).

75 For the complete interview, see "From Despair to Optimism: The Transformational Journey of Steve Grace, Author of *Grow!*" interview by Michael Brownlee, *Local Food Shift,* September 8, 2015, www.localfoodshift.pub/from-despair-to-optimism.

CHAPTER 13

76 Why do we settle for beliefs rather than pursuing our need to know?

77 We cannot be "placed based" until we know where and when we are.

78 My encounter with Teilhard began in 1964, the year *The Future of Man* was published. A copy somehow found its way to me that year—a gift from a distant relative—when I was a senior in high school. I could not comprehend the words then, but I knew this book and this gaunt priest were terribly important. In fact, that copy of *The Future of Man* resides on my primary bookshelf even today.

79 Carter Phipps, *Evolutionaries: Unlocking the Spiritual and Cultural Potential of Science's Greatest Idea* (New York: Harper Perennial, 2012).

80 By "God," Alexander means it in the same sense as Stuart Kauffman in *Reinventing the Sacred: A New View of Science, Reason and Religion* (New York: Basic, 2008), where he forges a common ground between religion and science by redefining *God* not as a supernatural creator but as the natural creativity in the universe.

81 John David Garcia, *Creative Transformation: A Practical Guide for Maximizing Creativity* (Eugene, OR: Noetic, 1991).

CHAPTER 14

82 Sibbet was a central member of Young's study group at the Institute for the Study of Consciousness, in Berkeley, studying theories of process.

83 Brian Thomas Swimme and Mary Evelyn Tucker, *Journey of the Universe: An Epic Story of Cosmic, Earth, and Human Transformation,* directed by Patsy Northcutt and David Kennard (Mill Valley, CA, Northcutt Productions: 2013) DVD.

84 At this stage, these particles cannot be called *subatomic,* because atoms do not yet exist.

85 Brian Swimme, and Thomas Berry, *The Universe Story: From the Primordial Flaring Forth to the Ecozoic Era—A Celebration*

of the Unfolding of the Cosmos (San Francisco, CA: HarperSan Francisco, 1992), 18.

86 Swimme and Berry, *The Universe Story.*

87 Tom Robbins, *Jitterbug Perfume* (Toronto: Bantam, 1984).

88 MIT's Jeremy England is exploring the possibility that "life is a consequence of physical laws, not something random." Some are already calling him the next Darwin. See Meghan Walsh, "Jeremy England, the Man who May One-Up Darwin," *Ozy,* April 20, 2015, www.ozy.com/rising-stars /the-man-who-may-one-up-darwin/39217.

89 The second law of thermodynamics, which decrees that entropy is positive. "Entropy is the tendency of the energies associated with inorganic substances to become more uniformly distributed—of stones to run downhill, and hot objects, emitting heat, to grow cooler—so that the total energy in a given area or system gradually becomes unavailable by averaging out. This tendency … is implied in the so-called billiard ball hypothesis, which conceives of the universe as a gradually subsiding agitation of lifeless objects," Arthur M. Young, *The Reflexive Universe: The Evolution of Consciousness* (New York: Delacorte, 1976).

90 At that time, oxygen was only 0.03 percent of today's levels.

91 Estimates for the total number of species of life on the planet vary widely.

92 See John Stewart, "The Evolutionary Manifesto," www.evolutionarymanifesto.com.

93 In *The Reflexive Universe,* Young demonstrates that each of the seven stages of the evolution of the universe has seven substages. It is beyond the purpose of this book to explore the principles of substages in depth, but interested readers are encouraged to consider these on their own.

94 John Stewart's phrase, in "The Evolutionary Manifesto."

95 It is perhaps limiting and even incorrect to speak about the universe as a "thing" or a being that is evolving through a process of emergence. We may more accurately say that something is emerging or being expressed through the evolution of the universe. It matters little whether we name it the Monad, Self, Great Mystery,

Wakan Tanka, God, Creator, or Primal Force. What matters is that there is a fundamental force underlying the evolution of the universe.

96 Stuart Kauffman, *Reinventing the Sacred.*

97 This is a radical, even revolutionary, shift from our previous understanding, which said that the universe is essentially fixed, serving as a mere backdrop for our drama.

98 Young, *The Reflexive Universe.*

CHAPTER 15

99 Daniel Quinn, "The Little Engine That Couldn't: How We're Preparing Ourselves and Our Children for Extinction," *3tags,* http://3tags.org/article/the-little-engine-that-couldnt-how-were -preparing-ourselves-and-our-children-for-extinction. This was originally an address delivered at the annual conference of the North American Association for Environmental Education, Vancouver, BC, on August 16, 1997.

100 Rob Wile, "A Venture Capital Firm Just Named an Algorithm to Its Board of Directors—Here's What It Actually Does," *Business Insider,* May 13, 2014, www.businessinsider.com /vital-named-to-board-2014-5.

101 It's possible to view the entire seven stages of the emergence of modern society as the Turn for humanity. This requires some contemplation. During this period, religion has been a major organizing principle. And now, in the twenty-first century, religion may finally fulfill its potential and become the primary catalytic force.

102 The sixth extinction, although how many species will become extinct—and over what period of time—is a matter of some disagreement.

103 Cuba's experience of shifting to an agricultural system largely free of fossil fuels is instructive.

104 Jared M. Diamond, *Collapse: How Societies Choose to Fail or Succeed* (New York: Viking, 2005).

105 Brian Swimme, *The Powers of the Universe,* directed by Dan Anderson (Center for the Study of the Universe, 2005), DVD.

106 Swimme and Berry, *The Universe Story.* Scientists believe that our own solar system had its origins in the explosion of a supernova,

see Charles Q. Choi, "Exploding Star May Have Led to Formation of Our Solar System," *NBC News,* August 6, 2012, www
.msnbc.msn.com/id/48531601/ns/technology_and_science
-space/#.UCfSTmOe530. Science writer Connie Barlow (wife of evolutionary evangelist Michael Dowd) suggests that we are composed of elements from more than twenty supernovas. And for what it's worth, supernovas only seem to occur in spiral galaxies.

107   "In every mass extinction, the world is changed forever—but over a short, terrifying two million years, rather than a slow billion." Annalee Newitz, *Scatter, Adapt, and Remember: How Humans Will Survive a Mass Extinction* (New York: Anchor, 2014).

108   Newitz, *Scatter, Adapt, and Remember.*

109   The science is far from settled on these matters. We invite the reader to explore the growing literature of extinction. In addition to the causes listed in this list of major extinctions, other triggers include cosmic gamma ray bursts, geomagnetic reversal, and disruption of thermo-haline ocean circulation.

110   This gives us a clue to the deeper meaning of *resilience:* the ability to withstand and recover from shocks. And it should give us a sense that, in evolutionary terms, the world can change very quickly.

111   Elizabeth Kolbert, *The Sixth Extinction: An Unnatural History* (New York: Henry Holt, 2014), 268–69.

112   Swimme and Berry, *The Universe Story.*

113   Paul Kingsnorth, "Opening Our Eyes to the Nature of This Earth," *Tricycle,* Spring 2015.

114   Baker and McPherson, introduction to *Extinction Dialogs.*

115   The Kindle version may be the most valuable, as it is replete with hyperlinks.

116   Ruppert committed suicide before the production was complete. "Apocalypse, Man: Michael C. Ruppert on World's End (Part 1)," YouTube video, 10:14, posted by "Vice," January 21, 2014, www.youtube.com/watch?v=aNVHbzlzUS8.

CHAPTER 17

117   That essay later became a key chapter in Stephenson's recent

book, *What We're Fighting for Now Is Each Other: Dispatches from the Front Lines of Climate Justice* (Boston, Beacon Press, 2015).

118 Bill McKibben, interview by Wen Stephenson, "Bill McKibben: Love and Justice," *The Roost,* March 21, 2012, http:// thoreaufarm.org/2012/03/bill-mckibben-love-and-justice.

119 Quoted by Stephenson in *What We're Fighting for Now Is Each Other.*

120 Naomi Klein, *This Changes Everything: Capitalism and Climate* (New York: Simon and Schuster, 2015).

121 Wen Stephenson, " 'I'd Rather Fight Like Hell': Naomi Klein's Fierce New Resolve to Fight for Climate Change," *Phoenix,* December 14, 2012, http://thephoenix.com/Boston /news/148879-id-rather-fight-like-hell-naomi-kleins-fierce.

CHAPTER 18

122 Our understanding of such matters is primitive.

123 Adbusters, November 22–29, 2010.

124 Chris Hedges, *Wages of Rebellion* (New York: Nation Books, 2015).

125 "A revolution is coming—a revolution which will be peaceful if we are wise enough; compassionate if we care enough; success-ful if we are fortunate enough—but a revolution which is coming whether we will it or not. We can affect its character, we cannot alter its inevitability." Robert F. Kennedy, "The Alliance for Prog-ress: Symbol and Substance."

126 Every major religion began as a small cult.

127 Wendell Berry, *Our Only World: Ten Essays* (Berkeley, CA: Counterpoint, 2015).

CHAPTER 20

128 Jack Kloppenburg's reference to *Thinking Like a Mountain: Towards a Council of All Beings,* by John Seed, Joanna Macy, Pat Fleming, and Arne Naess (New York: New Catalyst Books, 2007), a guidebook for deep ecology work originally inspired by Aldo Leopold's essay in *A Sand County Almanac.*

129 Compiled by Strolling of the Heifers (www.strollingoftheheifers .com/locavoreindex), the index is based on a comparison of per-capita direct sales, farmers markets, food hubs, and percentage of school districts with farm-to-school programs. Colorado's rank, sadly, is down from 19 in 2012.

130 We know this from our colleague Philip Ackerman-Leist, a farmer who teaches at Green Mountain College and is the author of *Rebuilding the Foodshed: How to Create Local, Sustainable, and Secure Food Systems* (Santa Rosa, CA: Post Carbon Institute, 2013). When he came to Boulder in 2012, he said that Vermont was then at 5 percent and that the next 5 percent was going to be a lot more difficult.

CHAPTER 21

131 Christopher Alexander, *The Timeless Way of Building* (New York: Oxford University Press, 1979), x–xi.

132 Alexander, *The Timeless Way of Building*, xii.

133 Christopher Alexander, Sara Ishikawa, and Murray Silverstein, *A Pattern Language: Towns, Buildings, Construction* (New York: Oxford University Press, 1977), xiii.

134 Christopher Alexander, Hajo Neis, Artemis Anninou, and Ingrid F. King, *A New Theory of Urban Design* (New York: Oxford University Press, 1987), 18–20.

135 Alexander, *The Timeless Way of Building*, 3–15.

CHAPTER 22

136 *Deadwood* was nearly the last thing I ever watched on television, and it was easily the best television I ever experienced.

CHAPTER 23

137 We see this happening in Colorado and Boulder County.

138 Permaculture teacher Adam Brock in Denver is currently writing a book, *People + Pattern* (Berkeley, CA: North Atlantic Books, forthcoming), which applies the principles of pattern language to social change, formulating an easy-to-understand, actionable set of solutions for "social design"—a compassionate and methodical approach to building better community. Many of the patterns Brock identifies are especially applicable to stage four.

139 Micah White, *The End of Protest: A New Playbook for Revolution* (Toronto: Knopf Canada, 2016).

CHAPTER 25

140 This reorientation puts us in some tension with our surroundings, which are largely industrialized and urbanized and do not support localization.

141 It's reasonable to consider that food localization is a gradual process. But in the face of global emergency, we may also need to quickly develop emergency measures.

142 David Holmgren, *Permaculture: Principles and Pathways beyond Sustainability* (Hepburn, Australia: Holmgren Design Services, 2002).

143 In 2016 they will also operate the Union Station Farmers Market in Denver.

144 Mark Shepard, *Restoration Agriculture: Real-World Permaculture for Farmers* (Austin, TX: Acres U.S.A., 2013).

145 Sir Albert Howard, *An Agricultural Testament* (London: New York, 1940).

146 Despite these important efforts, the rate of new farmers coming into Colorado agriculture has declined by 23 percent over the last five years (according to Dr. David Brown, Cornell University, and the Colorado Governor's Agricultural Forum, February 18, 2016).

147 At this stage, few can afford their own kitchen space and are forced to rent appropriately equipped kitchens on a part-time basis. Competition for such facilities can become intense.

148 "Accredited investors" are defined by the SEC as investors who are "financially sophisticated" and have a net worth in excess of $1,000,000 or an annual income of at least $200,000.

149 Some independent farmers and food artisans have benefited from Whole Foods' Local Producer Loan Program.

150 I'm avoiding the formal (capitalized) term *Slow Money* to distinguish the *mindset* from the Slow Money organization itself; "slow money" is a mindset, as is "food localization" or even "the local food shift."

151 Woody Tasch has called this a *Slow Muni.*

152 Monsanto, DuPont, and Syngenta dominate in this sector.

CHAPTER 26

153 Micah White's website is *Boutique Activist Consultancy,* http://
activist.boutique. See also his new book, *The End of Protest: A
New Playbook for Revolution.*

154 Douglas Gayeton, *Local: The New Face of Food and Farming in
America* (New York: Harper Design, 2014).

155 A project of Local Food Catalysts, LLC, a social venture we
started in December 2014.

CHAPTER 27

156 Christopher Alexander, *The Luminous Ground,* vol. 4 of *The
Nature of Order: An Essay on the Art of Building and the Nature
of the Universe* (Berkeley, CA: Center for Environmental Structure, 2004), 142.

157 Alexander, *The Luminous Ground,* 302–3.

158 Alexander, *The Luminous Ground,* 303–4.

159 Isn't this what we're doing in a foodshed, allowing the wholeness
to unfold?

160 Alexander, *The Luminous Ground,* 304.

161 Alexander, *The Luminous Ground,* 310–12.

CHAPTER 28

162 Robert Fritz, *Path of Least Resistance: Learning to Become the
Creative Force in Your Own Life* (New York: Ballantine Books,
1989).

163 Especially The Work That Reconnects (http://workthatreconnects
.org), and her recently updated book (cowritten with Molly
Young Brown), *Coming Back to Life: The Updated Guide to the
Work That Reconnects* (Vancouver: New Society, 2014).

CHAPTER 30

164 Dr. Albert Bartlett reminds us of journalist Eric Sevareid's declaration long ago that the greatest source of problems is *solutions.*

165 For more information about the film, see "GMO OMG! The Story behind the Movie," *Organic Connections,* http://organicco -nnectmag.com/project/gmo-omg-story-behind-movie.

166 "Fight the GM Food Scare" Science Agenda, *Scientific American* (September 2013), 10.

CHAPTER 31

167 David Robinson Simon, *Meatonomics: How the Rigged Economics of Meat and Dairy Make You Consume Too Much—and How to Eat Better, Live Longer, and Spend Smarter* (Newburyport, MA: Conari Press, 2013).

CHAPTER 32

168 The Colorado population is expected to soar to as many as ten million people by 2050.

169 Leo F. M. Marcelis, Wageningen Greenhouse Horticulture, The Netherlands.

CHAPTER 33

170 Charles Eisenstein, *Sacred Economics: Money, Gift, and Society in the Age of Transition* (Berkeley: Evolver Editions, 2011).

171 With apologies, I must admit that I've lost track of the source of this powerful statement.

CHAPTER 34

172 In most regions, channeling just one half of 1 percent of their monies tied up in nonlocal stocks, bonds, and various investment funds would provide sufficient capital to achieve 25 percent food localization (in Colorado that amounts to nearly $2 billion!).

AFTERWORD

173 "Interview with the Lunatic Farmer Joel Salatin," by Karen Pendergrass, *Paleo Movement,* October 18, 2015, http://paleofounda -tion.com/joel-salatin.

INDEX

ABOUT THE AUTHOR

A catalyst in food-localization efforts, Michael Brownlee is copublisher of *Local Food Shift* magazine, weaving together the saga of the awakening Colorado foodshed. He is also active in the effort to bring local capital into the growing local food economy, and he organized the first Slow Money investment club in Colorado. Previously, Brownlee was cofounder of Boulder-based Local Food Shift Group (formerly known as Transition Colorado, the first officially recognized Transition initiative in North America), a nonprofit organization with the mission of building community resilience and self-reliance through localizing the food supply. With partner Lynette Marie Hanthorn, he offers consulting and workshops for emerging evolutionary catalysts.